LITERATURE AND THE BODY

Selected Papers from the English Institute
New Series

Literature and the Body

ESSAYS ON POPULATIONS AND PERSONS

Edited by Elaine Scarry

THE JOHNS HOPKINS UNIVERSITY PRESS
BALTIMORE AND LONDON

Originally published in 1988 as Selected Papers
from the English Institute, 1986, New Series, no. 12
Johns Hopkins Paperbacks edition, 1990

The Johns Hopkins University Press,
701 West 40th Street,
Baltimore, Maryland 21211
The Johns Hopkins Press Ltd., London

The paper used in this book meets the minimum requirements of
American National Standard for Information Sciences—Permanence
of Paper for Printed Library Materials, ANSI Z39.48-1984.

Library of Congress Cataloging-in-Publication Data

Literature and the body.

(Selected papers from the English Institute;
1986, new ser., no. 12)
    1. English literature—History and criticism.
2. Body, Human, in literature. 3. Fertility,
Human, in literature. 4. Population in literature.
5. American literature—History and criticism.
I. Scarry, Elaine. II. Series: Selected papers
from the English Institute; new ser., no. 12.
PR409.B63L58 1988   820'.9'36   87-46308
ISBN 0-8018-3604-2 (alk. paper)
ISBN 0-8018-4109-7 (pbk.)

Contents

Introduction

Each of the seven essays in this volume is about literature and the body. Together they illustrate what Perry Anderson not unsympathetically calls "A sudden zest, a new appetite, for the concrete."[1] It is part of the work of this introduction to suggest what beyond this "zest for the concrete" is at issue in the present attention to the human body.

The body gradually comes forward in the course of this book in many capacities and attributes: its vulnerability to injury and disease, its erotic powers and fragilities, its capacity to enter states of sleep and work, to swim, to flirt, to discard class merely by performing calisthenics, its power to absorb the artifacts of culture into its own interior matter, its self-experience of gender and race, its endless separation into parts (hands, tongue, skin) and reacquisition of wholeness. What is steadily being looked at in the midst of all these attributes is the body's relation to the voice, to language. Only for a moment, however, does this simplify the question, since the introduction of the voice reintroduces multiplicity. The forms of speaking that gradually make their way into these essays are many (oath, riddle, prayer, curse, valediction, insinuation, gossip, declaration) as are the literary genres (scriptural narrative, elegy, song, sermon, meditation, ode, allegory, romance, novel).

It is useful, then, to begin with the simplest fact about the body, whether it is present or absent, and the verbal form in which this is most habitually registered, the act of counting. The different forms of speaking mentioned a moment ago each contain a different claim about the relation between language and the material world: the announcement that something is "an oath" and the announcement that something is "gossip" assert two very different quantities of material content. It would not be difficult to arrange the many verbal forms along a spectrum at one end of which language is loaded with referential obligations and at the other end of which it is nearly empty. If one were to make such a spectrum, the act of counting would probably be placed at both ends.

On the one hand, counting makes an extreme claim about its correspondence with the material realm. It asserts a one-to-one correspondence between itself and its subject matter: its vocabulary exists solely to register increases and decreases in the content it calibrates. Its proximity to the physical is also indicated by its inseparability from the body. The act of counting *is* an act, and was called this even before language came to be understood as speech acts. People who count tend to do so with their bodies (tapping a finger; bobbing the head; bouncing the entire body slightly as they number the people around the room); it is as though the existence of matter must be registered in matter itself. The fact that very young children find counting words wildly interesting and urgently important long before, for example, color words,[2] is suggestive of their physical primacy, as is the fact that people resort to counting in moments of bodily emergency. On the other hand, numbers and numerical operations are, presumably with good reason, habitually thought of as abstract, as occupying a space wholly cut off from the world. Even forms of counting that claim to have worldly content sometimes seem instead characterized by the complete lack of it: the "body count" in war is a notoriously insubstantial form of speech. Because numbers fall at both extremes of the spectrum, they provide a useful way of illustrating the more general capacities of language. In peace, as in war, the body count becomes a testing ground of the referential sturdiness of language; and the generic elaboration of the act of counting, the population tract, becomes a kind of skeletal model against which the materialist aims of other genres can be seen.

The "population treatise" is a useful model in several senses. In its self-announcing capacity for census-taking and speculation on bodily numbers, it becomes a demonstration of the way language both continually absorbs and empties itself of material content. It provides a stark background against which it is possible to see the more complex materialist reflexes of language as they habitually take place in elegy, in the novel, in biography, in historical narrative, even if "the problem of population" may now surface in the presence or absence of only one person (as in a love poem) or a small group of persons (the novelistic act of bringing into being a small population of characters, and then causing them to disappear or die). The human voice, the written word, continually regulate the appearance and disappearance of the human body. The population treatise makes this practice overt by making what is at stake inescapable.

The essay at the midpoint of this book—Frances Ferguson's "Malthus, Godwin, Wordsworth, and the Spirit of Solitude"—shows that population numbers may be stable reflections of the people counted, or may instead give way to a speculative, futuristic arithmetic, severed from any material reality other than the "actuarial terror" of the person doing the counting. Precisely how one counts (more specifically, how Thomas Malthus, or David Hume, or William Godwin performed the act of counting) depends in part on what the person envisions as the material attributes of "liberty" or of "consciousness." Philosophic debates about liberty and consciousness become debates about how much physical room these apparently nonphysical phenomena take up, especially when they belong to other people (it is as though consciousness has the capacity to swell matter itself, further magnifying the space-taking fact of the body). How one counts also depends on national pride and on what can be called a kind of "century pride"— present habits of self-replication are measured against both the fertility of ancients and the imagined incontinence of unborn descendants. What is poised in back of the pre-Romantic and Romantic numerical speculations is a speculative poetics, "the sublime," which also has depopulation, an emptying of the landscape, among its goals. Frances Ferguson makes dramatically visible the political volatility of the sublime: because it widens the realm of objects considered appropriate for aesthetic contemplation, it acts within perception as an equivalent to the widening of the franchise within the political realm; yet what it has designated aesthetic is an individual consciousness whose capaciousness requires the elimination of all other persons. The impulse toward depopulation in major Romantic texts such as Wordsworth's "Tintern Abbey" opens out into a more generalized impulse toward dematerialization. The emptying out of persons from the land leads to an eventual emptying out of all matter, even the soil and substance of the land itself. In the fragile precision of a phrase—"hedgerows, hardly hedgerows"—the material world is for a moment posited, then subtracted out again. Hedges, like persons, may be subjected to a linguistic fatality.

As we move from the spatial center of this collection to the periphery, the population model remains in place, for the opening and closing essays are also arguments about the pressure of corporeal additions and subtractions on the production of narrative. Throughout "The Rape of Narrative and the Narrative of Rape," Mieke Bal reminds us that the book of Judges is itself a population treatise: the problem of Judges "is the problem of fatherhood, the fatherline, and the construction of the people through it." Population tract and narrative are at this early time not yet severed texts that may be juxtaposed at our will; they are so fused that the narrative itself seems to come out of the act of numbering—specifically, the riddle of whether a woman should be numbered among those in the father's or instead those in the husband's household. Because the generation of both the nation and the narrative requires that women be eliminated, "violented," Mieke Bal must reposition them within the narrative, count them, confer standing upon them, in order to speak about them. Her account thus opens with, would be impossible without, her own act of census-taking: "The three young women who are murdered have no names, in spite of their crucial role in the narrative; this anonymity eliminates them from the historical narrative as utterly forgettable. I wish to speak about them and, in order to be able to do that, I will give them names. Jephthah's daughter, whose death is caused by her being daughter, will be referred to as *Bath*, the Hebrew word for daughter; Samson's first wife, killed because her status as a bride was ambiguous, will be called *Kallah*, which means bride but which also plays on *kalah*, destruction, consumption. The victim of chapter 19, who is dragged from house to house and gang-raped and killed when expelled from the house, will be called *Beth*, house." I cite this passage at length because of its beauty (and the same stately cadence of call and recall continues throughout), but also because it illustrates the interventionist impulse of materialist criticism, an impulse that will be briefly unfolded below and returned to more fully at a later moment.

A materialist conception of language ordinarily has two companion assumptions: first, that language is capable of registering in its own contours the contours and weight of the material world; second, that language itself may enter, act on, and alter the material world. The two tend to be inevitable counterparts: the first attributes to language the features it has to have in order to fulfill the claims of the second. Only the subtantiveness or weight accorded language by the first endows it with the force it must have to make an imprint on the resistant surfaces of the world. The inseparability of the two has, within philosophic conversation, a visible measure in the regularity with which the two words "materialism" and "practice" appear in one another's company. The insistent coupling recurs throughout the present volume and becomes especially striking in the opening and closing essays.

It is the weight of the hurt female body in scriptural narration that permits the conversion of words into speech acts: "the story is not told; it is *done*," Mieke Bal writes; "lineage and history . . . establish themselves." This issue of enactment—the capacity of the voice to shape the physical matter of history—returns in the closing essay, "The Souls of White Folk," where the identification of the Progressivist project "to save the souls of white folk" leads Walter Benn Michaels to assess the role of aesthetics in the formative policies of United States citizenship. Central literary texts of the 1920s—Fitzgerald's *The Great Gatsby* and *The Beautiful and Damned*, Hemingway's *The Sun Also Rises* and *A Farewell to Arms*—are positioned against two distinct sets of writings from the first quarter of the century: first, racially unstable writings addressed to a wide popular readership, such as Thomas Dixon's *The Clansman* and *The Leopard's Spots*, or again Lothrop Stoddard's *The Rising Tide of Color* and *Re-Forging America;* second, a more sober set of texts issuing out of the United States courts and Congress, such as the 1896 case, *Plessy* v. *Ferguson,* the 1898 case, *Williams* v. *Mississippi,* and the Johnson Immigration Act of 1924. The interventionist capabilities of language are visible in this double tiering of the historical frame: in the end, enactment, for Walter Michaels, is not aesthetics as politics but aesthetics as legislative practice.

The legal and literary writings from the American twenties together form a treatise on the birthing of a nation, a Progressivist "Essay on Population." The counting of persons takes place with loud alarm in the racial and political maps of Stoddard's *The Rising Tide of Color.* But the act of census-taking—the quietly reiterated, "Are you white? Are you black? Are you American?"—recurs steadily in all the books. Like other "essays on population," these texts become concerned with what within demography is routinely designated "reproductive practice." In passages both acute and painful, Michaels shows how a national absorption with "race," "breeding," and the "well-bred" is dispersed outward into a mystified idiom of skin color and eventually merged into the aestheticized vocabulary of Fitzgerald's "beautiful" and Hemingway's "nice."

Recommendations about "population" or "depopulation" (according to Bal, Ferguson, and Michaels) carry a fatal weight for women in the Hebrew Scriptures, for the poor in Romantic political discourse, for blacks in modern America: the stakes of counting remain high across the three historical periods. What also remains constant across the three historical moments is the entry of those recommendations into both aesthetics and ethics—into the beautiful and the sublime, as well as into the good, the free, the conscious, and the nice.

Insofar as a collection of essays may be said to have a structure, the attention to the birthing of nations forms a consistent concern at the opening, midpoint, and close of the book. But interspersed between these three "Essays on Population" are four others that might be called simply "Essays on Persons." John Donne. Again John Donne. Lord Byron. Eliza Wharton, and her historical counterpart Elizabeth Whitman. The body now comes forward in its monolithic singularity. Nonfictional language models still float in the background, but now we find not the population treatise but the letter, the biography, the life history, the medical case history, genres where the attempt to regulate the appearance and disappearance of a body is exercised in terms of a centrally locatable person.

This alternation between "Essays on Population" and "Essays on Persons" may seem to position "the collective" against "the individual," as though to present them as antagonistic sites. But this is not right. The error occurs in both directions. The essays about population are also about individual persons, often catching them at the moment when they disappear, as though to stop them from dropping off the edge of the page: Beth's mute hands straddle the threshold, the place of exit; and Homer Plessy is prevented from slipping back yet once more into the "stunning incoherence of *Plessy* v. *Ferguson.*" The converse is also true: to enter into the acutely individual terrain of Donne or Byron or Hannah Foster's Eliza Wharton is to reencounter populations and nations. John Donne, I try to show, "continually takes an inventory of the body—tongues, heart, arms, legs, eyes, and brain—and finds the often graphically described tissue coinhabited by towns, books, nouns, names, narrative, cross, lens, and compass." His poetry uncovers a wide cultural impulse practiced by art, religion, and medicine: the collective work of revising the essential nature of bodily matter by the inlaying of narratives and artifacts is visible in the drawings of Leonardo da Vinci as well as the writings of churchmen like Nicholas of Cusa and physicians like Leonardo Botallo, Athanasius Kircher, and Daniel Sennert. The title of Jerome Christensen's essay, "Setting Byron Straight: Class, Sexuality, and the Poet," announces an analogous concern. He proceeds by a sequence of intimate physical portraits: a man engaged in the display of calisthenic strength; two men swimming; a man and a boy separated by a sun-filled parasol; a husband and wife in the bedroom; a woman and her lawyer lost in hushed innuendo. Yet built into the intimate facts of sexual history is a wider cultural practice, the relation of Greeks to Turks, of British to both, of man to woman, of men to men, of aristocracy to bourgeoisie, of lawyer to client, of wife to reading public. And in Carroll Smith-Rosenberg's "Domesticating 'Virtue': Coquettes and Revolutionaries in Young America," we come full circle back through the individual to the birthing of a nation. By charting the intimate bodily fatality of the heroine in Hannah Foster's *The Coquette,* she shows the formation of the middle class through the revisionary narratives of republican political discourse and best-selling popular romance. Fascinating its public, the novel of seduction works to gender the body politic by anchoring central national texts in the substantive matter of economic and corporeal circumstance.

At the same time, the emphasis on singular, even monolithically singular, individuals has the important effect of reaffirming the possibility of human agency, about which we might grow sceptical in the population essays. Language does not, independently of us as agents, just happen to absorb us or empty us from its content. The users of language regulate the degree to which language describes or instead discards the material world. The deliberateness of this authorization—as well as the paths along which it is carried out—becomes especially visible in writers like Donne, and Byron, and Hannah Foster, who so directly concern themselves with problems of embodiment.

Human responsibility for the "materiality" of language has often been portrayed by directly tying language to the body itself, as when Sartre, echoing Marx, described the writer's voice as "a prolongation of the body."[3] Language, through this imagery, is made to honor its referential obligations to the material world. John Donne affirms the continuity between the materiality of the world and the immateriality of language by reconceiving language in terms of physical attributes: he imagines a word or sentence as something that can *contain*—or more graphically, as something that can be *wrapped* around—bodies and other substantive objects. He repeatedly speaks of language in terms of a "page" which, because made of cloth, rag, vellum, or even glass, itself has sensuous properties. The resulting hybrid of "body and cloth," "body and page," or "body and book" is central both to Christopher Ricks's argument in "Donne After Love" and to my own in "But yet the body is his booke." Somewhat remarkably, this fusion of material body and materialized voice reappears in the body-flower hybrids of Byron's botanical codes: in their exchanges of letters, Byron and Matthews create what Jerry Christensen identifies as "a class of equivocal beings, half boys, half flowers." And the process of hybridization then migrates from Britain to the United States where it now reappears not, as in Byron, in the object of desire but in the object of political envy.

"The gentry," writes Carroll Smith-Rosenberg, "had denied that commercial men, living in the fantastical, passionate and unreal world of paper money, stocks and credit, could achieve civic virtue. . . . [So, too,] middle-class men endlessly accused bourgeoise women of being untrustworthy and incapable of virtue because they lived in another fantastical, passionate, and unreal world of paper—the world of the novel and the romance." Access to representation is dismissed as the insubstantial tissue of passion and paper. But the complaint about men-into-paper and women-into-pages actually registers an anxious recognition of the newly acquired capacity for self-materialization. If paper has less substantive density than the body, it has far more than do words unheard, dissolving into thin air.

John Donne, Lord Byron, and Hannah Foster all affirm the individual's authorization over the space of passage between the physical and the verbal. They have for a moment been collapsed together under the rubric of "hybridization," the fusion of body with cloth, page, or petals. But the three provide very different models of the relation between language and the material realm—even disagreeing about whether the continuity is achieved by carrying the substance of the world into language, or instead by building the insubstantiality of language back into the world.

The model that emerges in John Donne—in the composite portrait given by Christopher Ricks and myself—recapitulates on an individual level the two-part rhythm of absorption and eviction by now familiar here. Donne lifts the body into language; he also (at the end of his poems) works to lift it out again. The lifting of the body into language, the subject of my essay, is visible across a broad sweep of his poetry and prose where language constantly aspires to bring about a mimesis of materiality. Words only acquire the material attributes of the world—mass, weight, substance—through their referential transparency out to that world, and Donne pictures this transparency as a cross-inhabitation of one another's interiors: matter inside the body (tears, blood, heart, brains) is relocated to the inside of some language-soaked artifact to whose material form it now contributes; alternatively, that language-soaked artifact will at times itself be transported back into the inside of the body. The resulting set of cultural repositionings can be summarized as "volitional" or "consentual materialism," a phrase which, as a description of Donne, has two distinct meanings, one philosophical, the other attitudinal. Philosophically, it means that Renaissance science, art, and religion together acted to revolutionize matter, revising it so that it would cease to be accidental and contingent, and become instead volitional, subject to the will—thus eliminating the medieval options of accepting the material world on its own (inevitably humiliating) terms, or rejecting it altogether through mystic disavowal. As a description of an intellectual attitude, "consentual materialism" also means that Donne does not merely happen to accept the body, but willfully accepts it, enters into it as though it were a contractual arrangement. He recognizes the ease with which he might divest himself of the material world and refuses to disavow or be repelled by it. The renunciation of the body is what he most forcefully renounces.

But it is precisely this bodily revulsion and renunciation that Christopher Ricks hears in the endings of the poems. In an essay that proceeds with the force of a legal brief, Ricks charges Donne with willful and repeated repudiation of the material world—or of, at least, one particular subzone of the material world, the sexual body. "Donne's poems, whether or not they are personal memories, record a dislike of having come. Postcoital sadness and revulsion are grimly seized, but what is more grim is that the poems are so often driven to bend this animus upon their own previous act of creative love." From this opening statement, Ricks moves in a rapid, tour de force declamation through the endings of an astonishing sequence of poems ("Farewell to Love," "Love's Alchemy," "Air and Angels," "The Curse," "Woman's Constancy," "Go, and Catch a Falling Star," "The Canonization," "The Triple Fool," "The Good Morrow," "A Valediction: Of Weeping," "A Fever," "The Second Anniversary," "The Cross," "Twicknam Garden") as well as through a several-century sequence of critical reactions to those endings (Samuel Johnson, Hazlitt, Coleridge, Swinburne, T. S. Eliot, William Empson, Helen Gardner, J. E. V. Crofts, Leslie Fiedler, Barbara Herrnstein Smith, Peter Brooks, Tilottama Rajan, Arthur Marotti, John Carey).

Donne, after love, disavows his own body, the body of the poem, and the generous materialism at the poem's center. The final lines damage all that comes before, lines that are not "more merely beautiful, but that . . . have a depth, a corporeal and spiritual grace, worth gaining." Ricks does not describe this dispassionately. In fact, he denounces it, using many ethical sites to bring to account the action of the final lines against the center: in the end, Donne is guilty of physical assault (he "rends" the earlier lines, "bends" them, cuts them with "acid"), verbal misrepresentation (he "libels his masterpiece"), adultery and infidelity ("the poem is more false to itself than any of its convenient women could ever be"), political appropriation (the endings "usurp entire rights over the poem"), and finally, cowardice ("the poems turn on their heels"). A more dispassionate description would merely reenact the disavowal; and it is precisely this disavowal that Ricks finds in the paraphrases by critics who rise above revulsion to make the last lines less corrosive, less cruel, more cheery and safe: the profession has "inured itself against joy and pain," forgotten the world that "hurts and kills."

The pair of essays on John Donne are at once starkly opposed and strangely compatible. It is as though having hurled himself into the text, Donne's body is so lodged there that when he tries to get it back out again (reclaiming for himself what he a moment ago lent to the poem) he cannot do it. So successful is his mimesis of material presence that he cannot disengage himself without severe forms of self-invalidation. "The trouble is Donne at times wrote more deeply than he meant or than he could bear." The model of language that results accommodates the extremes of absorbing and emptying itself of the material world.

A second model emerges in Carroll Smith-Rosenberg's analysis of the popular American novel in the late-eighteenth century. The body, according to this model, will always exist in relation to some text: that is a given. The only question is, "Which text?" In other words, achieving the capacity for self-authorization requires not, as in Donne, that the body be somehow lifted into language (that has apparently already happened), nor that it be gotten out again (that is not posited as a possibility). Rather, one must be able to shift it from one vehicle of representation to another. Hannah Foster's Eliza Wharton relocates the textual model for embodied experience. She shifts the reference for physical sensation away from the equally flawed models of "romance" and "sermon" to the Declaration of Independence. In doing so, she revises the nature of the body itself: it is still the acuity of sensory pleasure she seeks, but what gives rise to the thrill of pleasure is not the erotic (desire, deprivation, and dependence) but the immediate experience of bodily "independence" or physical "wholeness"—a kind of sensuous self-regard. Eventually Eliza "falls," not because she enters a prohibited sexual affair but because, unable to sustain the new textual model, she reverts to the old, now lethal, one.

Eliza Wharton's assumption that she can transport herself into the ethical space of a document about "life, liberty and happiness" is, Carroll Smith-Rosenberg argues, symptomatic of a widely felt assumption among middle-class women and men that the meaning and import of words like "liberty" and "virtue" were theirs to revise. The popular novel, like republican political discourse, catches these terms at the moment when they are being renegotiated by a wide public. The philosopher Thomas Nagel writes that "The ethical commonplaces of any period include ideas that may have been radical discoveries in a previous age," and he names "modern conceptions of liberty, equality, and democracy" as central instances. He designates ethical revision as among the most "democratic" of phenomena: "Because the questions are about how [people] should live and how society should be arranged, the answers [can't be pursued exclusively by experts but] must be accepted and internalized by many people to take effect."[4] "Domesticating Virtue" could have been entitled "Democratizing Ethics" for it finds in the "coquettes and revolutionaries in young America" the broadening of the definitional act, and the extreme risks entailed in the ethical work of inventing the commonplaces through which we now live.

Byron, in Jerome Christensen's account, provides a third, very different, model of the continuity between the material realm and language. Rather than carrying the substantiveness of the world into language, he forces the dissoluteness of language back into the material world, out of whose shattered surface then issues the genre of romance "pure and violent." The phenomenon of "equivocation" belongs to the verbal realm—the linguistic evasions of Mary Wollstonecraft; the codes and coded letters circulating among Byron, Hobhouse, and Matthews; the whispered legal conversations of Lady Byron and her attorney; the century-long practice of insinuation and critical gossip about the Separation Controversy ("the moment of greatest debate among biographers. What awful secret did Lady Byron tell?"). The dissolute verbal realm may at first seem opposed to the clarity or decisiveness of the very acts—murder, sexual transgression—rumored to have taken place, if only one could know them. And Christensen, wanting us to know them, does track the mystery.

But the solution to the mystery, which by replacing a question with an answer should work to dispel the element of equivocation, instead does the reverse. When the biographical narrative becomes clear, what becomes clear is that Byron practiced equivocation on the material world itself. Byron, argues Christensen, established his own difference from others not simply by passively disregarding the material principle of difference but by actively shattering it, acting violently against it, dissolving the ways of "East and West, past and present, boy and girl, pro and con, fore and aft." The last pair of terms provides the final test case: more elemental even than the willful confusion of gender (bisexuality), nationality (homosexuality), family (incest), or age (pederasty) is the "Byronic confoundment" of the front and back of the body (sodomy). If this series of confoundments gives rise to his monolithic individuality—his "genius," "sovereignty," and "aristocratic style"—it also returns us to the population treatise. Byron's rearrangements of matter approach the emptying out of matter in the Romantic sublime. So, too, his attempts to materialize the principle of "equivocation" in order to generate romance echoes the processes by which in Judges "the riddle" form is materialized in the female body in order to "restart" a historical narrative that has become "stalled" in its own immateriality.

The seven essays in this volume were not originally written as part of a book entitled "Literature and the Body" or to be framed under the subrubrics, "Essays on Population," "Essays on Persons." The 1986 English Institute program printed in the hardcover edition shows the panels and subjects separately addressed by Mieke Bal, Christopher Ricks, Elaine Scarry, Jerome Christensen, and Frances Ferguson, as well as the persons who in each instance designed those panels. In addition, Carroll Smith-Rosenberg has contributed the essay she originally gave at the November 1986 conference on "Tocqueville and Democracy" at Berkeley; and Walter Benn Michaels originally gave "The Souls of White Folk" as the 1987 Joseph Warren Beach lecture at the University of Minnesota.

While it would therefore be misleading to speak of a highly structured set of intentional relations among the essays, they together form a kind of morphology of materialist practice, two central attributes of which will be quickly summarized, and the third of which will be unfolded more fully.

First, language both absorbs the material world and empties itself of material content. To get "things" into words will be the project of some, to get "things" out of words the project of others. Materialist criticism simply observes the ways in which this may be done (as well as the costs in each direction) and avoids collapsing into a generalized state of scepticism each time an instance of emptying, or referential slipperiness, is encountered. It is the case that language sometimes bears very little reference to anything beyond itself; it does not follow that language is in general incapable of bearing reference, or that it is futile, or foolish, to work to extend those referential capacities. It is not clear why the fact that such efforts sometimes fail occasions the sense that such efforts should not have taken place. Conversely, the fact that language is sometimes highly referential does not obligate us to conclude that it must aspire to be so at all times; indeed, if language had no referential freedom or fluidity, many of its advantages, its ways of supplementing "the sensuously obvious," would immediately be gone.

The issue of cost leads to a second attribute: the fact that the human body is at the present moment a special site of attention and concern. As a historical phenomenon, there is nothing surprising about this: the very extremity of the scepticism about the referential capacities of language in the past decade made it almost inevitable that at the moment when language was finally reconnected to the world, the primary site of reconnection would be not just this or that piece of material ground but the most extreme locus of materialization, the live body. The body is both continuous with a wider material realm that includes history and nature, and also discontinuous with it because it is the reminder of the extremity of risks entailed in the issue of reference.

The continuity perhaps requires little elaboration: attention to the body constitutes a narrow band within the much wider spectrum of recent attention to history and naturalism, subjects that have themselves arisen as avenues of reclaiming the material world for literature. When at an earlier moment "history and literature" were placed side by side, what was being pondered had something to do with the juxtaposed categories of "truth" and "fiction"; what is now looked at in that juxtaposition is instead the relation of "material" to "immaterial." This is not to say that the question of whether language can be accurate, and the question of whether it bears reference to the material world, are two incompatible questions: a lie is both inaccurate and empty of material content. But neither are they precisely identical: asking whether language can be accurate is like asking if the train stays on the rails, whereas asking if language carries the contents of the material world is like asking whether the train carries any cargo. In either event it is moving through the landscape and if the answer to the first is no, then it is dangerous; and if the answer to the second is no, we have invented this danger for a tool without use. The turn to history and the body—the attempt to restore the material world to literature—has been in part inspired by a kind of collective regret at the very weightlessness, the inconsequentiality of conversation about literature. Contemporary political philosophy has charged the liberal democratic state with a progressive "thinning out" of the concept of personhood and the individual.[5] Even if we were to judge the contribution of literary studies to the creation of the liberal self as very small, it would at least be noticeable that the lack of aspiration toward linguistic consequence has been strangely compatible with the overall liberal retreat into the contentless and thin.

The severing of language and literature from the material world is, in the description above, problematic both because of a lack of consequence (thinness) and because of an overburden of consequence (danger). The two do go together, and concern about the body, like concern about history, works to redress both problems in a way—and it is here that it seems to differ from history—that makes prominent precisely what is at stake. The notion of "consequence," of "mattering," is nearly inseparable from the substantive fact of "matter." Or, phrased in the opposite direction, when "matter" goes from being a noun to being an active verb—when we go from saying of something that "it is matter" or "it has matter" to saying "it matters"—then substance has tilted forward into consequence. What matters (what signifies, what has standing, what counts) has substance: mattering is the impingement of a thing's substance on whatever surrounds it. This strange-sounding word, "mattering," creates the visual image of matter generating more matter, an association reinforced by its etymological association with the magnification or multiplication of physical substance in building (*materia*, the trunks of trees), in procreation (*mater*, the trunk of the reproducing female body), and in the action of the wounded body (the wound's production of matter).[6] When language and the body are placed side by side, the weightlessness of any language that has lost its referential aspirations becomes especially noticeable. But what becomes noticeable in addition to this problematic deficit of linguistic consequence is the problematic surfeit of consequence, the danger that results from excluding the material world.

Danger is so loaded a word that it should perhaps be revised down into one more tonally neutral. What can at least be said is that the present set of essays together show that language often bears reference to the material world even when the material referents are disowned. Further, the more invisible the material referents, the more possible that they are being put at risk (to be visibly at risk invites rescue and redress). Whether this is universal, very frequent, or only occasional is unclear. But enough instances occur to make it reasonable, when in the presence of nonmaterialist or antimaterialist recommendations about language, to wonder whether there is not some piece of the

material world lending those recommendations substance. The intrica-
cies of the phenomenon are traced by Walter Benn Michaels who
shows that the displacement of biology by culture in the race-free
aesthetics of American citizenship mimes the displacement of biology
by culture in the Ku Klux Klan where klan replaces biological clan,
reincarnation replaces physical reproduction, and white soul replaces
the white skin that has itself been lifted away from the body's surface
into the white sheets that obscure the person's physical color and
form. The result is a "rewriting of biology as ideology," an ideology
that claims to "transcend color while invoking its biological authority," in order to borrow its "immunity to cultural transformation."
Here and in the other essays in the volume, the missing body sponsors
the very verbal construct that itself carries only minimal physical
traces of what has disappeared: the female bodies missing from the narrative of Judges move that narrative forward; the bodies missing from
the sublime landscape contribute to the awe and terror elicited by the
starkness of the terrain that remains; and the body missing from Byronic romance makes possible "a particular kind of sexual experience
which because it cannot meet the eye underwrites everything that can."

Embedded in this description is a third attribute of materialist practice—its interventionist reflex. Because materialist practice assumes language acts on the real world and because it continually credits the possibility that literature acts on historical reality, it also gives rise to a genre
of criticism which itself acts to alter (rather than merely describe) the
literary text. But it may, and this is a separate point, even begin to operate as though it can, by changing the text, then move out through literature to alter, retroactively, the historical persons and events temporally
adjacent to that literature—a quite astonishing and immodest project.

The first of these two habits of intervention is immediately recognizable in the broad outlines of the essays summarized here: against
the patrilocal and virilocal census-taking of the book of Judges, Mieke
Bal provides a feminist countercensus; faulting Donne for his failure to
sustain his lyrical materialism, Christopher Ricks places before our
eyes the possibility of poems that bear through to the end feelings too
deep to long be borne; Frances Ferguson holds back for us the weight

of the hedgerows and persons as they slip out of late-eighteenth-century poetry and population treatises; Jerome Christensen shows the Romantic confoundment of the material realm by reconstructing the very material categories Byron so aggressively dissolves; and Walter Michaels restores to visibility the color and fragility of human skin made invisible in the aestheticizing of citizenship. These occasions of interference are not scattered across random points of the compass. The direction of the intervention is constant: in each, a material referent is restored to language on the edge of depletion. Only when the artists themselves undertake a revisionary materialism (as is true of Hannah Foster in Carroll Smith-Rosenberg's account, and as is true of Donne in my own) does criticism become descriptive rather than interventionist, celebratory rather than oppositional.

Beyond this, there is the second, more mysterious reflex of writing as though the persons and events contemporaneous with the literary text are themselves alive and subject to alteration – capable, in the three examples that follow, of being healed, or hurt, or educated. It is the eleven chapters habitually omitted from readings of Judges that Mieke Bal wishes to restore, but as she writes it is as though Beth, Bath, and Kallah themselves can be made to start breathing again. Jerry Christensen stops in the rich midst of his puns and verbal play to wince at the thought that the historical persons about whom he is speaking are at risk from the assessments being made: "It may seem cruel to vindicate Lord Byron's difference by blaming Matthews for drowning, but as his letters show, Matthews, like Keats, understood the profession of literature as a life of allegory – and Romantic careers, like Romantic poems, prove allegory's cruelty." The full force of this habit can perhaps be summarized by asking as a final question: "To whom is Christopher Ricks speaking?" In the very energy of its anger, Ricks's voice seems addressed to John Donne, a Donne who will mend his ways, cease to disavow poems and bodies, and produce within a fortnight a new set of poems with different endings. Donne is less spoken about than spoken to, and spoken to as one capable of arguing back with the same magnificent anger.

The restoration of "matter" to literature carries with it a heightened awareness of the impingeability of matter; and this sense of impinge-ability in turn makes it increasingly difficult to divest literary language of its ethical or political content. Although no one will confuse the term "materialism" as used here with any one political or ethical stance (such as marxism or feminism, each of which centers itself philosoph-ically in the reclamation of the material world), or with acts of advo-cacy (however much advocacy shares its extreme optimism about the referential abilities of language), or with an exclusive location on the right or left, it is clear that the recent immunity from such questions, what Perry Anderson calls the "political lability" of structuralist and poststructuralist writing,[7] ceases to be possible once language is again full of the world.

The impulse toward intervention is simultaneously continuous and discontinuous with materialism. The continuity was noticed earlier: only language endowed with the referential substance of the world has the force and weight to impinge on that world. But the discontinuity is equally striking. To be concerned about the referential obligations of language implies an acceptance of the material given of the world, as though to say, "It has standing, let it stand." But how can this im-pulse then give rise to a second which immediately contemplates inter-fering with that material given, and so subverts its very origins? The coupling of the two reenacts the way language absorbs and empties itself of the material world; it recapitulates the self-revising character of material culture at large.

A different way of understanding this peculiarity emerges if one places side by side the maximal, then the minimal, case for interven-tion. At its most extreme, one can say that intervention is not an at-tribute of, but coterminous with, materialism itself—the very heart of what it is. Pierre Macherey, for example, writes that materialism is "not a doctrine, not a theory, not a body of knowledge, but rather a manner of intervention, a philosophical 'position.'"[8] Regardless of how or why that intervention takes place, and even if demoted back to the status of mere attribute, entering and acting upon the world re-main essential to whatever materialism is or seeks to accomplish. Litera-ture acts on the world; criticism acts on literature and through it, the world. Art and criticism enter into line with ordinary craft in the perpetual continuity of construction and revision.

But this maximal account overlaps and is in the end strangely compatible with a minimal portrait according to which the "interventionist reflex" is dramatically visible precisely because it is so exceptional—holds so small a place—within the overall materialist project. A form of criticism unconcerned with, or having specifically disavowed, questions of reference would appear noninterventionist. It would not even raise the issue of interventionism, because it would have already bypassed material reality altogether. It could thus with equal accuracy be described either as "noninterventionist" or instead as an extreme version of interventionism where there is a complete displacement of world and literary text with whatever it is the person wishes to say. There would be no landmarks even to register the way the new voice impinges on what preexisted. In materialism, in contrast, enough of the material world is present that the artist's impingement on the world, and the critic's impingement on the art, are clearly etched. It is the very plenitude of the world as given that makes startlingly visible the intervenings, no matter how slender, how modest.[9]

ELAINE SCARRY

University of Pennsylvania

September 1987

NOTES

1. Perry Anderson, *In the Tracks of Historical Materialism* (Chicago: University of Chicago Press, 1983), 21.

2. Rochelle Gellman, Faculty Mellon Seminar on Human Nature, University of Pennsylvania, Fall 1986.

3. Jean-Paul Sartre, *What Is Literature?*, trans. Bernard Frechtman, introd. Wallace Fowlie (New York: Harper and Row, 1965), 7.

4. Thomas Nagel, "Ethics without Biology," in *Mortal Questions* (Cambridge: Cambridge University Press, 1979), 143–44.

5. See, for example, Michael Sandel, *Liberalism and the Limits of Justice* (Cambridge: Cambridge University Press, 1982), 92–95.

6. These etymologies are consistently cited in the *Oxford English Dictionary*, C. T. Onion's *The Oxford Dictionary of English Etymology*, Walter Skeat's *An Etymological Dictionary of the English Language*, and Eric Partridge's *Origins*.

7. Anderson, *Historical Materialism*, 56.

8. Pierre Macherey, "In a materialist way," trans. Lorna Scott Fox, *Philosophy in France Today*, ed. Alan Montefiore (Cambridge: Cambridge University Press, 1983).

9. A beautiful instance of this is Michael Baxandall's now classic account of the limewood sculptures of southern Germany. The very capaciousness of Baxandall's representation of the limewood itself makes stunningly visible the artistic entry into the wood by Hans Leinberger, as well as Michael Baxandall's own critical intervenings into Hans Leinberger's St. James the Great or his Virgin and Child (*The Limewood Sculptors of Renaissance Germany* [New Haven: Yale University Press, 1980]).

LITERATURE AND THE BODY

Fig. 1. Rembrandt, Samson Posing the Riddle to the Wedding Guests, 1638. Dresden, Gemäldegalerie. The bride takes the position of Christ in figure 2. The position as a sign includes the isolation, danger, and victimization involved for Christ in the Leonardo painting.

Mieke Bal

The Rape of Narrative
and the Narrative of Rape

SPEECH ACTS AND BODY LANGUAGE IN JUDGES

The book of Judges is a strikingly violent book. Men murder men, women murder men, and men murder women. I see all these categories of murder as related, but I contend that the man-woman murders are, narratively speaking, generative of at least the woman-man murders, if not of all. It is on the man-woman murders that I will focus. The young women who are the victims are, because of their sexual maturity and their institutional background, disruptive of the social structure as well as of the narrative; their rape or murder works to cure both—to bring about social order and to lead the narrative to its next phase. Although in general there are many nameless minor characters, it is striking that the three young women who are murdered have no names, in spite of their crucial role in the narrative; this anonymity eliminates them from the historical narrative as utterly forgettable. I wish to speak about them and, in order to be able to do that, I will give them names. Jephthah's daughter, whose death is caused by her being daughter, will be referred to as *Bath*, the Hebrew word for daughter; Samson's first wife, killed because her status as a bride was ambiguous, will be called *Kallah*, which means bride, but which also plays on *kalah*, destruction, consumption. The victim of chapter 19, who is dragged from house to house and gang-raped and killed when expelled from the house, will be called *Beth*, house.

Traditional scholarly readings define the topic of the book of Judges as the difficult establishment of the people in monotheism and in the land, and the wars against the native inhabitants this entails. The stories of the individual heroes, judges, or deliverers are supposed to enhance this overall political theme. This interpretation, on whose details I will not elaborate here, leads to the elimination of exactly

I

eleven out of twenty-one chapters from the "core" of the book: the two opening chapters, four of the Samson saga, and the so-called epilogue of five chapters. The majority of the chapters do not, by this interpretation, really count as "real Judges material." In a study that I have completed recently I argue that this view rests on an attempt to base the coherence of the book on political history, whereas a case can be made for social history as the main issue around which the stories evolve. If we take the social issues seriously, the rejected chapters become central. The crucial issue is the transition from what I call patrilocal marriage, the nomadic form of marriage wherein the woman remains in the house of her father, while the husband, whose relationship to her is much more casual and less permanent, visits her occasionally.[1] Disturbing as it is, the extreme violence of chapter 19 becomes, then, a central rather than a peripheral event. The intertribal war of the end is therefore not a side issue, not an accident meant to show that the people need a king, but a logical step in the struggle at stake. The set of wars against the natives is not the only problem the Hebrews had to face. "Going astray," the expression used for both religious and sexual "unfaithfulness," is a central issue confronting the fathers threatened with the loss of their daughters and the husbands who want their wives to live in their clan.

SPEECH ACTS: THE WORD BECOME FLESH

I would like to present one aspect of the narrative that is directly related to this social issue: the use of language for violence. Inspired by both Shoshana Felman's playful and seductive, brilliant analysis of speech acts,[2] and by Elaine Scarry's impressive and depressing, equally brilliant analysis of violence,[3] and worried by the more and more obvious limitations of narrative theory as I had myself contributed to construct it, I became interested in the relation between narrative structure and the characters' speech acts that both disturb and construct it. The central act of violence in the book of Judges is the rejection, rape, torture, murder, and dismemberment of the young woman, usually but fallaciously referred to as "the concubine," in chapter 19. She dies a violent death as a result of the competition between her patrilocal father and her virilocal husband. Eve Sedgwick's title *Between Men* applies here.[4] Sexual abuse is the form chosen for the revenge of the old institution over the new. Her death and the story of it are not only violent but also narratively ambiguous. She dies, we might say, several times, or rather, she never stops dying. The agents of her death are similarly unclear; the act keeps being displaced from one man to the next, until we reach the narrative situation of the end where all the male agents involved turn out to have contributed to her death. Not only is this woman raped to death (and is rape, as I will argue, an act of body language), her body is subsequently used *as* language by the very man who exposed her to the violence. Her dismemberment for semiotic purposes, a repetition of the gang-rape, can be seen as a miniature of the narrative of Judges as a whole. Where the narrative seemed to fail to construct history, rape becomes the generative event. The relations between language use in the book and the narrative that constitutes the book are what I would like to explore in this paper.

How can a dead woman speak? Why does she have to be dead in order to be able to speak? And what is speech in a book of murder? How does speech relate to action, affect lives, and bring about death; how does speech relate to the body; and how does the view that emerges from these questions affect the status of the text itself as speech?

As is typical of linguistic studies, speech-act theory has been developed around a few core examples. For J. L. Austin the favorite example is marriage, where the utterance of the word accomplishes the deed.[5] Felman works with the example of seduction. Similarly, in this paper there will be a central speech act that emblematizes both my reading of Judges and the view of speech I see in it. In memory of Beth's dismembered body, my core speech act is both one and many, it is both central and decentered, less clear as a case than seduction, although more "cutting"–the French would say: *tranchant*. The speech act I will focus on is the *riddle and the vow.* It is the one that questions meaning, while it is excessively meaningful; the one that is overmotivated and whose force is more central, as its meaning, than its meaning. It is a speech act that hovers between the two genres, while exploiting the ambiguity of both. On the one hand, Judges is full of riddles, the speech act of the *lacking* meaning. Riddles ask for meaning because without the answer, they don't have any. Samson's riddle at his wedding hardly conceals its sexual meaning, but it rests on a confusion—a "who is who?"—that questions this meaning. The subjects of the performance at stake in the riddle are anything but clear. And that lack of clarity is at the same time the riddle's force: the motivation of its utterance whose trace the riddle *is*. It is this disproportion between a lack of meaning and an excess of force that makes the riddle the emblematic speech act through which we will explore the power of language and its relation to events, to history, and to narrative.

On the other side, we have the speech acts based on an excess of meaning, acts that emblematize the power of words in the most radical way. Their meaning being death, they bring death, they kill. There is an opposition between the fatal word and the speechless, powerless character that is killed by it that drives the proportion between force and meaning into radical dissymmetry. But the excessive meaning that kills is at the same time motivated by a need to establish the overwhelming power of meaning that is the underlying force of the act. Again, there is no way to tell the force from the meaning.

The difference between riddle as a deficit of meaning and the fatal word as an excess of meaning breaks down in the case that will be the central and decentered example here: the *vow*. Denoting an as-yet-unknown, hence, nonexisting victim, the vow belongs on the side of the riddle. Killing that unknown victim, however, becomes its excessive meaning that at the same time instates the radical dissymmetry of power between speaker and victim. Hence, it is an act whose meaning is excessive but whose force is no less excessive. Thus, it challenges the assumption that the force and meaning of utterances can be somehow distributed or that they are different, distinct aspects.

Where seduction rests on the capacity and power of the victim to misunderstand,[6] hence, to participate, be it perversely, in the speech act, the vow, to the contrary, the promise of gift eliminates the victim from the linguistic process. The only function in the communicative process left open to the object, a function that the three victims of Judges each seem to cling to, is to become speech, in body language. Beth (formerly the "concubine") is again the most extreme case: She is conditionally given to many, the condition being that the rapists leave the husband alone. The gift is repeated after her death: her body is cut into pieces and sent to the tribes, as a letter containing a message. This is a case, if ever there is one, of the scandal of the speaking body.

SAMSON'S RIDDLE:
THE WORD BECOME WOMAN

During the seven days' party preceding his wedding, Samson "put forth a riddle" to the thirty Philistine companions of the feast. The riddle runs as follows:

> Out of the eater came forth food
> and out of the strong came forth sweetness.

> (14:14)

As a speech act, the riddle is based on a position of power. The subject who proposes the riddle knows the answer, while the addressee does not. Moreover, there is power in the initiative itself. It presupposes the right to be listened to, the obligation on the part of the addressee to invest the effort to find the answer. In the case of a stake, the power is betokened by the possession of the stake. There is a conditioned promise involved. All these aspects are explicit in the speech act that precedes the riddle itself, its staging:

> Let me now put forth a riddle unto you; if you can declare it me within the seven days of the feast and find it out, then I will give you thirty garments and thirty changes of raiment; and if you cannot declare it me, then you shall give me thirty linen garments and thirty changes of raiment.

> (14:12)

The companions accept the challenge. Thus they submit themselves to the power of the addresser; they hope or trust that they can reverse the situation.

When, later, the answer is revealed, it turns out to be a "bad" riddle, a riddle that cannot be "found out" at all by anybody else but the addresser. The riddle's answer/meaning is Samson's secret performance and transgression, the killing of the lion and the eating of honey out of the corpse's belly. The event is fraught with ambiguities, and so is the riddle that represents it, that assigns to it a core function in the narrative. The distinction between the general and the particular has not been respected. The riddle turns out to be based on an event that has been told by the narrator to the reader, not by Samson to the companions. Without that narrative act, the event remains particular and cannot be "found out." The riddle as a genre is based on another impossibility: although it must be understandable *after* explanation, it cannot be before. The explanation turns the arbitrary into the logical and the particular into the general.[7] Given these conventions and their transgression, we can at this point already predict that the companions need to appeal to resources other than their own inventiveness to find the riddle out. And, given the structure of power involved, we can foresee that the revelation of the riddle as an inaccessible one must cause a crisis.

The relation between riddle and vow is so far a simple one: a riddle with a stake contains a vow.[8] The vow, in this context, is the conditioned promise of something else. The stake is, typically, not the subject itself or the addressee, but a third object, or a third person for that matter. This introduction of the third person in the process is what distinguishes the vow from many other speech acts. The obligation it entails not only compensates the indeterminacy implied in its being conditional *and* future, but it is also in its turn compensated by the derivative third object, stake, or victim. Unlike the seduction through promise of marriage, the vow involves an objectification that excludes the object from the process, yet decides over her life and death. The victim of the vow does not have the possibility of accepting or rejecting the arrangement. Her collaboration in the speech act is not conditional for its "felicity." The asymmetry, then, becomes a dissymmetry, a power structure that radically separates the third party from the process as a nonparticipant, yet the most thoroughly affected one.[9]

Fig. 2. Rembrandt, Sketch after Leonardo's "Last Supper," 1635. The Metropolitan Museum of Art, Robert Lehman Collection. The Leonardo serves as a model for the composition of Rembrandt's Samson Posing the Riddle to the Wedding Guests.

The riddle predicts that dissymmetry. The stake proposed is, as we have seen, the symbol of the power structure that Samson tries to establish through the riddle. The all-male company in which the speech act is accomplished, together with the generic feature of unsolvability, and the future tense that points to the future wherein the wedding-to-come necessarily breaks the all-male unity by the introduction of the woman, the crisis that cannot but break out because of the dissymmetry of interests, all suggest a problematic of possession in the future where a woman is at stake.[10] Is she, also, the stake?

The riddle has a meaning that is its answer; it has a meaning as riddle, and the act of proposing it has a meaning. The analysis of these three semantic aspects shows not only that the distinction between force and meaning fails but also that its failure itself is thematized *in* the meaning. The answer to the riddle is given by the companions, who have used Kallah to get the answer through Samson himself. Hence, the riddle's meaning is self-referential. This self-referentiality is appropriate, as the answer reveals:

> What is sweeter than honey?
> And what is stronger than a lion?

(14:18)

Samson, the hero of strength, signifies himself in the riddle, his strength: force. Here, too, force precludes meaning.

A second feature of the meaning of the riddle-and-answer combination is the paradox in the riddle and the banality in the answer. Samson's extraordinary strength is the semantic core of the answer, as its concealment is of the riddle. There is an attempt to be someone very special that is encouraged by the hero's, the *gibbor*'s, encounter with the lion in the previous episode, and that suggests his power to him; hence the riddle.[11] The special power that his strength encompasses is, however, secret by definition, and not necessarily available in all circumstances. Proposing the riddle, then, is not only using that power; it is also a way to make it known. But, paradoxically again, the game depends on secrecy, and the revelation of the answer destroys the power. There is a logical conflict the subject is entangled in, and which leads, ultimately, to the failure of the act.

The answer, as already suggested, cannot be found out without the help of a mediator between subject and addressee. Samson has to reveal the answer himself, and the question is how this self-referentiality can be broken open, in order for the companions to have access to the knowledge. The meaning of the riddle as revealed in the answer is the combination of sweetness and strength. But the site of strength, its subject, is not, as is generally assumed, Samson himself; at least, not univocally. The lion, in the founding scene of the riddle, is not Samson but his antagonist. The one whose belly yields sweetness like honey is combined, conflated, with the strong one. The first meaning of the riddle is, then, the formidable woman. The identification with the lion does not predict much good for her; the lion can only yield sweetness when dead.

On the third level of meaning, proposing a riddle is, as we have already suggested, usurping a position of power that the subject may not (yet) deserve. The conflict that ensues from that usurpation is signified in the generic properties of the riddle itself. The companions, then, need to go and find access to the subject's mind. They go to the most obvious candidate: the woman. The choice is obvious not only because of the wedding situation, but also because the identification between sweet and strength in the riddle signifies marriage itself, and proposes that conflation as its meaning. It expresses, in fact, Samson's view of marriage. Samson will be subjected, then, to (part of) himself, in order to reveal instead of conceal it. The dialogic speech act that is the combination of riddle and answer requires a third party, an "excess" whose trace remains in order to betoken the force at stake. That violence will be used to erase that trace, a violence that, as another aspect of force, will leave its trace in its narrative account is therefore unavoidable.

But how can we talk about these meanings at all? We can do so on the basis of the presupposition that there exists a sequence of events that not only trigger, motivate, the speech act, but also determine its meaning. Without the event with the lion, known to us, unknown to the participants—hence, without its secret—there is no meaning possible in the riddle. There lies precisely its generic flaw: riddles are supposed to be generalizable. This narrative anchoring in the particular story of this particular *gibbor* is what makes it, as a riddle, both impossible and typical of the series of riddles in the book of Judges. It makes it the motor of the narrative.[12] It brings it close to the vow. The outcome of the riddle is equally embedded narratively in the whole story. It determines its status as a particular type of speech act: the one that lacks meaning. It has no meaning outside the sequence; hence, its motivation and meaning are but one. Narrativity produces the riddle and answer, and the latter requires the narrative. The metonymic relation between narrative and riddle is the *slip* of the speech act. As in psychoanalysis, the slip is not the excess of the narrative, it is its motor. As such, it motivates, energizes, it *is* the narrative. Hence, on this level, too, force and meaning are conflated.

If this is the case, then, we must conclude that the riddle, as the motor of the narrative, signifies already the end of its plot(ting): Kallah's death. The force of the speech act is motivated by the need to undo the woman who mediates between the subject and the addressee and who is, ultimately, the stake. The sequence that the riddle constitutes by linking the lion episode to the following one follows the line of increasing violence, only to end in Kallah's death. This linear movement is itself signified in nonlinear predictions; the meaning that is her death is predicted much earlier. The dead lion prefigures it, the companions announce it, and Samson triggers it. When they try to find out the riddle, the companions say to Kallah:

> Entice your man that he may declare unto us the riddle, lest we burn you and your father's house with fire. Have you called us hither to impoverish us?
>
> (14:15)

The first sentence here, signifies the conflation between Samson and Kallah; it is obviously she, not Samson himself, who must declare the riddle to them, after getting the answer from him. The second part of the sentence predicts Kallah's death, as the bride living in her father's house. The death, conditionally promised, equals the vow in the proposition of the riddle. The last sentence attributes responsibility to her, but if we look at the passage that precedes the wedding, we see that the subjects who "called them hither" are, again, both Samson and the Philistines. It is significant that, all through Kallah's story, the agents are thus conflated.

As in psychoanalysis there is no story without the motivation, the force that pushes the subject to tell it, and that lies both in the past and in the present of the speech act, similarly, there is, in Judges in general, and in this riddle episode in particular, no riddle without story, and no story without riddle; no present tense without a past that predicts the future. It is in the future that the word of the speech act becomes flesh, burned flesh; and the flesh is female.

THE RIDDLE AS VOW
AND THE VOW AS RIDDLE

We have seen that the riddle was proposed within the context of a vow: a conditioned gift. The basic feature of the riddle, its concealed meaning, made it possible for the narrative logic to produce the third party, the mediator, object of violence toward which the sequence leads, as the ultimate object of the conditioned gift. This turns the riddle into a vow, a vow like Jephthah's: one that promises to give what the subject does not *know.* To know and to possess, both expressions for the sexual encounter from the male perspective, are thus intimately related. One cannot possess what one does not know, for how can one know whether or not one possesses it? And one cannot give what one does not possess; hence, giving the unknown is a priori an act of abuse.

Riddles have a specific relation to the real in which they interfere. They pose, and dispose of, the unknown; so do vows. The first vow of the book of Judges is the case that the traditional readings of the book eliminate as part of the prologue: the conditioned gift of Achsah, chief Caleb's daughter, to the prospective conqueror of Kiriath-sepher, the city of books. This vow is the example of the "proper" vow: although it disposes of the daughter in a way we would, today, not rave about, it is in accordance with the tradition it signifies, and the following episode shows that it is, within the context, "proper" enough to serve as a model.[13] Unless we are extremely ethnocentric, we cannot refer to this gift as rape. Nor, for that matter, as history in the traditional sense. It does not generate the next episode, it does not relate to the rest of the book by continuity. The vow is fulfilled, and its beneficiary is generally considered to be the model of the ideal judge. The vow leaves no rest, nothing to regret, to blame, or to guess. Nothing to tell.

In comparison to Samson's riddle, this vow/riddle makes explicit what the other one tried to conceal: the identity of the third party, the stake, she who has no participation in the speech act while she is its object. The vow modifies the real in that it triggers a narrative sequence: first, the *gibbor* qualifies for the award, changing the situation of the city; then, he receives the award, changing the situation of the daughter. Achsah becomes, through this narrative, an *ʿalmah*. She accedes to the third of the three phases of female ripeness, and is thus separated from her father.[14]

Riddles have a specific relation to truth: they establish it. Truth is, let's say, a perfectly adequate relation between a statement and its referent, between language and the material reality it represents. Riddles conceal that reality, but their answers, which are always, typically, the only possible answer, are undeniably true. One does not challenge the answer to a riddle. The same holds for vows. The vow promises the gift of the unknown object; once the identity of the object is revealed, there is, at least within the biblical epistemology, no possible challenge to it, as Bath-Jephthah's fate sadly shows.

This feature of the riddle is interestingly exploited by Yael in verses 4:20–23. The exhausted chief Sisera, on his flight after the defeat of his army, is invited by Yael to seek refuge in her tent. He prepares to go and sleep, and then, Sisera gives Yael an order:

> Stand in the opening/door of the tent and it shall be, when any man comes and asks you and says: is there any man here? you will say: none.

Is this speech act a riddle, a vow, or something else? It is an order in the first place. But as an order, it misfires. Sisera's circumstances do not give him the authority required for ordering. The failed order embeds a question of identity that assimilates it to the riddle. The question is not, this time, *who* the man will be, but *what* he is: a man, or not a man? Typically, the negation allows for indeterminacy, and in the space created by that property, both characters respond to the speech act in a different way. For Sisera, the answer was obviously meant to deny his presence; it was an order to lie. For Yael, the speech act was a riddle, and riddles have perfect truth-value. Hence, the answer meant for her: no man. The riddle consists, then, of finding out how a man can be no man. Her answer is: as a dead man, and she acts upon it. This can be read as a response to Samson's riddle: how can a strong lion/woman yield pleasure? Answer: if she is a dead lion/woman. Sisera's involuntary riddle shares properties with the vow as well. It is emphatically phrased in the future tense, the object is not participating in the dialogue, and, as is systematically the case in the vows of Judges, it leads to death. Turning the misfired order upside down, Yael "obeys" it, but turns the lie into a question of identity.

Riddles have a specific relation to desire. They stage the desire to know which is the erotic desire of the Hebrew male. Proposing a question is proposing, for the addressee, the possibility of knowing: of knowing the object of the desire to know, of enjoying her, as the stake of the game. Samson's riddle—caught in the web of the narrative that produced and was produced by it—was about the desire to know what yields pleasure through violent appropriation, and that is precisely the view of eroticism that the book exclusively represents.

The riddle that becomes the interpretation of the negative vows, the threats that we also find in the book, has a similar relation to desire. Two examples suffice, here. When Barak does not take Deborah/Yahweh's promise of victory at face value, in 4:8, it is because, like Jephthah, he needs help from a real *gibbor*, someone unlike himself. Deborah turns his vow ("if you will go with me, I will go") into a riddle when she responds with the negative promise:

I will surely go with you; but the road you undertake shall not be for your
honor; for Yahweh will give Sisera into the hand of a woman.

(4:9)

As a reversal of the daughter-of-the-chief, Sisera, the chief of the enemy
army, will be given into the hand of the real victor: a woman. The riddle that ensues from this threat is, of course, the identity of the woman, who is, however, this time not the object but the beneficiary of the
gift. Again, the sexual aspect of the riddle is part of it. The woman can
only "get at" the fugitive through seduction, through the promise of
safety, comfort, in her tent, in her bed.[15] Giving him into the hand of
a woman is, then, nothing else than what custom prescribes: to give in
marriage.

The negative vow, toward the end of Judges, to give no daughters as
wives to the Benjaminites, leads to a question that provides another
striking example of the sexuality inherent in riddles. The vow threatens to exterminate the tribe of Benjamin, hence, to destroy the wholeness of the people. The riddle it entails is, then: how to provide wives
to the Benjaminites without breaking the vow not to give them? The
question of identity is implicit: who can these wives and nonwives be?
But again, the indeterminacy also allows for the other possible question: how can they be Israelite women, in spite of the vow? Again, the
truth of the riddle, the reality-changing aspect of the vow, cannot be
questioned. And again, the answer is logical in retrospect. The issue of
the riddle is not in the gift or in the identity of the object, both being
determined by the vow and the law. The issue turns out to be the question: how to avoid giving? The objects of the gift—women—and wom-
en who will guarantee ethnic purity through endogamy—will not be
given but stolen, abducted; in our understanding, certainly raped.[16]
The negativity of the description matches the negativity of the production: only by killing those who are *not* the objects of the riddle can
those objects come into existence.

If desire is acted out in such negative, destructive ways, and if the
narrative needs these actings-out in order to move on, we cannot but
draw the conclusion that between narrative, desire, and violence there

is a close bond. The violence the riddles in the book result in is the form taken by the appropriation that, according to Felman, is implied in seduction. The riddle-as-vow and the vow-as-riddle both explore the modalities of appropriation by language, by the power relations involved in speech acts. The playful reversal that seduction allows, and that Felman's own text illustrates, the reversal that gives the addressee the possibility of escaping the status of object and of gaining that of subject, is strictly impossible in the case of the fatal speech act, riddle and vow. The appropriation is performed outside of the object's participation. The appropriation is there radical, deadly.

THE DAUGHTER'S BODY LANGUAGE
AS A CHALLENGE TO FATHERHOOD

Samson's riddle causes Kallah's death just as much as Jephthah's vow causes Bath's. Apart from Samson, it seems to be primarily the father who, in Judges, performs the crucial speech act of the vow. Jephthah despairs over his cognitive failure. Not knowing whether or not he will qualify as a *gibbor*, he gives away what he does not *know*. It is his fatherhood that he gives away, showing that it is, in this sense, as insecure as is that of Manoah, Samson's failing father. Both fathers speak too much and are punished for it. If Manoah is corrected by the messenger, Jephthah, however, never learns the lesson. He seems to be a compulsive speaker, and, moreover, he seems pretty good at it. His success in the negotiations over his position as leader (11:6–11), his shrewd device to tell an Ephraimite from a Gileadite (12:5–6), and his tendency to negotiate before fighting, show that, for Jephthah, the mouth that utters words is closely related to what the Hebrew so happily expresses as "the mouth of the sword."[17] The lethal quality of his words adds to that effect. The question that arises from that relation is: is there a bond between speech and violence, and is that bond a polemical response to the failure, inherent in fatherhood, to reach material contiguity with the daughter? I will return to Jephthah's central role in the narrative of this problem, but, in order to assess the relations between the speaking killers and the language of their victims, we will first look at the daughterly speech acts which are, typically, acts of body language.

Body speech, like verbal speech, never stands alone; in other words, the sign is always part of a "text" and its utterance, of a sequence of utterances. Achsah's confrontation with her father, when she claps her hands to attract his attention, and then claims her due, is initiated by her nonverbal act that prepares her father for a surprising, yet respected desire. Her speech is successful; again, she provides a model against which the subsequent body speeches of the daughters stand out as its negatives. Within the limited focus of the present discussion, Achsah is not only a model as the daughter who, given away, yet assumes a subject position. Her story reveals that she is also a model of daughterly speech acts. Her request must be situated within the thoroughly patriarchal structure where daughters are promised as conditioned gifts, as stakes for military bravery, where they are the shifters between the two coherences of political and social history. She, too, is vowed away for the sake of the "higher" interests: war and "national" unity. But within those limits, she shows what language, if "properly" used, can perform: it can result in water, rather than fire. In the interpretations of her story, it is often assumed that it functions etiologically to explain the claim of Achsah's descendants, to the wells which "by their situation seemed naturally to belong to Caleb's descendants."[18] The assumption that there is a conflict at all between the two groups contradicts what is often taken to be the uncontested primacy of virilocal marriage and the patriliny that excludes the daughter's father. I suggest, indeed, that the claim for her own descendants must be seen in the light of the nonselfevidence of virilocy. If Achsah claims the wells, she seems to cause surprise precisely because it is not so "natural" that her descendants are different from Caleb's. The etiological function receives, then, a much more profound meaning: the claim is not just a matter of personal ambition but of social transition. Othniel has as much interest in this issue as has Beth's father in chapter 19.

If patrilocy versus virilocy is, indeed, the underlying issue of the conflict, the body of the daughter as the material mediator of the line of descent is the site of the struggle. It seems appropriate, then, that the language used is body language. Generating history—descendants—the body also generates narrative, but only if it is violented as is Beth's, not if it functions "properly" as does Achsah's. The daughter, by using body language in her address to her father, acknowledges the function that is assigned to her. Since the father, in his vow, disposes of her body, her distancing from him in following a husband is acted out in the semiotic use of the body. Speaking through it, she signifies its performative power: the force of the speech act. Thus recuperating, for her *as* body, a subject position, Achsah's gesture sets the limits to the father's absolute power. That limit is the body as producer of descendants: life. The water she claims is the indispensable material support of the life whose production saves her subjectivity. At the same time, the bodily nature of her speech act enhances the materiality of the daughter's way to establish descent, as opposed to the father's: through her body. Her daughterly submission also contains her future motherhood.

At the other end of the book, Beth's body language sadly echoes Achsah's. She also uses her hands, but she cannot forcefully clap them; rendered powerless by the men's abuse, she can only passively lay down her hands in a meaningful direction. Where Achsah's father responds to her gesture with the acknowledgment of her right to speak, to desire, to be, the husband of the already destroyed Beth responds with the opposite attitude. Instead of the question "what unto you?" (what do you want? 1:14) he gives the order: "Up!" Beth's gesture is not acknowledged as an initiator of the phatic function. The hands on the threshold that both accuse and implore are ignored by the husband to whom they are addressed. Beth's claim to safety in the house is countered by the husband's final attempt to take her to *his* house. In some sense, her gesture is similar to Achsah's, however. Both women are addressing the man who gave her away. Both choose to follow the husband, leaving the father. But while Achsah addresses her father from above, Beth addresses her husband from below. The gift of her was improper; it led not to marriage and descendants but to rape and death; instead of assessing her subject position, it destroyed it. While Achsah's father faces her, Beth's husband steps over her.[19] When in the morning he opens the door, the verb used is *jephtha*.[20] And indeed: "behold, the woman, his [patrilocal] wife." The language is that of visuality, of voyeurism, of one-sided power relations. It is here that the hands on the threshold, Beth's final, powerless act of body speech, are mentioned, and ignored. They misfire. Like Achsah, Beth speaks within the limits assigned to her: as body. But where Achsah, whose daughter position was "properly" acknowledged, could add verbal speech, Beth can speak no more.

Beth's story does not end on this gesture. It is one of a series of increasingly violent events generated by her rape. Her body is put to further semiotic use. The peaceful deal between Caleb and Othniel was possible because their blood relation allowed them to overcome, or rather to ignore, the virtual conflict between patrilocy and virilocy. It was mediated by Achsah's request for the life source. This deal is inverted into an ever-increasing mechanism of violence brought about by a deal that betokened the refusal to respect the bodily integrity of the daughter. Beth's body will be used to speak, but it is no longer Beth who speaks. Her body is

> divided, limb by limb, into twelve pieces, and he sent her throughout all the borders of Israel.
>
> (19:29)

The totally destroyed subject becomes the speaker to the whole nation. The obscure, anonymous husband gains, through the use of her body as language, a position that comes close to that of a *gibbor*. This act turns the domestic conflict into a major political issue.[21] But unlike Othniel, who also used Achsah to establish himself as a husband as powerful as the father, this man gains his position through the destruction of the daughter/woman whose body could have brought him life. Beth's dead body can speak, but by a perverse twist it is the man who totally subjected her, not herself, who speaks. In order to assess the meaning of this difference, let us return briefly to the body language that precedes the two discussed instances: the rape.

The meaning of the particular punishment inflicted on the attempt to establish virilocal marriage has been understood in various ways,

Fig. 3. Rembrandt, The Levite Finds His Concubine in the Morning (no date). Kupferstichkabinett, Berlin-Dahlem. Although the body lies still, the right hand seems to move. This enhances the sign-function of the gesture.

none of them satisfactory. Although the threat of homosexual rape is sometimes interpreted as a challenge "to standards of proper cultural civilized behavior, as the Israelites would define such behavior,"[22] as a symbolic gesture, its meaning in relation to the other body-speech acts of the story is not examined. The oblivion of these relations leads to astonishing gestures of repression. Robert Alter gives a clear instance of this repression.[23] He qualifies the story of Judges 19 as a "hetero-sexual companion-piece" of Genesis 19. The threat is here separated from the "real" act in a way that conceals the *language:* force and meaning together.[24] In a sense, rape is the body speech act par excellence. It is well known that rape victims experience the act as aggressive, not lustful; the rapist as a misogynist full of hatred not as the excusable frustrated loner. Homosexual rape is equally motivated by hatred of the object, and it is "logical" that it is often committed by heterosexual men. Rape being motivated by hatred, not by lust, men who hate and fear women and their attraction to them will rape women, while men who hate and fear men and their attraction to them will rape men. Homophobia and heterocentrism parallel gynophobia and androcentrism. To rape is to speak the hatred. Often, the act is accompanied by (or should we say: accomplished through?) offensive verbal language, as if the symbolic meaning of the act needed to be enhanced. It is also an act of cutting, of dividing the flesh, destroying its wholeness, hence the subject. It alienates the victim from herself *and is meant to do so.* Why, then, is there so much hatred, on the part of the inhabitants of Gibeah, and why is it addressed to the man? Why is the language chosen to express the hatred this particular body language of sexuality, and why is rape required to promote the narrative further? The rapists hate the man for challenging their institution of sexual relations. That the punishment has to be sexual is already motivated by this contiguity between crime and punishment. The issue is the "natural" right of physical property of the father over the daughter, in an attempt to make fatherhood "natural" by imposing bodily contiguity as its basis.

The language of rape can be seen in the light of this obsession. The aggression of rape is the speech act of contiguity par excellence. The hatred is spoken by one body into the other. But there is more to it.

The threat of rape of the husband is the threat to turn his body into anybody's property. Thus the rapists signify the insult on the father's property that the man is guilty of. The daughter belongs "naturally" to her father; this is the only accepted and culturally sanctioned contiguous bond. Going away to another man, going astray, is going to be any man's property. Any man, the arbitrariness of signification of relations that is so hard to accept, is understood as "every man." Between the "natural" owner and "any man" there is no difference as long as the daughter's choice is not acknowledged, her subject position ignored. It is the man who, by taking away the daughter, is responsible for her being anybody's, everybody's property. The gift of Beth, her rejection by the husband and delivery to the rapists, acknowledges that meaning.[25] It is the gesture by which the Levite submits to the other institution.

If the homosexual rape is thus the equivalent alternative to the heterosexual rape of Beth in the night-long torture session, the host verbalizes this equivalence very pointedly. To rape is to humiliate, and that is to be done not to the man but to the daughters. The reluctance to male rape occurs not simply because men are more valuable subjects and hence have a primary claim to protection, for the murder of men is not precisely shunned in the book of Judges. It is, more profoundly, because raping him would be a symbolic gesture, signifying the responsibility of the man for the daughter's alienation from the father, while raping her partakes in the contiguity that is so basic to fatherhood. That is why the rapists do accept the gift of Beth, while they refused the gift of the two daughters that was a simple compensation.

Judges 19 ends with an imperative: *speak*, a masculine-plural response to the mute speech of Beth's divided flesh. Just as the husband responded by a misfired order, since the circumstances were, to use Austin's happy term, "infelicitous," the tribes fail their response by abuse, since they address their order to speak not to the "speaker" but to the husband. The speaking body itself is ignored: the tribes blame the Benjaminites, not the husband and what he stands for. Thus, the speaking body fails to speak because it is not listened to. There lies the deepest scandal of the speaking body: it is not permitted to speak.

The daughters, in Judges, speak through their bodies, thus showing the materiality of speech in its specific, socially determined framework. Their speech acts reveal that it is the female body that is the stake of the speech act that circumscribes it. It produces, in the men between whom they are defined or divided, the identity that is indispensable to the construction of the *gibbor.* Full possession, full power of disposal over the daughter's body, is what they desperately try to come by. The materiality that their relations to their offspring seems to lack is produced by the contiguity they seek. Contiguity, and its linguistic figuration, metonymy, is the foundation of the speech of the daughters. The question that then arises is: how do the fathers act as speakers in their strife for materiality?

THE MOUTH OF THE S/WORD

At this point, we have to return to Jephthah, the hero of the cutting word. When he realizes that his word killed his daughter, he laments over himself. The confusion, signified not only in his "blaming the victim" but even in a so-called copist error,[26] points to the basic problem of Judges, which is the problem of fatherhood, the father line, and the construction of the "people" through it.

One of Austin's favorite metaphors is fire; one of Don Juan's characteristic assets is his sword. Felman points out that the interesting challenge to truth implied in fire is that it is undecidable whether it is a thing or an event.[27] The same can be said of the sword-in-action, the instrument of "rupture," the breaking off of relations, and of "*coupure,*" the cutting: penetrating and dividing. The same can be said of words: are they things, to be placed in a sequence and to be read by innocent bystanders, or are they events not that *are* things but that *do* things? Jephthah is the master of manipulation of the sword, word, and fire. His cutting sword kills, in close collaboration with his cutting language. His fatal words are motivated by the same conflict that caused the murder of Beth: insecurity about lineage, history; an insecurity that generates the narrative, using rape and murder as its device.

The language of the fathers is a language of power. It is through that language that Jephthah establishes himself as the head of the Israelite people, in his negotiations with the elders of Gilead (11:6–11). The central element and the stake of the negotiations are Jephthah's sword: he requires appointment, not as a temporary, military *katsin*, but as permanent head, *rosh*, after the victory. But negotiation is not only about or for power, it is also based on power. Thus Jephthah negotiates his own status as leader over the people that had expelled him as the son of "another woman," a "harlot" or patrilocal wife, on the basis of his power as a master of the sword. The term "head" seems appropriate for the hero of the mouth: to be "head" compensates on more levels than one for the expulsion from the father house, from history, from contiguity with forefathers and offspring. The fatal vow, utterly futile since the Judge has sent his spirit already, displays Jephthah's addiction to negotiation, the speech act of and for power. We may wonder why the repetition compulsion is so insistent. Negotiation is based on power; who has none, has nothing to negotiate with. But it is also a recognition of the limits of power; the negotiator has something, and lacks something. Jephthah, the to-be head of the people, hero of might, has the power of his s/word, but he lacks some other power, the power that would give him security, certainty about his victory. If the divine Judge is appealed to here to decide, first, to accomplish, next, the victory Jephthah is hired to perform, it is because the negotiator, the man of speech, realizes that fundamental lack.

Like Don Juan, Jephthah is a master of "rupture" and *"coupure."* Breaking away from the father's house, he later breaks with his only child, a break that costs him his identity—and her, her life. His attempts to counter this movement of "rupture," of breaking, by reinserting himself in the line, use *"coupure,"* killing, just as in the case of the rapists in chapter 19. The weapon of negotiation, the mouth that must provide him with the position in history that he strives for, is replaced with the weapon of killing that must materialize the delicate, insecure position he thus conquered: the mouth of the sword. His basic insecurity betrays itself doubly in his fatal vow: not only does he show himself to have no confidence in his own *gibbor*-ship, he also proposes a riddle with a stake that is contiguous to himself. The "comer-out of his house to meet him" is also the materialization of his relationship to his (father's) house. The daughter's body that can either secure the line or destroy it, according to his power over her, is his "exclusive possession."

It is precisely the exclusivity of that possession[28] that can never be secured. Fatherhood is never certain, the father line is always doubtful, and Jephthah, the son of the "other" woman is well placed to realize it. The use of the s/word that he seems to master so well is itself not a clear-cut enterprise. The *shibboleth* episode in 12:5–6 is, in its ambiguity, a *mise en abyme*[29] of Jephthah's problematics which in its turn is that of the whole book. It parallels the rape scene of 19 in that function. The situation is war; we are in the middle of the political coherence. The mouth of the sword, not the mouth of the word, is the appropriate weapon in the circumstances. But Jephthah abuses the word; he uses it in inappropriate circumstances. Killing, as he now has learned, is tricky; the sword can kill the self. It is crucial to tell—to know—a Gileadite from an Ephraimite, a member of the father house from the others. The trick Jephthah devises to "judge," that is, to distinguish, is verbal: a riddle, again. The question is: who belongs to the father line? The criterion is the "proper" pronunciation of the word *shibboleth*, "proper" being according to the pronunciation in the father's house. Language determines the father line. The mouth of the word enables the mouth of the sword to be effective, not the other way around. As such, the episode signifies the priority of language over the body, while at the same time proclaiming the materiality of language, its bodily effectiveness and foundation: its basis in contiguity.

Derrida relates *shibboleth* to circumcision, the cut that divides and defines. Circumcision is not an issue in Judges, but it is replaced. Two cuts take over its function: the rape that kills the inappropriately appropriated woman, and the cut of the mouth of the s/word. It is, then, not the male member that is circumcised, but the male word. Derrida formulates it as follows:

> The circumcision of the word must also be understood as an event of the body, in a way essentially analogous to the diacritical difference between *Shibboleth* and *Sibboleth*. It was in their bodies, in a certain impotence of

their vocal organs, that the Ephraimites experienced their inability to pronounce what they nonetheless knew ought to be pronounced *Shibboleth*. The word *Shibboleth*, for some an "unpronounceable name," is a circumcised word.[30]

That the impotence or potency is situated not in the male member but in the male head, the site of knowledge, of symbolization, but also the site of the knowledge of the insufficiency of symbolization, is quite appropriate. Jephthah has learned, in his long career as *gibbor*, how to become a hero of masculinity, of paternity: of memory. Memory, the historization of language, is another form of its materialization. Master killer, he is also the master speaker of the book of Judges. It is through his story that the narrative of the deliverers and that of the judges, so obstinately separated by many philologists, are convincingly linked together.[31]

There is yet another relation between the mouth that utters speech and the body. It is represented in the material satisfaction of the mouth par excellence, food, and it is used to express bondage. Bonding it does indeed, not only between father and husband but also, in the narrative, between the two major "cuts": rape and murder. Bread, *lehem*, the material consecration of bonding that the messenger, in chapter 13, refuses to accept from Samson's prospective father, is again the object of rejection and temptation in chapter 19. In his attempt to keep his daughter, Beth's father confronts the husband in his own house, in Beth-lehem, the house of bread. The site of the exclusive possession of the daughter is also the site of the father's speech. After three days of hospitality, the husband prepares to leave the house, but the father will not let him go. He retains him with the words:

> Support your heart with a morsel of bread, and afterwards you shall go your way.

> (19:5)

The noun "heart" recalls the expression "to speak to her heart" in verse 3, misinterpreted today as kind concern.[32] It refers to the site of reason. The expression in 3 means "to persuade her." If we take it that the heart has a similar function here, the father's words may suggest that the husband be more reasonable, that he accept the house of bread as a better place to be, and the father house as the appropriate place for the daughter to be, for lineage and history to establish themselves.

The last part of this speech seems a failure through abuse: the next episode shows that the father had no intention to let the man go; the promise is no promise-with-a-future. But this may be yet another case of a failure, not of the speaker but of the addressee, a failure to understand the force rather than the meaning. The question—or the riddle—implied in the speech act is: what will the husband's "own way" be, after having strengthened his heart with the father's bread? Like Manoah's invitation, the father's invitation to share a meal is an attempt to establish the group, the community of the father house. After eating the father's bread, the man is expected to have "his own way" within the father house. The speech act is meant to establish, through bread, the contiguity that only the daughter can provide. The failure, then, is misfire: the circumstances are inappropriate. The father does promise with the intention to carry out his promise, but the riddle is not acknowledged by the addressee. Food, then, is more than the material satisfaction of the mouth. It is also what relates the word to the body. Bread is spoken rather than eaten; as spoken attempt to establish who belongs to the father's house and who does not, the offer of bread is the offer of contiguity, of participation in the material symbolization of fatherhood. Taking the daughter away from the father without providing his own "way," his own house of bread, the husband cannot but fail to replace the father. Once arrived at his house, there will be no bread for the mouth, only the mouth of the knife that will cut and separate, not bond and share.

The mouth of the s/word is, in Judges, the site of the materiality of language as a mediation between symbolic fatherhood and its material anchoring in the daughter's body. Bread, or corn,[33] or the water that allows it to grow, is virtually the positive side of the contiguity to be established, but it is unsuccessful because the speech act misfires. The sword as well as the penis of the rapist is the negative side of the same attempt: one group, line, contiguity is established through separation from the other. The priority of the word itself uttered by the mouth of the father who is so forcefully motivated to use force as speech, is betokened in the core speech act of the failing father: Jephthah's vow, which does not feed the mouth, but kills through it.

Jephthah's *shibboleth* device was an attempt to tell one group from the other. To tell, in this sense, is to differentiate, to discriminate. The act is the one that gave the book of Judges its title, explicit in the Greek version: *krittein*, to judge. It is also, to differentiate, the etymological meaning of critique. The more usual sense of "to tell" is: to produce narrative, to recount. *Shibboleth* seems, in this light, a failure to match the speech act of judgment, of differentiation, with the speech act of narration that is the speech act par excellence of memory; the speech act, also, that brought forth the book of Judges. If memory is the asset of maleness, if knowledge is the token of fatherhood, judgment is the decisive speech act that arbitrates between failed and successful attempt to actualize, to materialize, fatherhood. Judgment is the ideal that is replaced, by the powerless father, with the mouth of the s/word. In this sense, the *gibbor* is not a judge, in spite of his status as head. *Gibbor*-ship as represented by Jephthah is, rather, a reversal of judgeship—its impotence.

The cutting quality of the word that is meant to establish contiguity, the contiguity of ideal fatherhood and that, like fire, hovers between being thing or event, is linked to, placed in contiguity with, the site of "true" or "proper" contiguity: the house. The house is the word's other side, the materialization of the word whose materiality can only cut, not bond. It is the word's stake, as the site of fatherhood, betokened by the daughter's bondage in it. And it is the word become stone, its unavoidable realization, the hard aspect of the fugitive word used to produce meaning, permanence, memory. The narrative of Judges is, if about anything, about building the house, an enterprise that turns out to be highly problematic since the social structures that are to be its foundation are shaken.

This meaning of the book is generated by the characters' speech acts, not by the narrator's discourse. The story is not told; it is *done*. Beginning with Achsah's gift and gesture, the story becomes a story proper, a story with a future, at the moment of Samson's riddle. Kallah's death,

Bath's sacrifice, and Beth's utter destruction string the episodes together. Beth's rape is the climax of the violence and of the narrative. If we can conceive of the final composition of the book as one narrative at all, it is thanks to, not in spite of, chapter 19—the chapter that critics tend to eliminate, teachers to skip, and believers to disbelieve.

NOTES

I am grateful to the Gemäldegalerie, Dresden, the Metropolitan Museum of Art, Robert Lehman Collection, and the Kupferstichkabinett, Berlin, for permission to reproduce the Rembrandt works.

1. This form of marriage is known in anthropological literature under different names, all equally mystifying. As early as 1929, Julius Morgenstern enumerates all the cases he sees in the Hebrew Bible, without however discussing the consequences of his discovery for the interpretation ("*Beena* Marriage [Matriarchat] in Ancient Israel and its Historical Implications," *Zeitschrift für die Alttestamentliche Wissenschaft* 47 [1929]:91–110; see also "Additional Notes on *Beena* Marriage [Matriarchat] in Ancient Israel," *ZAW* 49 [1931]:46–58). I contend that the words traditionally rendered as "concubine" (*pilegesh*) and "prostitute" (*zonah*) refer to a patrilocal wife. Although I object to Morgenstern's idealizing term "matriarchy," the integration of this type of marriage in biblical interpretation has far-reaching consequences. See my *Death and Dissymmetry: The Politics of Coherence in Judges* (Chicago: University of Chicago Press, 1988).

2. Shoshana Felman, *Le scandale du corps parlant: Don Juan avec Austin ou la séduction en deux langues* (Paris: Editions du Seuil, 1980).

3. Elaine Scarry, *The Body in Pain: The Making and Unmaking of the World* (New York: Oxford University Press, 1985).

4. Eve Kosofsky Sedgwick, *Between Men: English Literature and Homosocial Desire* (New York: Columbia University Press, 1985).

5. J. L. Austin, *How to Do Things with Words* (Cambridge: Harvard University Press, 1975).

6. The power to misunderstand is crucial not only because it entails a position of participation in the communication process. Misunderstanding is, as

Jonathan Culler argues, a central aspect of semiosis (*On Deconstruction: Theory and Criticism after Structuralism* [London: Routledge & Kegan Paul, 1983]). Where Umberto Eco defined signs as everything that can be used in order to lie (*A Theory of Semiotics* [Bloomington: Indiana University Press, 1976]), Culler stresses the other side of the same definition: it is everything that can be misunderstood. The Bible provides a good case.

7. For an analysis of Samson's riddle, see O. Eissenfeldt, "Die Rätsel in Jud 14," *Zeitschrift für die Alttestamentliche Wissenschaft* 30 (1910):132–45.

8. In the literature on vows in the Hebrew Bible, no connection is established with the riddle, while all the vows have arguably such a relation. See, for example, Steven J. Brams, *Biblical Games: A Strategic Analysis of Stories in the Old Testament* (Cambridge: M.I.T. Press, 1980), and the popular G. Henton Davies, "Vows," *The Interpreter's Dictionary of the Bible* 4 (1962):792–93.

9. The distinction between asymmetry and dissymmetry is crucial for this essay. The word asymmetry refers to an absence of symmetry, while dissymmetry refers to a relevant relation wherein the expected and "logical" symmetry is replaced with a distortion of it that allows power to take its place between the two related subjects.

10. For those who doubt this deep involvement of the "woman problem" in the episode, I refer to Rembrandt's painting of Samson Posing the Riddle to the Wedding Guests (figure 1). The work is modeled on Leonardo da Vinci's *Last Supper*, which is a significant choice. The woman is isolated in the all-male company, and depicted as utterly alone. She has the position of Christ; Rembrandt's interpretation of her victimhood is strikingly sympathetic compared to the commentaries that massively blame this victim. Rembrandt's Sketch after Leonardo's "Last Supper" (figure 2) shows his interest in the spatial features of the work and his repetition of them in the Samson painting.

11. The noun *gibbor* is usually translated as *hero*. I argue in an earlier work that the concept needs more careful analysis. Briefly, it holds within it the ideas of power, physical power and/or political power, violent behavior, and maleness. The frequent combination *gibbor havil* is best translated as *hero of might*. The concept of hero is arguably different for each culture. Hence my decision to leave it untranslated. See my *Death and Dissymmetry: The Politics of Coherence in Judges*.

12. For this concept, see Peter Brooks, *Reading for the Plot: Design and*

Intention in Narrative (New York: Knopf, 1983). Although Brooks tends to by-pass the role of women as motors of the narrative, his idea if elaborated in that direction can be useful precisely for a gender-specific approach to traditional narrative.

13. We have here an obvious case where neither ethnocentrism nor cultural relativism can solve the problem; the event is clearly in accordance with social traditions and can only be criticized when distance from the context is acceptable. I do not want to argue that it should not be criticized; it should be, however, on a different level than the other events that I call "improper." It is only when a distinction such as this is carefully made that we can establish the system of values inscribed in the book, which is a prior condition even for beginning a critique.

14. The three phrases are *na'arah,* young girl, approaching physical ripeness yet in full possession of the father; *bethulah,* the state of transition, of full ripeness, ready to be handed over from father to husband; and *'almah,* just married, not yet pregnant, handed over to the husband. The very existence of these three concepts shows that the handing over of the daughter from father to husband is a crucial event that influences not only the lives of the young women but also the social structures that define the power relations between men.

15. See for a typical interpretation of the scene as repressed sexuality, Yair Zakovitch, "Siseras Tod," *Zeitschrift für die Alttestamentliche Wissenschaft* (1981) 93:364–74. The article is interesting also for the blindness it displays. Focusing on a possible sexual interpretation, the author fails to notice the *problematic* aspects of sexuality—its less glorious aspects, like a fixation on the mother—that his very evidence clearly suggests. See my *Murder and Difference: Gender, Genre and Scholarship on Sisera's Death* (Bloomington: Indiana University Press, 1987).

16. There is here again a question of the evaluation of a different cultural practice. The first of the two abduction scenes implies so much violence, however, that the negative value judgment, if implicit, is not impossible. For the problem of evaluation free of ethnocentrism, see Johannes Fabian, *Time and the Other: How Anthropology Makes Its Object* (New York: Columbia University Press, 1981), and Ton Lemaire, *Over de waarde van culturen* (Baarn: Ambo, 1978).

17. Given the subject of this essay, it seems appropriate to translate the

expression literally and replace the more usual English expression, "the edge of the sword," by its Hebraic counterpart.

18. A. Cohen, *Joshua. Judges: Hebrew Text and English Translation,* with introductions and commentary (London: Soncino Press, 1980), 160.

19. Jephthah's visual confrontation with Bath at the moment of the revelation of the identity of the victim can be compared to these two other scenes of focalization. Jephthah does also, in a way, ignore his daughter, since he says that he himself is destroyed. He then blames her for his destruction. This confusion of self and other points to a problem that we also see at work in Freud's "Taboo of Virginity": the incapacity to separate, as both the cause and the acting out, in the writing, of the taboo. See *Death and Dissymmetry.*

20. Patrick D. Miller, Jr., drew my attention to this verb, whose significance for the construction of the "countercoherence," the social interpretation, is considerable. His thoughtful and sympathetic response to a previous version of this analysis has been an important encouragement to me.

21. Explaining the story of Beth as etiological, as an explanation a posteriori of the intertribal war, is an act of manipulating the political coherence into a position of dominance that is by no means justified. The fallacy it rests on is betrayed by the "rest" the interpretation leaves out: it does not explain why intertribal war is integrated into a narrative claimed to be about external war.

22. Susan Niditch, "The 'Sodomite' Theme in Judges 19–20: Family, Community and Social Disintegration," *Catholic Bible Quarterly* (1982):367–68.

23. Robert Alter, *Motives for Fiction* (Cambridge: Harvard University Press, 1984), 132.

24. In *La volonté de savoir* (Paris: Gallimard, 1976), Michel Foucault convincingly argues the inseparability of language and sexual experience, indeed, the formative effect of the former on the latter. It is obvious that Alter misses this relation. As a result, he comes close to the illogical, and actually homophobic, assumption that the entire population of the town of Sodom was driven by homosexual desire. The repression of the linguistic presence of homosexual rape in Judges 19, on the other hand, is also evidence of the realistic fallacy.

25. In a certain sense, the rejection of her can also be seen as abjection. See Julia Kristeva, *Powers of Horror: An Essay on Abjection* (New York: Columbia University Press, 1982).

26. The narrator says: "besides *him* he had son nor daughter," and the commentators are quick to "correct" the error into "besides her." Too quick; they miss the point of the whole book.

27. Felman, *Le scandale*, 151.

28. The idea of "exclusive possession" of a woman comes from the opening sentence of Freud's "Taboo of Virginity" (1918): "The demand that a girl shall not bring to her marriage with a particular man any memory of sexual relations with another is, indeed, nothing other than the logical continuation of the right to exclusive possession of a woman, which forms the essence of monogamy, the extension of this monopoly over the past" (1957, Standard Edition 11:191–208). This statement and its "logic" are the best formulation of what is at stake in Judges.

29. See Lucien Dällenbach, *Le récit spéculaire. Essai sur la mise en bayme* (Paris: Editions du Seuil, 1978), for a theory of this figure that denotes the miniature within a narrative. For a critique of that theory, see Mieke Bal, *Femmes imaginaires. L'ancien testament au risque d'une narratologie critique* (Paris: Nizet, 1986), chap. 4.

30. Jacques Derrida, "Shibboleth," in *Midrash and Literature*, ed. Jeffrey Hartman and Sanford Budick (New Haven: Yale University Press, 1986), 344.

31. In *Murder and Difference*, I have analyzed the theory of Wolfgang Richter (*Traditionsgeschichtliche Untersuchungen zum Richterbuch* [Bonn: Peter Hanstein Verlag, 1963]), which is generally accepted (see, for example, A. D. H. Mayes, *The Story of Israel between Settlement and Exile: A Redactional Study of the Deuteronomic History* [London: SCM Press, 1983]). The theory is not only based on a circular argument, but is also clearly devised in order to get rid of the disturbing case of Deborah. It is interesting that Jephthah is presented not as a counterargument, since he "cuts through" the distinction, but as central evidence.

32. Phyllis Trible, *Texts of Terror: Literary-Feminist Readings of Biblical Narratives* (Philadelphia: Fortress Press, 1984).

33. It is interesting that two of the many possible meanings of the meaningless word *shibboleth* are "ear of corn," which relates it to Samson's destruction of the crop that kills Kallah, and "stream of water," which recalls Achsah's claim and, by antithesis, Bath's sacrifice as a burnt offering.

Christopher Ricks

Donne After Love

Donne's poems, whether or not they are personal memories, record a dislike of having come. Postcoital sadness and revulsion are grimly seized, but what is more grim is that the poems are so often driven to bend this animus upon their own previous act of creative love. The old criticism of Donne was that he did not create whole poems; for me, this takes shape in the recurrent phenomenon of how unhealthily the poems end. Of the half-dozen essential instances, "Farewell to Love" may be the starting point, an extremity.

Farewell to Love

Whilst yet to prove,
I thought there was some deity in love
So did I reverence, and gave
Worship; as atheists at their dying hour
Call, what they cannot name, an unknown power,
As ignorantly did I crave:
Thus when
Things not yet known are coveted by men,
Our desires give them fashion, and so
As they wax lesser, fall, as they size, grow.

But, from late fair
His highness sitting in a golden chair,
Is not less cared for after three days
By children, than the thing which lovers so
Blindly admire, and with such worship woo;
Being had, enjoying it decays:
And thence,
What before pleased them all, takes but one sense,
And that so lamely, as it leaves behind
A kind of sorrowing dullness to the mind.

Ah cannot we,
As well as cocks and lions jocund be,
    After such pleasures? Unless wise
Nature decreed (since each such act, they say,
Diminisheth the length of life a day)
    This; as she would man should despise
        The sport,
Because that other curse of being short,
    And only for a minute made to be
Eager, desires to raise posterity.

    Since so, my mind
Shall not desire what no man else can find,
    I'll no more dote and run
To pursue things which had endamaged me.
And when I come where moving beauties be,
    As men do when the summer's sun
        Grows great,
Though I admire their greatness, shun their heat;
    Each place can afford shadows. If all fail,
'Tis but applying worm-seed to the tail.[1]

The poem's ending is an act of revulsion, and in me it then inspires
a revulsion, not only from its repudiation of love and sex but also from
its repudiation of the poem's own deepest apprehendings. The point is
not just that the preceding lines were more merely beautiful, but that
they have a depth, a corporeal and spiritual grace, worth gaining; the
preceding lines are unsentimentally comfortable in their sexuality,
even in the act of imagining the relief and release of freedom from it:

And when I come where moving beauties be,
    As men do when the summer's sun
        Grows great,
Though I admire their greatness, shun their heat;
    Each place can afford shadows. If all fail,
'Tis but applying worm-seed to the tail.

"If the worst comes to the worst, I can always clap an anaphrodisiac to my penis": is that an ending worthy of the poem's reconciliation to age's unobtrusively castrative rescindings?

What is at issue is not effectiveness; Donne's ending is entirely effective, and all the more so because "applying worm-seed"—as against the lenitive gloss "an anaphrodisiac"—so cruelly applies to the emissions that are sex and death, food for worms and limp as a worm. So effective is the ending that it usurps entire rights over the poem, and becomes its point. But the success of the ending is the failing of the poem, since it demeans.

The issue is not contrariety of mood, or of thought and feeling, or heterogeneity of ideas, but the incompatibility—for an integrity of response—of the depth of the poem at its best with the shallowness of such final repudiatory bitterness. William Empson's cheery paraphrase—"It tells us never to bother about women, because a man gets bored with a woman as soon as he has enjoyed her"[2]—is a mercy, but the poem is merciless. The poem had contemplated the pincer beliefs that in the short run ("that other curse of being short") sex dulls and revolts you while at the same time lethally affecting your chances of a long run: "since each such act, they say, / Diminisheth the length of life a day." It is under the pressure of these double diminishings that Donne is then driven to diminish, to demean, and to endamage his poem.

Arthur F. Marotti, in *John Donne, Coterie Poet*, is given no offense by the poem, which is for him an "exercise in an established form performed for an audience of sympathetic, knowledgeable males, gentleman-amorists"; the poem is "mischievous, iconoclastic," and indeed altogether hygienic: "He demystifies courtly Petrarchan and Neoplatonic amorousness by pointing out that it has no proper object." Marotti can speak here of "the familiar Donnean fantasy that love hurts or kills,"[3] as if that were a fantasy (has he never noticed that love does hurt and kill?), and as if "familiar Donnean fantasy" were words of sufficient weight for the poem's centric—uneccentric—gravity.

The professionalizing of literary studies, of which our culture is the victim-beneficiary, has brought with it the price paid for all professionalism: an induration against its own central human imperatives. Doctors become not only more but also less sensitive to suffering than others are; judges, to justice; journalists, to truth; soldiers, to slaughter. And critics to the apprehensions of joy and pain both within a poem and reached by a poem. It suits the professionalized critic to suppose that, contrary to what used to be believed, a poem of any energy not only need have no problem about reconciling gravity with levity but also need not even have any difficulty in doing so. The fierce truths for which T. S. Eliot fought are now bromides. Donne's imperious wit need fear no challenge from such suppliant criticism; and yet, as "Love's Alchemy" shows, a poem itself may contain along the way a resistance to the poet's imperiousness, only to be finally overborne.

Love's Alchemy

Some that have deeper digged love's mine than I,
Say, where his centric happiness doth lie:
        I have loved, and got, and told,
But should I love, get, tell, till I were old,
I should not find that hidden mystery;
        Oh, 'tis imposture all:
And as no chemic yet the elixir got,
        But glorifies his pregnant pot,
        If by the way to him befall
Some odoriferous thing, or medicinal,
    So, lovers dream a rich and long delight,
    But get a winter-seeming summer's night.

Our ease, our thrift, our honour, and our day,
Shall we, for this vain bubble's shadow pay?
        Ends love in this, that my man,
Can be as happy as I can; if he can
Endure the short scorn of a bridegroom's play?
        That loving wretch that swears,
'Tis not the bodies marry, but the minds,
        Which he in her angelic finds,
        Would swear as justly, that he hears,
In that day's rude hoarse minstrelsy, the spheres.

> Hope not for mind in women; at their best
> Sweetness and wit, they are but mummy, possessed.

Marotti underestimates the end of the first stanza so that he may over-estimate the end of the last. "Some that have deeper digged love's mine than I": there is to my ears a depth at the end of the first stanza which is lost in Marotti's words, "the tone of personal disappointment, if not of self-hate" (M, iii):

> So, lovers dream a rich and long delight,
> But get a winter-seeming summer's night.

The lines are hauntedly vacillatory, though not restless or restive, and they are unexpectedly at peace with what can be got, a summer's night that does outlast the words "winter-seeming." Is it possible to say the lines with a merely personal worldly disappointment or self-hate?

> So, lovers dream a rich and long delight,
> But get a winter-seeming summer's night.

They have the cool compassion of an angel's gravity. But the poem ends in the scrannel levity of a fallen angel:

> Hope not for mind in women; at their best
> Sweetness and wit, they are but mummy, possessed.

For Marotti, the poem is "an exercise in outrageous paradox" (M, iii), and he has no difficulty in smilingly swallowing the last lines: "Donne uses a kind of facile antifeminism (e.g., 'Hope not for minde in women') to demythologize the *donna angelicata* of spiritual lovers." That "e.g." is distinctly placating, as is the curbing of the misogyny in question (tailored as "antifeminism" throughout Marotti) to the half-dozen words "Hope not for mind in women":

> Hope not for mind in women; at their best
> Sweetness and wit, they are but mummy, possessed.

Helen Gardner's word "insulting" is to be preferred to "demytholo-gizing." Empson speaks of "a rather nasty brash boyishness"[4] in the

poem; but the nastiness is worse than boys', it is *the* boys (those "gentleman-amorists"). Donne's lines speak of wit, but are they themselves
truly witty? They are certainly crushing, especially in that final com-
pacting in "possessed," but like all brutally crushing retorts, they are
inadvertently self-indicting and self-demeaning. "Ends love in this"?
One may even sympathize with Leslie Fiedler's hunger to import something deeper than this routine misogyny into the poem's last words by
hearing "mummy, possessed" as the deeply accredited old oedipality.

Donne is often witty, but he often isn't, and Marotti is altogether
too lavish with the word. "Air and Angels" is rangingly ruminative,
wondering and wonderful, about men and women and love, and then
what is the upshot?

>   Just such disparity
> As is 'twixt air and angels' purity,
> 'Twixt women's love, and men's will ever be.

Tilottama Rajan praises this as "cleverly epigrammatic";[5] what exactly
is clever and epigrammatic, as against flatly brusque, about it? Marotti
says that these lines "engage in some witty antifeminist teasing" (M,
221), but again what exactly is witty about them? And is "teasing" (a
word with which Marotti persistently teases us out of thought) quite
the word? "The teasing antifeminism of the conclusion of this lyric—
one more example of Donne's strategy of literary surprise . . .": oh,
that's all right, then, for what, these days, could be less assaulting, or
insulting, than a strategy? But the end of "Air and Angels" strikes me
as an offense—against women, against men, against love, and against
the poem which it wantonly degrades. I appreciate the candor of John
Carey: "'Aire and Angels', in which the girl is spoken of with transfig-
uring wonder, ends up with a cheap crack about the inferiority of
woman's love to man's"[6]—except that I'd rather a critic didn't highly
value something he himself calls cheap. Which means appreciating
J. E. V. Crofts, who said of women's inferiority to men: "This doleful
notion . . . runs through the poems of Donne like spilt acid, producing
the oddest effects of corrosion and distortion, yields, for instance, that
quiet insult at the end of 'Air and Angels.'"[7] But the corrosion and

distortion are produced by what for Donne comes to spilt acid: spilt semen. Coleridge's marginal note on "Air and Angels" said: "The first Stanza is noble . . . the 2nd I do not understand."[8] What has to be understood is not just what Donne meant but what he meant by it, by being so de-meaning. For not all agencies of the supreme prefix *de* should be esteemed; we may, or may not, welcome Rajan's welcoming of all that deconstructs or destabilizes, or Marotti's unqualified pleasure in that which demystifies, deromanticizes, demythologizes, and desentimentalizes; but what of that in Donne's poetry which debases, demeans, and degrades?

The better the best things in his poem, the more Donne is driven to rend it with his ending. So "The Will," engaged throughout at no serious level, was in no danger, whereas "The Curse," just because it is alive with the profoundest acts of Donne's noticing, was doomed to an upshot that would take it down a peg or two, or—in the terms of Iago's Donne-like cynicism—"I'll set down the pegs that make this music."

The Curse

Whoever guesses, thinks, or dreams he knows
Who is my mistress, wither by this curse;
  His only, and only his purse
  May some dull heart to love dispose,
And she yield then to all that are his foes;
  May he be scorned by one, whom all else scorn,
  Forswear to others, what to her he hath sworn,
  With fear of missing, shame of getting, torn:

Madness his sorrow, gout his cramps, may he
Make, by but thinking, who hath made him such:
  And may he feel no touch
  Of conscience, but of fame, and be
Anguished not that 'twas sin, but that 'twas she:
  In early and long scarceness may he rot,
  For land which had been his, if he had not
  Himself incestuously an heir begot:

May he dream treason, and believe, that he
Meant to perform it, and confess, and die,
    And no record tell why:
    His sons, which none of his may be,
Inherit nothing but his infamy:
    Or may he so long parasites have fed,
    That he would fain be theirs, whom he hath bred,
    And at the last be circumcised for bread:

The venom of all stepdames, gamesters' gall,
What tyrants, and their subjects interwish,
    What plants, mines, beasts, fowl, fish,
    Can contribute, all ill which all
Prophets, or poets spake; and all which shall
    Be annexed in schedules unto this by me,
    Fall on that man; for if it be a she
    Nature before hand hath out-cursed me.

The point of the poem turns out to be the old jibe at women, altogether without wit, since if it is in a way surprising, after all those curses, that none of them is so bad as the curse of being a woman, it is surprising only in that a great poet should have thought this adequate even as misogyny. Such an ending manages even to demean misogyny (which is not the same as "questioning" it); one recalls T. S. Eliot's speaking of Donne's "scoffing attitude" toward the fickleness of women as perhaps "hardly more than immature bravado; it comes to me with none of the terrible sincerity of Swift's vituperation of the human race."[9] The revenge that is the poem's end is not against the tattler of the beginning, a stalking-horse; or really against women, its mere butt; but against sex and against the poem itself, the poem having had the noble effrontery to imagine at a depth that Donne then feared and repudiated. There was the imagining of desire at a depth that rivals Shakespeare's sonnet on lust in action.

May he be scorned by one, whom all else scorn,
Forswear to others, what to her he hath sworn,
With fear of missing, shame of getting, torn.

And there was the imagining of the nightmare world of suspected treason's damnation, at a depth that rivals or outdoes Kafka:

> May he dream treason, and believe, that he
> Meant to perform it, and confess, and die,
>   And no record tell why.

How could such apprehensions—lines of lamination that press, with
hideous levelness, upon *and* until it is the torture of "peine forte *et*
dure"—not be suffocated by a poem the point of which turns out to be:

> Fall on that man; for if it be a she,
> Nature before hand hath out-cursed me.

The answer is that they couldn't; Donne treats them treasonably, and
we are forced to practice our own snatched violation of the poem's
integrity, to rescue them, if we would resist Donne's corrosive violation. For what we should have responded to, in the hiding places of
the poem's power, is something in an entirely different world from
anything that Marotti's unmisgiving words would suggest: "After wishing an inventively varied series of ills on the hypothetical male . . ."
(M, 81).

"Woman's Constancy" is an instance of the poet's inconstancy. Coleridge turned the woman addressed into a whore, one way of making
the end not inappropriately meretricious. Marotti has the poem addressed by a woman to a man, and licks its boots for being on the
other feet. But then he hears merely "a series of hypothetical excuses"
(M, 74), much as Carey observes Donne's "turning round and dispar-
aging the arguments he has fabricated" (C, 231).

Woman's Constancy

> Now thou hast loved me one whole day,
> Tomorrow when thou leav'st, what wilt thou say?
> Wilt thou then antedate some new made vow?
>   Or say that now
> We are not just those persons, which we were?
> Or, that oaths made in reverential fear
> Of Love, and his wrath, any may forswear?

Or, as true deaths, true marriages untie,
So lovers' contracts, images of those,
Bind but till sleep, death's image, them unloose?
       Or, your own end to justify,
For having purposed change, and falsehood, you
Can have no way but falsehood to be true?
Vain lunatic, against these 'scapes I could
       Dispute, and conquer, if I would,
           Which I abstain to do,
For by tomorrow, I may think so too.

The trouble is that Donne at times wrote more deeply than he meant, or than he could bear, and what we then engage with is not Carey's "fabricated arguments" or Marotti's "hypothetical excuses," but imaginings which—beyond the poet's final digestive powers—the poem is forced to spit out and spit upon. The airy hauteur of the end is a spurning of the poem's previous precious magnanimities:

Or, as true deaths, true marriages untie,
So lovers' contracts, images of those,
Bind but till sleep, death's image, them unloose?

With how true a love knot, even at such a time, does "unloose" gather the insinuatingly interrogative syntax, plaiting it and plighting it even in the prospect of rupture. This, "hushed into depths beyond the watcher's diving" as it contemplates what it is to sleep together (dissolved in sleep, perhaps to be dissolved by sleep)—this outdoes even that other great conjunction of death and sleep in Donne, the hours when "the condemned man" "Doth practice dying by a little sleep."[10]

"Song: Go, and catch a falling star" is likewise quintessential Donne, something rich and strangely cheapened.

Song

Go, and catch a falling star,
   Get with child a mandrake root,
Tell me, where all past years are,
   Or who cleft the Devil's foot,
Teach me to hear mermaids singing,

Or to keep off envy's stinging,
  And find
  What wind
Serves to advance an honest mind.

If thou be'est born to strange sights,
  Things invisible to see,
Ride ten thousand days and nights,
  Till age snow white hairs on thee,
Thou, when thou return'st, wilt tell me
All strange wonders that befell thee,
  And swear
  No where
Lives a woman true, and fair.

If thou find'st one, let me know,
  Such a pilgrimage were sweet,
Yet do not, I would not go,
  Though at next door we might meet,
Though she were true, when you met her,
And last, till you write your letter,
  Yet she
  Will be
False, ere I come, to two, or three.

Empson judged that "the song had aimed at being gay and flippant but turned out rather heavy and cross";[11] but though the end may be heavy, it is of no weight, being the most attenuated of old jeers. This leaves the field open for Marotti, for whom the poem is a "sportful literary exercise," to claim that the poem isn't really about love and sex but about "a topic of more genuine concern to Donne and his Inns readers" (M, 79–80) (or in-readers): worldly advancement. So Marotti locates the poem's central impulse in the lines—

Or to keep off envy's stinging
  And find
  What wind
Serves to advance an honest mind.

—lines which I find rhythmically and syntactically inert and senten-
tious in comparison to what is for me the poem's centric happiness of
conception:

> If thou be'est born to strange sights,
>   Things invisible to see,
> Ride ten thousand days and nights,
>   Till age snow white hairs on thee.

"Things invisible to see" is at once straightforwardly an unperturbed
redundancy and—with the inverted syntax—a miraculous accomplish-
ment; and what follows has been exquisitely praised by Carey: "Hair,
and its greying, are as distinct from our conscious life, and as unknow-
able, as the weather" (C, 140). But what, then, of the smart and smart-
ing intrusion of Donne's conscious life, the knowingness beamed at
the boys in the poem's unworthy ending?

> Though she were true, when you met her,
> And last, till you write your letter,
>   Yet she
>   Will be
> False, ere I come, to two, or three.

The poem is more false to itself than any of its convenient women
could ever be.

Coleridge noted in the margin either of "The Canonization" or of
"The Triple Fool,"

> One of my favorite Poems. As late as 10 years ago, I used to seek and find
> out grand lines and fine stanzas; but my delight has been far greater, since
> it has consisted more in tracing the leading Thought thro'out the whole.
> The former is too much like coveting your neighbour's Goods: in the latter
> you merge yourself in the Author—you *become He.*—[12]

But becoming He (while grammatically superb) is misguided, since
without difference and distance there couldn't ever be a meeting of the
poet's consciousness and conscience with our own. The nub, on this
reading, is not Johnson's complaint that the metaphysicals "broke

every image into fragments"; Johnson's own procedure here in the life of Cowley was to break every metaphysical poem into fragmented images, and not once to attend to a whole poem—even while he turned propitiatingly to the crucial word: "their whole endeavour"; "as they were wholly employed"; "is never wholly lost." Nor is the nub what is usually meant by "unevenness," since it is not effectiveness but the nature of the effect, the divisive effect, which is at issue. Coleridge, who is Donne's greatest critic, is so partly because he is authentically provoked by division in Donne, and often provoked to criticize him. It is Coleridge who needs the word "deep" to get at both Donne's powers and his abuse of them. Of the end of "The Good Morrow": "Too good for mere wit. It contains a deep practical truth—this Trip-let." This is itself a deep praise, not least because it is instinct with the warning that elsewhere a deep truth might be too good to be subservi-ent to "mere wit," especially if the wit were "concupiscence of wit." It is Coleridge who speaks of "a substrate of profound, tho' mislocated, Thinking," and who is unable to resolve his pained perplexity of praise and blame, again in depth. Of "The Undertaking": "A grand Poem; and yet the Tone, the *Riddle* character, is painfully below the dignity of the main Thought." It is Coleridge who points to something damagingly (not delectably) paradoxical about Donne's art; alongside lines 25–28 of "A Fever," Coleridge wrote:

> Just & affecting *as dramatic*, i.e. the out-burst of a transient Feeling, itself the symbol of a deeper Feeling, that would have made *one* Hour, *known* to be *only* one Hour (or even one year) a perfect Hell! All the preceding Verses are detestable. Shakespere has nothing of this. He is never *positively* bad, even in his Sonnets. He *may* be sometimes worthless (N.B.: I don't say, he *is* but no where is He *un*worthy.

When Donne is unworthy, this is—as Coleridge saw—a matter of what violates "a deeper Feeling." One may dissent from Helen Gardner's judgments as to what is worthy, but this would be a more limited dis-sent than is involved when the critical procedure is such as to preclude the whole question of unworthiness or any such judgment as she passes when she says of the variant endings of "The Good Morrow," "Neither version provides a close worthy of the poem's opening."[13] Or there is Hazlitt, who was sensitive to intertextual erotics: "This is but a lame and impotent conclusion from so delightful a beginning."[14] Empson once feared that he had gone too far in suspecting an insensitivity in the close of a Donne poem, but he did not exactly retreat: of "A Valediction: Of Weeping," "The language itself has become flattened and explanatory: so that he almost seems to be feeling for his hat. But perhaps I am libelling this masterpiece. . . ."[15] Donne himself libels his masterpieces. Empson (it is a fault usually on the right side) is sure that any fault must be the critic's, not the poet's. "It is true that the words are not explicit. But when such a master has used all his resources to present an astonishing turn in his logic and his story, the usual presumption is that he means something adequate to the occasion he has created."[16] But the "usual presumption" may not fit the fiercely unusual Donne, who takes perverse delight in meaning in the end something not only inadequate to, but unworthy of, the occasion he has created.

There survives only one interesting critical statement by Donne about the art of poetry; it furnishes the clinching conclusion to the introduction to Barbara Herrnstein Smith's *Poetic Closure*, and John Carey, who cannot bring himself to ignore it, affects that it makes for his sense of Donne.

> And therefore it is easie to observe, that in all Metricall compositions, . . . the force of the whole piece, is for the most part left to the shutting up; the whole frame of the Poem is a beating out of a piece of gold, but the last clause is as the impression of the stamp, and that is it that makes it currant.[17]

Carey gives the thought his audacious setting:

> Even when, in a sermon, he discusses metrical composition more generally, he retains a view of poems as unstable processes. "The whole frame of the Poem," he asserts, "is a beating out of a piece of gold, but the last clause is as the impression of the stamp, and that is it that makes it currant." The emphasis on the ending looks a bit exaggerated here, especially if applied wholesale to poetry, but it fits in well enough with Donne's own insistent modification and development of his material throughout a poem, and

with the sense he gives us that it would be unwise to conclude anything about it until it's concluded.

Or when it's concluded, come to that. For the conflicts of attitude within Donne's poems relate to irresolvable confusions within the human personality.

(C, 192)

This is perverse. First, the impression of the stamp is the authoritative termination of any "unstable processes." Second, Carey finds the "emphasis on the ending . . . a bit exaggerated" only because he would prefer Donne's poems to be open-ended since their endings resist Carey's resolute allegiance to unresolvability. And third, though it makes sense to say that Donne's emphasis on the ending fits Donne's not wishing us "to conclude anything about it until it's concluded," it is a rhetorical sleight to continue: "Or when it's concluded, come to that." People may now prefer—to the point of nullifying Johnson's witty stubbornness—conclusions in which nothing is concluded, but the stamp of Donne's conviction is firmly upon the last clause, "the impression of the stamp, and that is it that makes it currant." Donne resolves his poems, even when—or rather, especially when—the poem turns on its heels. But Carey is in hock to the idea that conclusions are not last impressions. "As the final stanza counteracts the rest of the poem, so the rest of the poem counteracts the final stanza, making its briskness seem blustering."[18] *As . . . so? Seem?* This is a sentimentality of simultaneity and a pretense of equipollence.

Barbara Herrnstein Smith is entirely persuasive on the power, within poems, of "closural allusion," "references not to termination, finality, repose, or stability as such, but to events which, in our nonliterary experiences, are associated with these qualities—events such as sleep, death, dusk, night, autumn, winter, descents, falls, leave-takings and home-comings."[19] And comings, nowhere mentioned by her but no less apt. As with all endings, there is an equivocation as to how final they are; after orgasm, something takes its course, but then after what does it not? "Allusions to any of the 'natural' stopping places of our lives and experiences—sleep, death, winter, and so forth—tend to give closural force when they appear as terminal features in a poem."[20] It is a pity about the cagey quotation-marks round "naturally," since those stopping places are indeed natural. Another natural stopping place is orgasm, perhaps the most serious rival to death, whom it wedded and bedded in the pun on "die"; death, which is for Smith "more than sleep, winter, or the permanence of the fixed stars, the most personal and ultimate of ultimates."[21] It is not willful of Smith not to mention erotic closure, but it would have provided warrant for her staunch footnote: "The question . . . is whether or not we can assume a universal psychology of closure—and I can only answer that I do not know, but that I am assuming it anyway."[22]

Frank Kermode does not make too much of this sense of an ending, but there are erotic energies in the opening chapter of his inaugurative book:

> Men, like poets, rush "into the middest," *in medias res,* when they are born; they also die *in mediis rebus,* and to make sense of their span they need fictive concords with origins and ends.[23]

For, prior to our being born, there is our origin; there is—as Tristram Shandy knew—an act of rushing into the middest; Sidney, whom Kermode is quoting, went so far as to say "thrusteth into the middest"— not that "rush" lacks eroticism, of the white rush and of this:

> Let us not then rush blindly on unto it,
> Like lustful beasts, that only know to do it.[24]

Kermode later speaks of "biology," saying that "the End is a fact of life and a fact of the imagination, working out from the middle,"[25] where his words are decently open to the vulgarism "the facts of life," and to the sexuality of the middle, the waist/waste and middle of the night. A reconsideration by Kermode in 1978, "Sensing Endings," says: "The rules are culture-specific; as to that, one would expect rules about endings to be culture-specific, though I have no doubt that the interest in them is species-specific, having to do with our understanding that our time is not the time of the world, nor is the time of our culture."[26] Having to do as well with doing, since for any species the one thing

necessary is that we (in Donne's words) "propagate our kind." Kermode
in this essay is respectfully wary of John Kucich's theory of concentration and release: "Certainly the view that this concentration and release
is related to orgasm and to death is intuitively acceptable; Milton's last
word is 'spent,' and the notion of a cathartic discharge is very persistent.
But all the evidence is surely against the opinion that it is only to be had
at the end. And the notion of orgasmic or cathartic dispersal is not one
that I find it easy to hold."[27] One could easily maintain a scepticism
about the general applicability of orgasmic endings (and penultimata)
while remaining confident that for Donne, alive to the pun on "die," a
poem's ending is likely to relate to, though it may not reproduce or
mimic the timing of, orgasm's affiliation to death. "Death and conception in mankind is one";[28] and the resurrection—since "Only in heaven
joy's strength is never spent"—is the only consummation devoutly to be
wished by Donne, devoutly and wholeheartedly since it will be the consummation to end consummations and though spoken of as the "last
great consummation" will be essentially the first:

> Joy that their last great consummation
> Approaches in the resurrection.
>> "The Second Anniversary: Of the Progress of the Soul"

The rhyme of "consummation" / "resurrection" is itself both a consummation and a resurrection (a reprise and reprieve for "We die and
rise the same" in "The Canonization"); and "Approaches," with its
sense of gathering tinglingly for the great consummation, assures that
here at last there comes the one orgasm which will not issue in revulsion and disappointment.

"Textual erotics," whether or not prosecuted as in Peter Brooks's
Reading for the Plot (1984), is clearly not limited to such art as is patent-
ly erotic. But textual erotics may gain a warrant from Donne's preoccu-
pations and from his finding it natural to write of poems in relation to
"strange adultery" and to "concupiscence of wit." Donne meant his as-
servation in Paradox XI, "I say again, that the body makes the minde."
A letter on letters invokes ecstasy as the conjunction of that which is
supremely erotic with that which supremely is not:

I make account that this writing of letters, when it is with any seriousness, is a kind of extasie, and a departure and secession and suspension of the soul, which doth then communicate it self to two bodies: And as I would every day provide for my souls last convoy, though I know not when I shall die, and perchance I shall never die; so for these extasies in letters, I often times deliver my self over in writing.[29]

But Donne was no more at ease with delivering himself over in writing than in sex, "the poor benefit of a bewildering minute." Donne's disparagement of his poetry is notorious, and crucial to the arguments of Carey and Marotti. Yet they avert an eye from the extremity of it, assimilating Donne to the usual deprecations, regarding "his poems as trifles," and wishing to be thought "a literary amateur" (M, x). But it was not just "the stigma of print" from which he shrank, and to speak of "his characteristic aversion to becoming a publishing poet" (M, 341) is to elide his aversion from having consummated poems at all. For, as Marotti himself concedes, Donne "tried to foreclose the possibility that it [his writing] would travel further by the normal means of manuscript transcription" (M, xi). Donne did think it unpardonable in himself to have "descended to print anything in verse,"[30] but this is something of a disguise—not in the usual sense of false modesty but rather as insufficiently repudiatory. He craved from his friend "assurance upon the religion of your friendship that no copy shall be taken for any respect of these or any other my compositions sent to you."[31] The coterie insouciance is indeed germane, but is not Donne's case. Coleridge acknowledged the courtly context–"The idea of degradation & frivolity which Donne himself attached to the character of a professed Poet, & which was only not universal in the reigns of Elizabeth & James"–but Coleridge's terms, "degradation and frivolity," suppose a deep entwining, not a social affectation. The entwining is that of the poetic act and the sexual act. Donne writes about his writings as if they were intimate with the act of love and its issue. Those which he permitted to circulate were called by him, in the decent obscurity of a learned language, "virgins (save that they have been handled by many)," and those which he kept private were "so unhappily sterile that no copies of them have been begotten."[32] Marotti quotes the fa-

mous words about the Paradoxes, "To my satires there belongs some
fear and to some elegies, and these perhaps, shame" (M, 41); but where
Donne speaks of shame, his critic speaks at once of embarrassment—
and of the "dissemination" of his lyrics without remarking that for
Donne both disseminations are an expense of spirit in a waste of
shame. *Fear . . . shame.* The pincer-jaws are those which Donne saw
sharp in lust: "With fear of missing, shame of getting, torn."

For Donne, the expense of spirit in a waste of shame is *love* in action.
Contempt for sex, or for poetry (Carey's phrase), is not quite it, for perfect contempt casteth out fear. A double shame moves the poems to
suicide; *Biathanatos* admired this forethought consummated, "As De-
mosthenes did with poison, carried in a pen." Donne wrestled there
with the text "No man hateth his own flesh" (exquisitely equivocal),
confident that it did not "yield an argument against self homicide." The
poems, after love, imagine hating their own flesh, and they turn their revulsion upon the body of the poem, their own flesh. If the body is his
book, then the book will be his body. The terms of the sonnet "To Mr.
B.B." are those of textual erotics pricked by sexual and textual dismay:

> If thou unto thy Muse be married,
>> Embrace her ever, ever multiply,
>> Be far from me that strange adultery
> To tempt thee and procure her widowhead.
> My Muse (for I had one,) because I am cold,
>> Divorced herself: the cause being in me,
>> That I can take no new in bigamy,
> Not my will only but power doth withhold.
> Hence comes it, that these rhymes which never had
>> Mother, want matter, and they only have
>> A little form, the which their father gave;
> They are profane, imperfect, oh, too bad
>> To be counted children of poetry
>> Except confirmed and bishoped by thee.

That last line is wistful beyond belief. Donne, in the days of his sexually unsatisfied Muse (accusing him of frigidity), had often committed
his own form of "strange adultery," unfaithful to his love, his self, and

his poem, all at once: "To invent, and practise this one way, to annihi-
late all three," he writes in "The Will."

It is not simply that wit may be concupiscent but that wit is concupiscence, and concupiscence wit, each an utterance (and it is men,
not women, who disseminate).

> So when thy brain works, ere thou utter it,
> Cross and correct concupiscence of wit.
>
> "The Cross"

The younger Donne did not so much cross and correct concupiscence
of wit as cross and corrode it. He knew about corrosiveness, and about
its being the ingrate's suicidal revenge; in the words of the poem "To Sir
Edward Herbert, at Juliers":

> We do infuse to what he meant for meat,
> Corrosiveness.

No longer meat, and not meet.

The uncorrosive genius is Byron's: T. S. Eliot was exactly right in
setting up the Donne/Byron choice (not simply a comparison), and the
recovery of Byron since Eliot's heyday has gone with the partial eclipse
of Donne. To Eliot, Byron—unlike Donne—offers merely "the substitution of one mood for a wholly different one": "Byron's 'effective' change
here is not only a theatrical effect: it is callowness masquerading as
maturity of cynicism; it represents an uninteresting mind, and a disorderly one."[33] But those who value Byron as the greatest comic poet in
the language may retort that it is Donne who is retrospectively cynical,
and may urge the praise given to *Don Juan* by Swinburne: "There is in
that great poem an especial and exquisite balance and sustenance of
alternate tones." Thomas Moore told Byron that he always felt about his
art "as the French husband did when he found a man making love to his
(the Frenchman's) wife—'Comment, Monsieur,—sans y être obligé!'"
Byron (*noblesse oblige*) at once assented and dissented: "I feel exactly as
you do about our 'art,' but it comes over me in a kind of rage every now
and then, like * * * *, and then, if I don't write to empty my mind, I go
mad."[34] But emptying his mind, and his body, was for Byron a generous

pleasure, even in retrospect. "Oh pleasure, you're indeed a pleasant thing," this Scotsman found it necessary to insist not to himself but to the English.

That Donne's poems practice some form of self-destruction has long been recognized. What Hazlitt saw as a wanton dissolution ("The scholastic reason he gives quite dissolves the charm of tender and touching grace in the sentiment itself"),[35] Carey might see as a due recognition of life's wantonness ("The poem dissolves itself,"[36] he therefore says gratefully). These days, critical practice often sounds like sub-Empson with a cold in the head: subversions of pastoral. Tilottama Rajan finds the *Songs and Sonnets* of self-consuming interest, since they are so self-compromising, self-defeating, self-emptying, and self-reversing. (It is something of a relief when the grizzled ruffian "undermining" puts in an appearance.) Rajan says that she "would argue, without making a value judgment, that all Donne's lyrics are in a sense evaporations,"[37] but her critical allegiances do not permit of not making value judgments, and in any case it is clear from every page that she highly values Donne's lyrics exactly as evaporations. One trouble with Rajan's "hermeneutics of suspicion" (which explicitly consigns the rest of us to a limbo of naïfs called the "hermeneutics of immediacy") is that it is insufficiently suspicious. It expends so much suspicion on New Critics and other traitorous clerks that it has none left for Donne. But there is something missing from any account of Donne which implies that only a buffoon, or someone suckled in a creed outworn, would ever have been moved to cry, as an anonymous critic did in 1823, that Donne's poems are "so completely *irritating* to the imagination, as well as to the taste."[38]

No doubt there have been traitorous clerks, but Donne is the one who matters most.

> But O, self traitor, I do bring
> The spider love, which transubstantiates all,
> And can convert manna to gall.
>
> "Twicknam Garden"

And so he did. It is a shocking blasphemy, and one ought to pay it the compliment of being shocked by it. The poems are not beamed at the self-consumer society; they are tortured into becoming self-traitors. They then mean their contaminating conversions. "And confess, and die," though *some* record tells why. Their unmistakable power partakes of the venomous irresponsibility which Donne feared:

> for hearing him, I found
> That as burnt venomed lechers do grow sound
> By giving others their sores, I might grow
> Guilty, and he free.
>
> "Satire 4"

This should not be an art conducive to equanimity, and I am mildly shocked by such criticism as is even less than mildly shocked. Rajan makes the love poems amenable not only by the abstractions of deconstruction but also by giving their sores to "personae." Carey makes the love poems amenable by having them not really be about love at all but about religion: "the love poems are a veil for religious perturbations" (C, 38), and Carey himself writes as one quite unperturbed by religion since for him it is nothing but the expression of psychological "preferences." Marotti makes the love poems amenable in two ways: either (one more example of the critic's strategy of surprise, surprise) by having them be meta-poems, "virtually 'self-consuming artifacts,'" "virtual meta-poems," "virtually a meta-poetic statement" (M, 22, 71, 74) (much virtue in that "virtually"); or by having them be not just the products, but statements, of worldly ambition's socioeconomic frustrations. This insistence that the poems are really not about sex but about politics has its calmative side, but it regularly entails a slighting of—among other things—sexual politics.

The poems may be said to be marked by a vengeful infidelity to their own deepest apprehensions; they may also be said to commit the infidel's supreme act, suicide. Donne's inordinate respect for suicide was lifelong. *Biathanatos* was "A Declaration of that Paradoxe or Thesis, that Selfe-homicide is not so naturally Sinne, that it may never be otherwise." One of the Paradoxes had been devoted to the thesis "That all things kill themselves." Even plants, with their vegetable love, kill themselves by an expense of spirit in a waste of shamelessness: "This they spend their Spirits to attaine." As for men, "we kill dayly our bodyes with Surfets," for instance "Of affections, Lusting our Lust." This cruel love knot, tightening its lusts and luxuries, twists about the poems. Carey describes "A Nocturnal Upon St. Lucy's Day" as "suicidal"—is this its mood or its act? His good jokes about "Donne's suicidal longings" sharply differ from Donne's mood: "Suicide drill, like fire drill, reduces the chance of a fatality." Carey is persuasive on Donne's penchant for valedictions—"His partings are miniature suicides" (C, 93, 173, 215-16)—but "miniature" comes across as endearing. The question is less that of Donne's staving off his own suicide ("the kind of poem which helped to keep Donne alive by giving scope to his suicidal fantasies" [C, 215]) than of his inciting his poems to commit this act of darkness.

Just as Carey's page on death in the *Songs and Sonnets* never mentions the pun on "die," so his pages on death *tout court* never mention Donne's recurrence to the fear that every act of sex "diminisheth the length of life a day." Marotti keeps his spirits up by being still the coterie votary.

> The truth of the remark "We kill our selves, to propagate our kinde" lies as much in the context of the careerist hampered by "hostages to fortune," as in that of the (hardly serious) belief that orgasms shortened one's life span.
>
> (M, 237)

"Hardly serious" is too much of a nub to be tucked within those prophylactic brackets. Marotti pooh-poohs "the flimsy folk belief that every orgasm costs a day of one's life" (M, 239). Donne's accents, though, are not sportive, or s'pportive:

> For that first marriage was our funeral:
> One woman at one blow, then killed us all,
> And singly, one by one, they kill us now.
> We do delightfully ourselves allow
> To that consumption; and profusely blind,
> We kill ourselves, to propagate our kind.
>   "The First Anniversary: An Anatomy of the World"

Wishing for a Donne of sprightliness, Marotti says: "He cannot resist puns and other comic elements as he points to the self-destructive-
ness of mankind, jokingly referring to 'new diseases' (like syphilis)."
But puns are not necessarily comic, and comedy not necessarily joking,
and joking not necessarily tousling; venereal disease—again those prophylactic brackets, "(like syphilis)"—is treated by Donne with grim
horror, and itself constitutes, as D. H. Lawrence argued, a central impulse in the revulsion from sex in Donne and his age. ("Lust-bred
diseases rot thee; and dwell with thee / Itchy desire and no ability.")[39]

> With new diseases on ourselves we war,
> And with new physic, a worse engine far.
>
> > "The First Anniversary"

"New diseases," critick'd to a joke; "new physic"—ah yes, iatrogenic
. . . But Donne was infected by the sinful perversity he so imagined:

> Of nothing he made us, and we strive too,
> To bring ourselves to nothing back.

Donne strove to bring his poems to nothing back, and he warred on
them diseasedly.

"Self murder" is not just exploited in the love poems and explored
in the religious ones, but is poetically prosecuted. The conviction did
not change, and it lethally animates Donne's "Epitaph on Himself":

> Whilst in our souls sin bred and pampered is,
> Our souls become worm-eaten carcases;
> So we ourselves miraculously destroy.

"Miraculously" is stingingly salty. And if we destroy ourselves, why
not those other carcases?:

> Sickly, alas, short-lived, aborted be
>   Those carcase verses, whose soul is not she.
>
> > "A Funeral Elegy"

Like Walton, and unlike his modern critics, Donne does not use the
word "aborted" blithely, acclamatorily.

Sex can be, in its quiet incremental way, murderous. Empson speaks with level dismay of Donne's killing his wife by giving her a baby every year (she died, at thirty-three, just after the birth, the stillbirth, of their twelfth child); but Empson urged, too, a historical mitigation:

> I should warmly agree that he was a bad husband to give his wife so many children, if this is what is at the back of the editor's [Helen Gardner's] mind; but the idea seems to have been unknown at the time, and besides, Donne was becoming more under the influence of the Church throughout his married life; we may be sure that the clergy would have denounced any relief for child-birth, then as later. Donne says nothing in verse about his children because he found them merely a nuisance, but this didn't keep him from being devoted to his wife; I expect Blake and D. H. Lawrence would have felt the same, if they had not been spared.[40]

Donne may have been insufficiently sensitive to this domestic aspect of sex as murderous (though there are in his letters about his wife and children what sound like whinges of guilt), but he was exacerbatedly sensitive to sex as suicidal, killing us daily by "Lusting our Lust":

>   freely on his she friends
> He blood, and spirit, pith and marrow spends,
>   Ill steward of himself, himself in three years ends.
>
> Else might he long have lived;
>
> Yet chooseth he, though none of these he fears,
> Pleasantly three, than straitened twenty years
>   To live, and to increase his race, himself outwears.
>
>   "The Progress of the Soul"

Carey's dismissal of "the worn Elizabethan pun on 'die'" (C, 43) would be telling only if "worn" were taken this seriously ("himself out-wears"), just as it would be right of him to speak of "the boring old Elizabethan sexual pun on 'die'" (C, 176) only if he were triplicating "boring" (Beckett: "And they talk of stiffs being bored!"). But the pun on "die" does need its "substrate of profound, tho' mislocated, Think-ing" in the fear that in the sexual act man "himself outwears."

We are tapers too, and at our own cost die.

We can die by it, if not live by love.

"The Canonization"

The timbre, elsewhere, of the end of Elegy 9, "The Autumnal," is unique in Donne (as "Marina" is unique in Eliot) in its quietude of hope, its aspirations disowning all "panting." Here the tacit pun on "die" is muted to an acquiescence which is the opposite of Joyce's panting ahquickyes; is muted to a making friends with the twofold necessity of dying.

> Since such love's natural lation is, may still
>   My love descend, and journey down the hill,
> Not panting after growing beauties, so,
>   I shall ebb out with them, who homeward go.

"I shall ebb out with them, who homeward go": it is Donne's "Crossing the Bar"; and a coming that is for once a homecoming.

The occasions when Donne conquers the itch to violate his poem are those when the poem suffers no orgasm. The act of love may be still to come—"I shall ebb out . . ." It is so in "The Dream," which—whatever it may say—prefers this being unsatisfied (escaping "The greater torment / Of love satisfied"). "The Dream" ends:

> Thou cam'st to kindle, goest to come; then I
> Will dream that hope again, but else would die.

"That hope again," it had a dying fall. "The Ecstasy" is all in prospect, nothing in retrospect. Sometimes the love is not just not consummated "as yet," it is supreme because it never was or will be. "What miracles we harmless lovers wrought": the poem itself is less harmed than is Donne's wont, for if "The Relic" had not been the story of two lovers who had escaped the act of love and its ashy fruits, it is likely that the sexual revulsion would not have been the merely distasteful and labored aside of the first stanza—

> (For graves have learned that woman-head
> To be to more than one a bed)

—but the upshot, the last word. Even in "The Good Morrow" the terms of undying love are those of unacted desire, for desire after action must "slacken." The sense of chastened chastity in "slacken" ("none do slacken, none can die") is the benign, albeit strict, counterpart to the sardonic further detumescence in "The Apparition":

> Will, if thou stir, or pinch to wake him, think
>   Thou call'st for more,
> And in false sleep will from thee shrink.

Perhaps the sharpest of the occasions when Donne claims to be making the best of things when actually he is enjoying what is for him the best of things (the *not* enjoying love's fruition), is Elegy 10, "The Dream." It gives unforgettable expression to the cruelest of imagination's distempers, the conviction that, whereas joys are imaginary, pain is true; and then it expresses its gratitude for the best of mercies, the smallest one:

> So, if I dream I have you, I have you,
>   For, all our joys are but fantastical.
> And so I 'scape the pain, for pain is true;
>   And sleep which locks up sense, doth lock out all.
>
> After a such fruition I shall wake,
>   And, but the waking, nothing shall repent;
> And shall to love more thankful sonnets make,
>   Than if more honour, tears, and pains were spent.

The thankfulness, the reprieve from repentance, "after a such fruition," depend upon the flagrant omission from that last line, "Than if more honour, tears, and pains were spent." No expense of spirit, no waste of shame; then, I "nothing shall repent."

Relatedly, the very beautiful high spirits of Elegy 19, "To his Mistress Going to Bed," are a consequence of the act of love's being all in prospect; the sadder usual tale would be "To his Mistress Coming from Bed." Empson misrepresents the poem in describing its last two lines:

> To teach thee, I am naked first, why then
> What needst thou have more covering than a man.

as "the jolly remark at the end, after all is won";[41] for it stanches the act of love to suppose that "all is won" once the lady is in this sense won. This would herald the cult of the simultaneous nonorgasm; in some ways easier but less jolly. Elsewhere Empson, fiercely repudiating the reading in the penultimate couplet "Here is no penance, much less innocence," turned to the general question, "Why is this not simply a dirty poem, please?": "I think it becomes very dirty if you make the poet jab his contempt into the lady at the crisis of the scene of love."[42] Empson's fierceness is properly erotic (against a demeaning of the erotic such as jabs contempt into her), and he is right about the poem's being pure of contempt; but in using the words "at the crisis of the scene of love," he is premature (at Yale, the praecox trope), since the crisis of the scene of love must be securely off the end of the poem, still to come, and it is exactly this which disarms in Donne the rage to jab his contempt into a poem.

"There is no penance due to innocence": this (the manuscript reading preferred by Empson) is said before the act and may recall the close of Ben Jonson's translation of Petronius, where amorous unconsummation is revered as serenely endless:

> There is no labour, nor no shame in this;
> This hath pleased, doth please, and long will please; never
> Can this decay, but is beginning ever.

In the Bridgewater manuscript, about 1625, an unknown reader wrote beside a line from "To his Mistress Going to Bed" ("To enter in these bonds, is to be free"): "Why may not a man write his owne Epithalamion if he can doe it so modestly."[43] It is a beautiful question because it is not just a rhetorical one. "All that belongs to love . . . is to desire, and to enjoy; for to desire without fruition is a rage, and to enjoy without desire is a stupidity . . . nothing then can give us satisfaction, but where those two concur, *amare* and *frui*, to love and to enjoy."[44] But if, in these terms of Donne's, to enjoy without desire is a stupidity, what is it to enjoy without then having enjoyed? "To desire without fruition is a rage":

> After a such fruition I shall wake,
> And, but the waking, nothing shall repent.

"If he can do it so modestly": Donne's name—*nomen est omen*—notoriously announced the sibling pun to "die." Do and die. Done as consummated. That the other intimate name on which he grounded and ground his puns, that of his wife, More / more,[45] incarnates the opposite impulse to "done," entrenched his siege of contraries. "More" is the unsatisfied, perhaps the insatiable ("think / Thou call'st for more"); "done" ought to be the quietus of satisfaction but is for John Donne the revulsion from satiety. In the words of Jonson's translation from Petronius,

> Doing, a filthy pleasure is, and short,
> And done, we straight repent us of the sport.

Yet the delivery of himself over in a verse letter to Sir Henry Wotton permitted Donne a final gracious bow of social solicitude, the name pun a firm signature:

> But, Sir, I advise not you, I rather do
> Say o'er those lessons, which I learned of you:
> Whom, free from German schisms, and lightness
> Of France, and fair Italy's faithlessness,
> Having from these sucked all they had of worth,
> And brought home that faith, which you carried forth,
> I throughly love. But if myself, I have won
> To know my rules, I have, and you have
>
> > > > Donne.

Donne's dear equanimity here comes from his confidence that his love for Wotton is entirely without carnal consequence, so that words which would elsewhere be erotically charged ("faithlessness," "sucked," "I throughly love") manifest such a "white integrity" as to permit the name Donne, for once, both to pun, and not to pun on *sexual* doings.

His friends could of course play more blithely with his name. Why did Thomas Pestell write as if the verse letter "Written by Sir H. G. and J. D. *alternis vicibus*" were written by Goodyer and Donne not—as it clearly was—in alternate stanzas but in alternate lines? Because this permitted Pestell a further flight of textual erotics, since seventeenth-century loins are lines too:

'On the Interlinearie poëme begott twixt S*ͬ* H. Goo: & D*ͬ* Donne'

Here two rich ravisht spirrits kisse & twyne;
Advanc'd, & weddlockt in each others lyne.
Goode-res rare match with only him was blest,
Who haes out donne, & quite undonne the rest.[46]

When Donne delivered himself over to Wotton, he and his name—"have Donne"—could bow; when he delivers himself over to the supreme patron, he and his name kneel:

Wilt thou forgive that sin where I begun,
    Which was my sin, though it were done before?
Wilt thou forgive that sin, through which I run,
    And do run still: though still I do deplore?
        When thou hast done, thou hast not done,
            For, I have more.

"A Hymn to God the Father"

Kneeling, this shudders at the primal parental shudder in the loins, for "that sin where I begun, / Which was my sin, though it were done before" is not only Adam's implicating sin but also the lethal act of love which was to issue in John Donne. "Death and conception in mankind is one": "is"—not "are"—compounds the pun on "die," and it issues in something deeper than the earlier flat revulsion of

Think further on thy self, my soul, and think
How thou at first was made but in a sink.

"The Second Anniversary"

Carey says of Donne and bodies, "We are reminded, yet again, of Lawrence" (C, 164); but Carey is not moved to remind us of what

Lawrence said about Donne in "Introduction to These Paintings": "Man came to have his own body in horror, especially in its sexual implications . . . Donne, after his exacerbated revulsion-attraction excitement of his earlier poetry, becomes a divine." "Pornography is the attempt to insult sex, to do dirt on it." "Do dirt on" is, in Lawrence, something more than the dictionary's "to harm or injure maliciously," partly because the earlier instances lack any preposition (and "doing dirt *to*" is then the more usual form); doing dirt on—ugly, unignorable—is excremental. Donne, doing dirt on his poems, insults sex. It was à propos of Donne that Coleridge invoked The Filter: "To eject is as much a living Power, as to assimilate: to excrete as to absorb. Give therefore honor due to the Filter-poet."[47] Honor due: how much is that? "Just so much honor."

Marotti praises Donne for insulting sex: "Sex is portrayed in the most imaginatively energetic sections of the piece [Elegy 8, "The Comparison"] as nauseatingly filthy. The perspiration on the antagonist's mistress's brow is 'Ranke sweaty froth' 'Like spermatique issue of ripe menstruous boiles.'" (M, 49). "Perspiration" there is a touch decorous. Carey goes the whole hog, praising "The Comparison" as "a rich, ingenious and medically informed physical experience—especially the disgusting parts, such as the description of the other woman's sweat."

> Rank sweaty froth thy mistress' brow defiles,
> Like spermatic issue of ripe menstruous boils.

Here we can see Donne pursuing his interest in the body's excremental secretions, and speculatively blending four of them—sweat, pus, sperm, and menses—in order to gain something more satisfying than mere sweat" (C, 141). Even Carey underrates Donne's pursuit of excremental secretions, for to sweat, pus, sperm, and menses should be added spittle ("froth"), bile (*defiles / biles,* the rhyme and the manuscript spelling), and—the monstrously spermatic *issue* of the menstruous, and the supreme excremental secretion—a baby. There is something disconcerting about Carey's being so undisconcerted, as there is about Marotti's equanimity as to how Donne here uses "the aesthetics of disgust." Do Carey and Marotti bring these lines into relation to their own

bodies, or to anyone's really? "A Hell for the *other people*":[48] that is how
Eliot repudiated Pound's "aesthetics of disgust." Honorably, Eliot himself did not publish his most extreme feats here, such confected and cun-
ning (*con* and *cun*) revulsions as might have graced "The Comparison":

> Odours, confected by the cunning French,
> Disguise the good old hearty female stench.[49]

Undisguised disgust, not now to be disguised by the professionalized
antisepsis of "the aesthetics of disgust": what does it minister to?

It is one of the strengths of Empson's criticism of Donne that he not
only conceives of it in moral terms but also concedes that there could
be principled moral objections to the poet. Against Carey's unimped-
ed consciencelessness should be set Empson's acknowledgment: "Many
people, I should say, have at the back of their minds a real moral objection to the earlier Donne love poems because they regard the poet as
a cad who boasts of getting girls into trouble."[50] But even this protects
Donne, for "cad" ("the cad needs taking down a peg or two,"[51] Empson
says elsewhere of Donne) and "getting girls into trouble" come out as
too charmingly archaic; anyway it isn't so much that Donne is a cad
to women (who may now find the concept of the cad more insulting
than the behavior of such), but that he is corrosively unfaithful to his
poems.

Postcoital sadness is something other than revulsion, though the
two may make common cause. For Empson, attirelessly resourceful in
defense of Donne ("Donne may have invented knickers, as a final ob-
stacle on the overdressed lady"),[52] Donne was decently reluctant: "He
accepted the cynicism of Christianity about love, along with all the
rest of its horrors, because he could not otherwise feed his wife and
children."[53] But Donne did not accept, he relished; and with "profound, tho' mislocated, Thinking" he then fiercely eroticized his revulsion from the erotic. "Between the excremental jelly that thy body is
made of at first, and that jelly which thy body dissolves to at last; there
is not so noysome, so putrid a thing in nature."[54]

Since sperm is men's, not women's, Donne is fleetingly able to imagine a postcoital mood that has less self-revulsion; but this, since it is

women's remission not men's, is then another strike against women. Carey writes with beauty, though with exorbitant liberality, about the moment in Problem VII when Donne broods on why the most beautiful women are always the falsest:

> Doth the minde so follow the temperature of the body, that because those complexions are aptest to change, the mind is therefore so? Or as Bels of the purest metal retain their tinkling and sound largest; so the memory of the last pleasure lasts longer in these, and disposeth them to the next.

Carey has his own resonance when he comments: "Something within the woman, as Donne imagines it, remains quivering and resonant, like a struck bell, after love-making is over . . . orgasm fills the body like a musical note setting up its lingering whispers" (C, 139). But the resonance is Carey's own. For Donne's "tinkling and sound" is less generous than Carey's "quivering and resonant," "like a musical note setting up its lingering whispers"; and that this is "within the woman" breeds its own resentment, so that the use to which Donne puts his momentary concession that orgasm may not always be dismaying is punitive and vengeful; the point, after all, is that women are not only false but also insatiably and lethally demanding, too well remembering their "last pleasure."

But it is in the end incumbent on someone who finds that Donne's postcoital malaise degrades the poems' own deepest understandings to give a hostage, a contrastive poem such as deeply imagines something other than a sadness colluding with revulsion. The twentieth-century poet most, and best, influenced by Donne is also his best twentieth-century critic, and Empson's poem "Camping Out" (thanks to "Donne the Space Man") has its rocketing climax and then at the end rises above being aggressively *anti*-climax:

Camping Out

And now she cleans her teeth into the lake:
Gives it (God's grace) for her own bounty's sake
What morning's pale and the crisp mist debars:
Its glass of the divine (that Will could break)

Restores, beyond Nature: or lets Heaven take
(Itself being dimmed) her pattern, who half awake
Milks between rocks a straddled sky of stars.

Soap tension the star pattern magnifies.
Smoothly Madonna through-assumes the skies
Whose vaults are opened to achieve the Lord.
No, it is we soaring explore galaxies,
Our bullet boat light's speed by thousands flies.
Who moves so among stars their frame unties;
See where they blur, and die, and are outsoared.[55]

"See where they blur, and die, and are outsoared": this, in its surprising, and gratefully surprised, unenvious awe, shows the achieved possibility of an art of postcoital gladness.

NOTES

1. John Donne's poems are quoted from *The Complete English Poems,* ed. A. J. Smith (Harmondsworth: Penguin Books, 1971).

2. William Empson, "Donne in the New Edition," *Critical Quarterly* 8 (1966):272.

3. Arthur F. Marotti, *John Donne, Coterie Poet* (Madison: University of Wisconsin Press, 1986), 111–13. Subsequent references will appear in parentheses as M, followed by the page number.

4. Empson, "Donne in the New Edition," 276.

5. Tilottama Rajan, "'Nothing Sooner Broke': Donne's *Songs and Sonets* as Self-Consuming Artifacts," *ELH* 49 (1982):817.

6. John Carey, *John Donne: Life, Mind, and Art* (London: Faber & Faber, 1981), 190. Subsequent references will appear in parentheses as C, followed by the page number.

7. J. E. V. Crofts, "John Donne: A Reconsideration," *Essays and Studies* (1937); reprinted in *John Donne,* ed. Helen Gardner (Englewood Cliffs, N.J.: Prentice-Hall, 1962), 79.

8. All quotations from Samuel Taylor Coleridge, except that at note 47, are

from *Marginalia,* ed. George Whalley (London: Routledge & Kegan Paul), 2 (1984):213–338.

9. T. S. Eliot, "Donne in Our Time," *A Garland for John Donne,* ed. Theodore Spencer (Cambridge: Harvard University Press, 1931), 10.

10. Donne, "Obsequies to the Lord Harrington."

11. William Empson, "There Is No Penance Due to Innocence," *New York Review of Books,* December 3, 1981, 42–50.

12. Coleridge, *Marginalia,* 2:220.

13. Helen Gardner, ed., *The Elegies and the Songs and Sonnets* (Oxford: Clarendon Press, 1965), 199.

14. William Hazlitt, on "The Blossom," *Lectures on the Comic Writers* (1819); reprinted in *John Donne: The Critical Heritage,* ed. A. J. Smith (London: Routledge & Kegan Paul, 1975), 311.

15. William Empson, *Seven Types of Ambiguity* (London: Chatto & Windus, 1930; 2d ed., 1947), 145.

16. Empson, "Donne in the New Edition," 280.

17. John Donne, *Sermons,* ed. George R. Potter and Evelyn Simpson (Berkeley & Los Angeles: University of California Press, 1953–62), 6:41.

18. Carey, on "A Valediction: Of My Name in the Window," 196.

19. Barbara Herrnstein Smith, *Poetic Closure* (Chicago: University of Chicago Press, 1968), 175–76.

20. Ibid., 102.

21. Ibid., 182.

22. Ibid., 32.

23. Frank Kermode, *The Sense of an Ending* (New York: Oxford University Press, 1967), 7.

24. Ben Jonson, translating Petronius.

25. Kermode, *The Sense of an Ending,* 58.

26. Frank Kermode, "Sensing Endings," *Nineteenth-Century Fiction* 33 (1978): 153.

27. Ibid., 155.

28. Donne, "Upon the Annunciation and Passion falling upon one day. 1608."

29. Letter from Donne to Goodyer; quoted by R. C. Bald, *John Donne: A Life* (Oxford: Clarendon Press, 1970), 169.

30. Letter from Donne to "G. G." (April 14, 1612); quoted by A. J. Smith, *John Donne: The Critical Heritage*, 2.

31. Letter from Donne, possibly to Wotton (c. 1600); quoted in A. J. Smith, *John Donne: The Critical Heritage*, 3.

32. Letter from Donne to Goodyer (1611); quoted by Marotti, *John Donne, Coterie Poet*, 16.

33. T. S. Eliot, "John Donne," *The Nation and the Athenaeum* 33 (June 9, 1923):10.

34. Letter from Moore to Byron (January 2, 1821); *Letters and Journals*, ed. Leslie A. Marchand (London: John Murray), 8 (1978):55.

35. Hazlitt, on "The Funeral," in A. J. Smith, *John Donne: The Critical Heritage*, 311.

36. Carey, on "A Lecture upon the Shadow," 181.

37. Rajan, "Nothing Sooner Broke," 828.

38. *The Retrospective Review* (1823), in A. J. Smith, *John Donne: The Critical Heritage*, 328.

39. Donne, "Elegy 11: The Bracelet."

40. Empson, "Donne in the New Edition," 274.

41. Empson, "No Penance Due," 42.

42. Empson, "Donne in the New Edition," 259.

43. "Marginalia on the Bridgewater Manuscript," in A. J. Smith, *John Donne: The Critical Heritage*, 77.

44. Donne, *Sermons* 1:237; quoted by Marotti, *John Donne, Coterie Poet*, 135.

45. Harry Morris, "John Donne's Terrifying Pun," *Papers on Language and Literature* 9 (1973):128–37.

46. Quoted by Bald, *John Donne: A Life*, 168 n.

47. Coleridge, *Notebooks*, in A. J. Smith, *John Donne: The Critical Heritage*, 276.

48. T. S. Eliot, *After Strange Gods: A Primer of Modern Heresy* (London: Faber & Faber, 1934), 43.

49. T. S. Eliot, *The Waste Land: A Facsimile and Transcript of the Original Drafts*, ed. Valerie Eliot (New York: Harcourt Brace Jovanovich; London: Faber & Faber, 1971).

50. William Empson, "Rescuing Donne," in *Just So Much Honor*, ed. Peter Amadeus Fiore (University Park: Pennsylvania State University Press, 1972), 117.

51. Empson, "No Penance Due," 42.

52. Ibid., 43.

53. Empson, "Donne in the New Edition," 275.

54. Donne, *Sermons* 3 (1957):105, quoted by Carey, *John Donne: Life, Mind, and Art,* 135.

55. William Empson, *Collected Poems* (New York: Harcourt Brace, 1949; London: Chatto & Windus, 1955). Reprinted by permission.

Elaine Scarry

Donne

As evening began to fall on Easter Day, 1625, the men and wom-
en of Saint Paul's entered the church and listened as John Donne spoke
to them at length on three subjects: the torture of the Inquisition, the
nature of fornication, and the consecration of the dead. What emerged
in the half-light of evening were three successive representations of the
human body at the moment of that body's being touched by the hand
of another person: first, the body tortured and put in pain; second, the
body desired and caressed, sometimes inside and sometimes outside
the boundaries of Church law; third, the undesired body, undesired
because dead, decomposing, and in its decomposition, repelling the
touch required for consecration.

Donne insists on the obligation to touch the human body, whether
acutely alive or newly dead, with generosity and fierce decency; and
what is most remarkable and perhaps also most moving about this insistence is that he locates the precedent for the generous reflexes of the
hand in what he identifies as the willful materialism of the Judeo-
Christian God. God, says Donne, has not only repeatedly "dignified"
and "crowned" the human body, but (invoking the word that becomes
nearly electric in its ethical resonance) "associated" himself with it: he
created the body in His own person; he took it as his own in the person of Jesus; he inhabits it in the person of the Holy Ghost. "That
God, or Angels, or our Soules, which are all Spirits, should be in
heaven, *Ne miremini*, never wonder at that. But . . . *Miramini hoc*,
wonder at this; That God, all Spirit, served with Spirits, associated to
Spirits, should have such an affection, such a love to this body, this
earthly body, this deserves this wonder."[1]

What inflames Donne's imagination, what takes hold of his mind, is
not the fact of God's materialism per se (however miraculous that is;
and it is, of course, the Easter miracle of the resurrected body that

provides the materialist premise of the whole sermon). It is instead the fact that that materialism is wholly willed: it is volitional and freely chosen. How easily might God have dissociated Himself from the body; yet how consistently he chose to be associated. How at liberty to disavow; hence how breathtaking the refusal to disavow.

This refusal to disavow, and the volitional materialism it entails, characterizes John Donne as well as John Donne's God. In fact, if we have any difficulty recognizing this mental habit in his work, it is perhaps because he seems so little tempted to disavow that we can hardly credit him for valiantly refusing to do so. To be human is to be at once body and soul; but, like any pair of friends, the two are forever tilting out of balance, overbalancing and rebalancing, and that split second of being off balance creates the pressure to choose between the two. Donne in such moments as often as not comes down on the side of the physical. Thus, among the *Paradoxes and Problemes* of the *Juvenilia* is his high-spirited and winning argument that "The Gifts of the Body [which "strike us *suddenly*" and "possesseth us (so) immoderately"] Are Better than Those of the Minde."[2] They are so primarily because our physical perceptions provide the ground of all subsequent enablement, whether intellectual or ethical: thus, it is only because of the body that we can be, not merely brave and strong, but also brilliant and good. Donne aims here to be brilliant and good; and fragments of the same argument periodically reemerge, often in more sober and lovely forms, throughout all his later writings. As late as 1627, six years into his deanship at St. Paul's and several years before his death, he will still be identifying the body as that "which I have loved better than my soul,"[3] even if it is now the intonation of confession rather than spirited bravado that rounds out the arc of comparison.

There are, of course, an equal number of moments where the balance suddenly tilts in favor of the soul, moments when Donne either is, or imagines himself to be, at liberty to repudiate the material realm. But here again what becomes visible is the force of his refusal to do so. Thus, in the suspended metrics of the first two-thirds of "The Extasie," man and woman slowly grow all soul and mind; in the final third, the last twenty-six lines, Donne negotiates his way back to the body through a series of "but" constructions: "But O alas, so long, so farre / Our bodies why doe wee for beare?" and a few lines later, "On man heavens influence workes not so, / But that it first imprints the ayre, / Soe soule into the soule may flow, / Though it to body first repaire," and finally the lines that will lead into the poem's close, "Loves mysteries in soules doe grow / But yet the body is his booke . . . "[4] The continually re-emerging word "but," "though," "but Yet" is there to make palpable, to provide an identifiable verbal site for, the fact of turning back. Twenty-six lines are required not because Donne needs twenty-six lines mentally to reenter the body, but because by moving though a set of metaphors that define with ever-greater precision the exact relation between body and soul, he is able to prolong the moment of standing outside the body, and hence dramatize the deliberateness and the deliberation with which the body is reembraced. The poem's large-souled mysticism (with its pregnant banks, proliferating violets, fiercely clasped hands, and gazing eyes) thus provides the capacious stage for the dramatization of his volitional materialism.

Similar moments recur throughout the later writings, as at the end of *Devotions Upon Emergent Occasions,* where, now through the agency of death rather than ecstatic passion, Donne once more imagines himself at liberty to step away from the body, a liberty that we might have guessed would seem to him acutely sweet, since for the last hundred pages he has been chronicling, often in alarmingly concrete clinical detail, the inner vagaries of his 1624 illness. Instead, Donne at this moment imagines the soul taking one step away from the body, looking toward heaven, looking back toward the body, and being overcome with homesickness: "That body," he writes, "which scarce three minutes since was such a house, as that that soul, which made but one step from thence to heaven, was scarce thoroughly content to leave that for heaven."[5]

Physical disease, plague, fever, accident, the risk of childbearing— these loom large in the background of all the poetry and prose; for Donne sees himself forever moving though a world "where in every street / Infections follow, overtake, and meete,"[6] and many of his works are written on what he believes to be the eve of his own death.

His animus against disease, far from entailing an animus against the body, is based precisely on an affection for the body that makes its appropriation by foreign agency intolerable. It is this same unequivocal commitment to the body that makes medicine the very model of Renaissance science for Donne, as Don Cameron Allen has shown in his exhilarating, and now classic, 1943 account of Donne's knowledge of anatomy, physiology, and pathology.[7] Thus the necessity of making an even temporary choice between the home of heaven and the home of the body is a pain-filled one: "This man," Paul Valéry once wrote about Leonardo da Vinci in an essay that might instead have been about Donne, "this man who would dissect ten cadavers to follow the course of some veins thinks to himself, The organization of our body is such a wonderful thing that the soul, though a thing divine, is deeply grieved at being separated from the body that it inhabited. *And I can well believe,* says Leonardo, *that its tears and its sufferings are not without reason.*"[8]

At no point was John Donne in danger of an overt repudiation of the material realm, but he does seem to have perceived himself to be steadily in danger of a more quiet form of disavowal, for he was acutely aware of the ease with which the material realm can simply fall away from language. What puts him at liberty to separate himself is not the dissolution of the body in ecstasy or illness but his own devotion to writing. His accounts of God's authorial acts of speaking and writing are revelatory because in them he announces so clearly his own sense of what is most difficult, and what is most to be emulated; he therefore exposes his own aspirations as a writer. For Donne, language achieves its greatest triumph when it is inclusive of the material realm. Thus he frequently moves in his sermons to the biblical passage describing the approach of the Holy Ghost: a rush of wind filled the house, and there "appeared . . . cloven tongues, like as of fire" (Acts 2:1). As is true of any scriptural passage, this one permits several different emphases. The tongues of fire can be understood as purely figurative, an expression of the force and immediacy with which God's presence is felt. Alternatively, one may take the passage literally, envisioning the flames as the physical phenomenon that actually appears: the word "tongue" is in this case only adjectival; the flames of fire are "tonguelike" in their shape. The third alternative is that tongues, the purplish organs of speech, enter the room, and now it is the word "fire" that slips to the position of adjective, describing the temperature, the heat, of the bodily organ. It is always this third alternative to which Donne is drawn: when "fiery" appears at all, it does so only as an attribute of the tongue, and often it simply drops out altogether, as in this passage from a sermon in 1627: "Every good person in the Congregation . . . feeles *This Spirit of the Lord, this Holy Ghost,* as he is *this cloven tongue,* that sets one stemme in his eare, and the other in his heart, one stemme in his faith, and the other in his manners, one stemme in his present obediance, and another in his perseverance, one to rectifie him in the errours of life, another to establish him in the agonies of death . . . "[9]

This same attention to the material possibilities of language recurs when Donne praises God's written word. Thus, a passage in *Devotions Upon Emergent Occasions* starts by crediting God's attention to the literal plane; it then moves quickly away from the concrete to the figurative, and begins to unfold a complicated list of ever-more-difficult and remote feats of language; but suddenly, at the climactic moment, it swings back to reinclude the material realm:

> My God, my God, thou art a direct God, may I not say a literal God, a God that wouldst be understood literally and according to the plain sense of all that thou sayest? but thou art also (Lord, I intend it to thy glory, and let no profane misinterpreter abuse it to thy diminution), thou art a figurative, a metaphorical God too; a God in whose words there is such a height of figures, such voyages, such peregrinations to fetch remote and precious metaphors, such extensions, such spreadings, such curtains of allegories, such third heavens of hyperboles, so harmonious elocutions, so retired and so reserved expressions, so commanding persuasions, so persuading commandments, *such sinews even in thy milk, and such things in thy words,* as all profane authors seem of the seed of the serpent that creeps, thou art the Dove that flies.[10]

God soars through the air while all other authors creep along the ground, but what enables Him to soar above the material realm is precisely the climactic capacity of his language to include not simply the body, but the body redoubled, and double gendered, "sinews in your milk," and finally, most simply and perhaps most beautifully, his capacity to get "things" in his words.

There are "things in John Donne's words" as well, as has been consistently recognized by his readers, both in decades when he has been resisted and in those in which he has been widely read.[11] That his poetry successfully incorporates the material realm and, in particular, the human body, can for the present, be assumed as a given, and what I will instead look at is the way in which Donne thinks about the issue, what he sees as being at stake in it. Donne in fact halfway solves the problem of material representation by the very way in which he formulates it. Rather than conceiving of fitting an object inside a word, or wrapping a sentence around the human body, he reformulates the issue in terms of the page, something that because it is cloth or paper or rag or leaf or vellum itself has sensuous properties. Donne often refers to the material attributes of the page, sometimes even overtly transferring them to language as when, in the seventh Elegy, he speaks, not of torn pages but "torn sentences."

He thus bypasses the problematic immateriality of language by thinking in terms of something that already has material standing in the world, no matter how slender and two-dimensional that material standing is. Much less difficult than imagining an object folded into a word is to imagine the object enfolded into a paper or cloth, an image that one finds continually in his letters. Thus he writes to his friend Tobie Mathew, "SIR, At *Ratisbone* I had your Letter from *Brussel's;* and, in it, you,"[12] as though the paper were folded around a minature Tobie Mathew. Similarly, in a letter written in 1621 to George Villiers, Duke of Buckingham, Donne says, "I most humbly beseach your Lordship to afford this ragg of paper a room amongst your evidences [a characteristic opening, for he often contemplates the space-taking fact of the letter and speculates about the particular drawer or cabinet in which the recipient will put it] . . . I deliver this paper as my Image; and I assist the power of any Conjuror, with this imprecation upon my self, that as he shall tear this paper, this picture of mine, so I may be torn in my future, and in my fame."[13] In his satiric verse celebration of Thomas Coryat's book, *Crudities*, he designates the bound volume as a "voluminous barrel," full of wares from the east; he then begins to unbind the book, and now envisions each dismembered page as wrapped around a parcel of currants or figs, "Medicinall and Aromatique twigs," that fill the stalls of the fairs and marketplace. Donne invents this ingenious image in order to permit himself the following lines: "Then thus thy leaves we justly may commend, / That they all kinde of matter comprehend" (ll. 47, 48). The "matter" in question here is not yet the human body; though that will enter later in the poem. But even here the paper packets of vegetable matter are on the verge of life: they have become "warm" with handling and are described as being about "to hatch." The fact that Donne calls the pages "leaves" underscores the continuity between them and their vegetable content. By extension, it also asserts a broader continuity between language and the material realm it seeks to represent.

Thus the verbal unit (word, sentence) is reconceived as a material unit, the page. But the whole page in turn must now be reconceived as capable, beyond its own material fragility, of somehow bearing the record of the material world. Although Donne thinks about this problem in many different ways, two ways of picturing it recur persistently. In the first, he lifts the interior of the body directly onto the surface of the page. In the second, he repositions the page back in the interior of the human body. The two together begin to make visible what is at stake in the issue of volitional materialism with which we began or what will be called "consentual materialism" by the time we end.

The material realm might ordinarily be thought of as the realm of nonnegotiable contingency and accident, a realm in which one's alternatives are either to be wholly subject to its claims or to distance oneself from it altogether by some form of mystical repudiation. To thus reconceive of materialism as voluntary is in some sense to revolutionize or reinvent it altogether, and though this labor belongs collectively to Donne's age rather than to Donne personally, his poetry excavates that shared cultural motivation as it takes place in medicine and the other sciences, and in religion as well. Donne in his sermons continually questions the material reality of hell: that is, he never questions the *reality* of hell; in fact, he periodically encourages his congregation to be quite alarmed about it; but however urgent its reality, it is not, he suspects, a *material* reality. How could it be? Since heaven, by virtue of the incarnation, is the final destination for the physical body, then hell, which exists at an absolute distance from heaven, cannot itself concern the physical body and must be immaterial. All this is a way of saying that though the shift to volitional materialism can quite rightly be thought of as taking place in the rather glacial change from a religious to a secular and scientific world, the pressure of that same shift can, within religion itself, be felt in the repositioning of the material realm from the space of the inferno to the space of heaven.

The first of the two models, the lifting of the body out onto some surface of display, has many examples: it may be an anatomy table, or instead a cross, or instead a miniaturized surface like the fingernail on which the commingled blood of man, woman, and flea is displayed. But the capacity of page, paper, or cloth to absorb into its own surface the interior matter of the body finds its most representative example in Donne's account of the relic at the Cathedral of Turin, the white cloth or sheet that, says Donne, was either loosely wrapped around Christ's body in order to carry him from the cross to the sepulchre, or was instead the actual winding sheet bound close around him. Donne thinks that it must have been the second, because of the precision with which the image of the body is inlaid into the cloth: "it appeares, that that sheet stuck so close to his body, as that it did, and does still retaine the dimensions of his body, and the impressions and signatures of every wound that he had received in his body."[14]

Of the many things that might be said about this translation of body into cloth, three are relevant here. First, the transfer is literal: there is an actual "thing" lifted from body to cloth. In that satiric verse on Thomas Coryat's book, the surfaces of the pages take on the temperature of the living substance they contain. So, too, Donne's verse letter to Magdalene Herbert tells her that the paper she is holding will absorb into its surface the redeeming heat of her warm hand (l. 17). Now, again in this passage about the Savoy cloth, an interior substance of the body (this time not heat, but blood) is directly lifted onto the white surface, a transfer so direct that Donne imagines the difficulty the attending women must have had pulling the cloth away: "It would," he writes, "have been no easie matter for those women to have pulled off that sheet, as if it had no other glue, no other gumme, but his owne precious blood to hold it."

Second, the page or cloth (and by implication language) is thus conceived of as supple and receptive to content. Whether it was loosely wrapped around, or tightly bound to, its content, it now presents the precisely etched outline of what it once held—and is thus like the many Renaissance studies of drapery, cloth drawn on cloth, falling into the shapes and folds that somehow become the back of Leonardo's Mary or the impossibly generous lap of Ann (figure 1). Leo Steinberg, calling attention to the visibility of Christ's genitals beneath the covering cloth, writes that it was "the special pride of Renaissance painters to make drapery report subjacent anatomical events."[15] Or again one thinks of Leonardo's topographical maps, where the folds and falls of the terrain, like a cloth that has picked up the shape and weight of the material world, are now draped over the page to map the world. For Donne, as for Leonardo, the identification between garment and body, or cloth and land, is so close that he often uses the two words interchangeably.[16]

Third, the body on the cloth hovers between substance, picture, and word. There is actual substance; the literal blood that makes the two, for the attending women, almost inseparable. Simultaneously, the representation is pictorial: the cloth contains the outline of the body. And finally, it is linguistic: the "signature" of the wound is, if not a word, at least the ghostly anticipation of a word. Throughout the poetry and sermons, Donne is forever tracing and retracing the passage between the material and immaterial worlds: as is shown by poems like "Aire and Angels," or "The Dream," he finds many alternative ways of envisioning how one gets from one to the other. The passage from body to voice, or body to language is itself one instance of the spectrum that leads from the material to the immaterial, and that passage in turn can be charted by including a thing, a picture of the thing, and a name for the thing within the space of a poem or passage.

Fig. 1. Leonardo da Vinci, Drapery Study on Canvas, Louvre, Paris.

The cloth at Savoy is an instance of, and model for, Donne's habit of lifting the interior of the body out onto the surface of the page. The second model is visible in many poems but can be illustrated with one particular poem, "A Valediction: Of My Name, in the Window." It is the opposite since the page is now itself placed into the interior of the body. It is as though Donne cannot allow body and voice to become separated from one another: thus language, in the first model, moves beyond the perimeter of the body, but takes the body with it, lifting it out into the world beyond its own original boundaries. Now, conversely, the body reclaims language, reabsorbing it back into its own interior as though to remind us that this is the original site of all lyrical utterance.

Donne's contemplation of the Savoy cloth occurs in an Easter-evening sermon at St. Paul's, this time in the year 1630. The specific scriptural passage he had taken for that night was Matthew 26:6: "He is not here, for he is risen, as he said; come, see the place where the Lord lay." Thus the entire frame for the sermon is the problem of material absence—"He is not here, for he is risen"—and the reassurance provided by the residues of materiality—"come, see the place where the Lord lay." The framing circumstance for this sermon, and perhaps for the whole set of Easter-evening sermons, is therefore very close to that which underlies the four Valediction poems ("A Valediction: Of the Booke"; "A Valediction: Of My Name, in the Window"; "A Valediction: Of Weeping"; "A Valediction: Forbidding Mourning"), all of which arise out of the anticipated disappearance of the beloved, and all of which seek to establish some form of representing the body during that temporary absence.

Ultimately, the vehicle of representation is language, since the poem itself is offered as a place holder, occupying the person's space until he returns. Even within the poems, writing is designated as having this function, and in each instance language is portrayed in terms of some material counterpart such as a book or a page. In "A Valediction: Of the Booke" this is immediately visible in the title alone. "A Valediction: Forbidding Mourning" culminates in the objects of page and pen, but page and pen each raised to the ninth power; for the page is now not rag or leaf or paper or vellum but the gold leaf; just as the pen has become the ultimate Renaissance agent of creation and inscription, the pair of compasses. In "A Valediction: Of Weeping" the image of a face suspended in a spherical tear permits a shift to the image of terrain draped across a spherical atlas, and this in turn allows Donne in the final stanza to reclaim material reality by displacing the topographical representation with actual rocks and tides.

In the last of the four, "A Valediction: Of My Name, in the Window," the inscribed name suspended in the sheet of glass becomes a magnified analogue for the translucent tear with its miniature representational cargo. It is this noun, this name (which I assume we can refer to as John Donne, or Johannes Donne) which gives the surface its solidity, its material substantiveness; and makes this page more authoritative than the merely paper pages with which it may have to compete, the rival letters his young wife is likely to receive from other men while he is gone. Windows, at the time Donne was alive and looking through them, were often still made of "oiled paper or muslin,"[17] in other words, of material whose overt resemblance to the materials of letters or books allows him to play upon the analogy in many ingenious directions: thus he worries that she may carelessly fling open the casement, distancing herself from his self-memorialization the way an imperious mistress might fling down an unwanted letter or turn over, with impatience, the page of a book. This page, however, is made not of "oiled paper or muslin" but of glass; and Donne opens the poem with the notion that it is the noun, the name, now inlaid into that vertical surface, that has given it, or at least contributed to, its "firmness," making it as "hard" as that which engraved it. While, in other words, the suppleness and receptivity of the Savoy cloth made visible the capacity of language to absorb the material world, the glass window is the reminder that that material world, once absorbed, is all that gives language its substantiveness. It is only its transparency out to the world (is "through-shine" as Donne calls it), its inlaying of nouns and names (or what we would call its referential capacity), that gives it standing in the world.

The substantiveness of language—its capacity to mime, and perhaps eventually acquire, the actual weight of what it describes—is at issue throughout the Valedictory poems. "A Valediction: Of Weeping" is in many ways the closest counterpart to "A Valediction: Of My Name, in the Window" since the tear (with its captive face) is such a clear analogue for the window (with its captured noun). The window is a magnified version of the tear which itself represents language as a fragile transparent envelope containing nouns or name, or picture. The tear in this poem, as is the way with tears in Donne's poetry, turns into a

coin with an engraved picture on it before it completes its fall; a transformation that indicates, less Donne's preoccupation with economics
than his preoccupation with the way a vehicle of representation acquires the material form and force of the object represented—that is,
acquires the negotiating power of the material world. The substantiveness of language is again in question in "A Valediction: Of the Booke"
since the book will survive and outlast invasions by the Goths and
Vandals. And, finally, in "A Valediction: Forbidding Mourning" the
compasses are the "stiffe twins"; the final assertion of "fixity" and
"firmness" brings simultaneously into play the erotics of erection, the
ethics of constancy, the moral psychology of loyalty, and the philosophy of materialism. While the weight of language is a special preoccupation of the Valedictory poems, it is by no means limited to them.
Donne is always attentive to verbal forms—such as curses or prayers—
that aspire to bring about a visible alteration in the physical surface of
the world; as he is equally attentive to verbal forms, like promises and
oaths, that aspire to acquire the substantiveness of the physical world;
thus, for example, the long prose work *Pseudo-martyr* centers on the
issue of oath-taking.

As important as the solidity of the window is its location. When at
the poem's opening, Donne invites Ann More to look at the name, he
stands on the other side of the glass, so that she can see noun and embodied person overlaid on one another. But there is simultaneously a
third layer because, as she looks at man and name, she sees, superimposed over the other two, her own reflected image. Thus, as was true of
the Savoy cloth, Donne brings together the actual material object (the
live body, himself), a pictorial representation of the body (Ann More's
reflected image), and the verbal equivalent, noun or name divested of
both sensuous matter and pictorial image. The inclusiveness of this
word-image-object triad is not subverted by the fact that there are two
persons present, since, within the fiction of the poem, man and woman
are one: "Here you see me, and I am you" (l. 12) and it is perhaps relevant
to mention that Donne's habitual way of spelling his name—Johannes
Donne—ensured that the name Ann Donne was present whenever his
was. The identificaton of the two is elaborated throughout the poem.

In the fifth stanza, for example, each becomes the other's interior. She bears their children (between the age of seventeen when she married Donne and thirty-three when she died, Ann More was pregnant twelve times); thus, he grows within her; and she grows within him because she stands in the room whose walls and rafters contain his bodily labor; thus each is "emparadis'd" within the other.

But the suspension of this name in a glass envelope between Donne on one side and Ann More's reflected image on the other means that that glass envelope appears to be itself enveloped in bodily substance, that the window is inserted into the physical interior of the composite body of Ann and Johannes Donne. When they step away, the noun becomes a "ragged bony name," a skeleton divested of its surrounding matter, a "ruinous Anatomie" awaiting the return of that enclosing body. The startling positioning of the glass in their physical interior is in part a restoration of the voice to the site of origin, at once establishing the standard by which the success of material representation is measured, and at the same time making labored forms of representation unnecessary. This restoration of the voice is reenacted at the poem's end when Donne, as though exhausted by his own display of genius, announces that "our firme substantiall love" has no need for this strange talk about "glasse and lines" which was, after all, only a man murmuring on the edge of sleep, into which he now presumably falls. Thus, in the silence of the poem, speech dissolves back into and is enclosed within the body, the site of all word-making.

The act of repositioning the translucent noun or picture or page inside the interior of the body is one that Donne performs many times in the course of his writing, though it takes many different forms and acquires a range of tones. Eventually, for example, one page of Thomas Coryat's book is wrapped around a pill and another becomes gunshot wadding, both pages thus making fateful entries into the body (ll. 61, 62). A stray noun or picture or page may turn up in almost any part of Donne's own vulnerable interior. Thus he announces in "The Dampe," "When I am dead, and Doctors know not why, / And my friends curiositie / Will have me cut up to survay each part, / When they shall finde your Picture in my heart . . . ," and so the poem

continues with Donne's speculations about the doctors' response to
finding this artifact in his heart. In the first sermon he ever preached
before the congregation of St. Paul's, he spoke of the devout Christian
as one who "hath [not now a page but] a whole *Bible*, and an abundant
Library in his own heart,"[18] nor does he use the word "heart" casually.
Two pages later he elucidates the command *Scrutari Scripturas* as entailing *exquisita scrutatio;* not a mere "ruffling" of the pages (the wonder-
fully impatient word "ruffling" is of course Donne's), but a graphic
manipulation of the tissue of the physical interior: "Turne over all the
folds, and plaits of thine owne heart, and finde there the infirmaties,
and waverings of thine owne faith." It is of course only by the agency
of that same "exquisite scrutiny" that that bodily matter comes itself to
be recognizable as an endless sequence of layered tissue, as in Leonardo
da Vinci's drawings of a torso where across the horizontal expanse of
the page different depths of breast, heart, veins, and lung are brought
successively into view as though it were the layers of a book with all
pages simultaneously open (figure 2). Donne's "mystick book," as he
calls it in Elegy XIX,[19] can be found in any part of the body deserving
exquisite scrutiny, and since so many parts of the body deserve exquisite scrutiny, it turns up quite often.

By carrying language into the body, Donne participates in a collective project whose work is shared by religion and science. As the name
John Donne is carried there in the glassy envelope of a lyric poem, the
name "Adam" and the noun "apple" are already thickly located in the
human throat; just as the name and narrative of Jesus line a woman's
womb, and the name and narrative of Eve, a man's chest—precedents
which Donne elaborates in one of his sermons on the penitential
psalms, in "La Corona," and in his first epithalmion sermon. A name
or noun is never a solitary word, but enfolds within it an entire narrative; it is in part for this reason that Donne can imagine not just a
name but whole pages of text, indeed whole books and libraries, entering there. The same is true of medicine: when a small slippery piece of
arterial matter is named "the duct of Botallo,"[20] the history of that
sixteenth-century Italian physician is carried there as well. So, too, the
name "Tulp's valve"[21] carried into the center of the heart an evolving

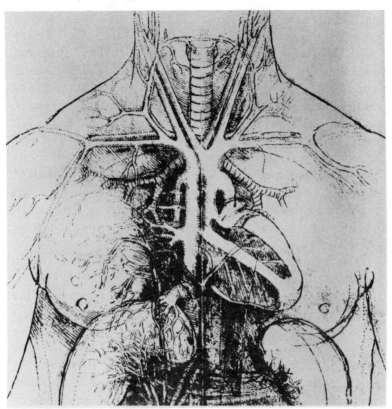

Fig. 2. Leonardo da Vinci, Organs of the Chest, Anatomy Notebooks, vol. 1, fol. 12 recto, Windsor Castle.

medical ethic requiring that the accuracy of diagnosis begin to be checked by means of postmortem dissection; and it perhaps carries there as well the image of Rembrandt's painting of Dr. Tulp, opening the body that would eventually hold his name. What the sixteenth- and seventeenth-century anatomical charts display is the insertion of name after name into part after part—this is a tongue, this is a heart— and those solitary words sometimes become whole paragraphs of text, as in Leonardo's anatomical drawings, where dense passages of language hovering on the margins of an open arm, eye, or chest often slip into and begin to coinhabit the interior of the drawing, without subverting the precisely rendered, material content of that thought-laden tissue (figure 3). It is indeed the very compatibility of the two that Leonardo's pages announce. As Donne repeatedly observes, and as is registered in the very form of the medical treatises written during the Renaissance,[22] it was precisely the work of the omnipresent plague, typhus, syphilis, and sweating fever to appropriate the body away from its inhabitant, and to do this by making the recitation of parts impossible, by shutting out language; making it no longer seem the human body but instead what Donne calls a "pestaduct," a vehicle of contagion that is not simply mentally unenterable but actually active-ly repels mental attention, the human touch needed for consecration. The inlaying of names and narratives is in part the attempt to keep the pathways open.

Donne's sense that the cultural work of the lyric itself excavates a wider cultural motive is visible in his incorporation of the material tools of religion and science into the body. So, in the poem called "The Crosse," the shape of that material artifact is absorbed into the gestures of the body as Donne stretches his arms in conscious imitation; then it is absorbed into the preconscious mimesis of the swimmer's stroke, "Swimme, and at every stroake, thou art thy Crosse" (l. 19); from the arms it migrates to the sutures of the skull and is eventually incorpor-ated into the gestural reflexes of the brain: "And as the braine through body walls doth vent / By sutures, which a Crosses forme present, / So when thy braine workes, ere thou utter it, / Crosse and correct concupiscence of witt" (ll. 55–58). In "The Canonization" the lovers are revered as ones "Who did the whole worlds soule contract, and drove / Into the glasses of [their] eyes . . . Countries, Townes, Courts." The parenthetical interruption—("So made such mirrors, and such spies, / That they did all to you epitomize")—on a technical grammatical level, works to make the image explicable and relatively harmless, inviting the gloss which explains that countries, towns, and courts enter the eyes only as objects of perception. But the actual effect of that paren-thesis is to heighten rather than diminish the sense of forceful entry, since it provides concrete objects that, by their habitual proximity

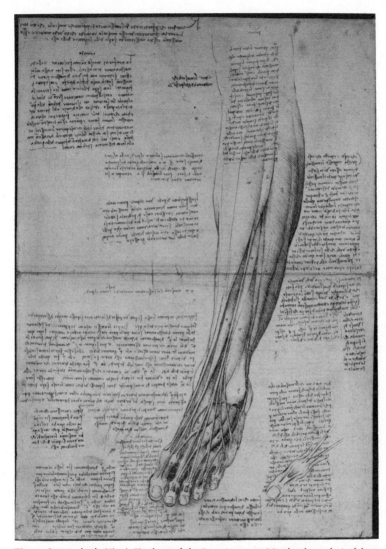

Fig. 3. Leonardo da Vinci, Tendons of the Leg, Anatomy Notebooks, vol. A. fol. 18 recto, Windsor Castle.

to the eye, make disarmingly palpable the asserted trespass through that most sensitive of regions.

For Donne, touch is the model for all the senses. Within the phenomenology of perception, different modes of perception are ordinarily recognized as existing at different distances from the body: thus the objects of vision, those windows, exist at a distance a hundred feet away; the object of audition, the voice in the hallway, exists twenty feet away, but the object of touch, the wood beneath my fingers, is immediately in contact with me, materially present. For Donne, sight, sound, touch, all have, not simply the immediacy, but the proximity of touch: as the wood rubs against his fingertips, the window rubs up against his eyes, and the voice in the hallway, as in the passage about the Holy Ghost, is felt along the passage in his ear. The gloss on "The Canonization" makes a startling set of lines seem for a moment normal, but only for a moment, after which we are likely to be as struck and startled by this account of perception as we originally were. Over a full array of instances, Donne's habit of interiorizing objects cannot be explained as a mimesis of perception, since it is not natural objects, but only humanly created ones, whether verbal or material, that enter the body this way. A catalogue of perceptual objects would presumably include a more promiscuous mixture of natural and artificial unless it is, and I believe it is, the very nature and destination of perception itself that is in the midst of being re-created.

The artifacts so far named here are ones Donne explicitly positions within the body, sometimes even, as in this last instance, making visible not only its site of occupancy, but also its arrival there, its passage from the outside to the inside. But the regularity with which we encounter these interiorized artifacts begins to establish within us the perceptual reflex of recognizing metaphor as precisely this act of interiorization, even when that spatial positioning is not explicit. When in "The Second Anniversarie" the spasmodic contortion of the beheaded man is compared to "a Lute, which in moist weather, rings / Her knell alone, by cracking of her strings" (ll. 19, 20), the body and neck of the lute seem not simply set down beside the trunk of the man, or superimposed over it, but absorbed into it, assisting the generous interpretation that those twitchings are the reflexes of a body beckoning its soul to return. The man's soul may not have reentered his body, but Donne's lute has, and in doing so, it works to hold the man steadily within the field of human perception.

This perceptual reflex of seeing the artifact absorbed into the body even when Donne has not himself positioned it there is probably encouraged in this instance by the fact that the body itself is open; but it seems equally in play where the surface of the body is not only not open, but also not even named or outlined in substance or shape. Thus the compasses in "A Valediction: Forbidding Mourning" have taken the breath away from several centuries of readers in part because, though not explicitly identified as residing within the interior of the body, or themselves containing within them sentient matter, the poem, with its forceful refiguring of the lovers, stands on the very edge of this assertion. Discussions of Donne's compasses seem eventually to end by directing attention to other Renaissance invocations of this most potent of objects, which is an appropriate reminder of how widespread the cultural investment in this object was, appearing both in verbal texts and (as the recent exhibition of the Bibliotheca Palatina makes clear)[23] on cover after cover of sixteenth- and seventeenth-century books about technics and architecture.

But what emerges in these other invocations is not just the compasses but their interiorization. The theologian and cultural philosopher Nicholas Cusanus, at least some of whose works Donne had read,[24] includes in his philosophy on the nature of artifacts—wooden spoons, glass prisms, a children's hoop, an ikon of God—an insistence that the act of such invention is simultaneously an act of measurement. To make a wooden spoon, to originate any object, is to bring into the world something which has no precedent in nature; thus it provides, in the most literal way possible, a visible measure of our mental and spiritual capacities of the human interior. One of the motives of invention is precisely to perform the act of interior measurement. Thus making and measurement, art and science, become a shared cultural enterprise. Although Cusanus sees the artifact as originating from within us, and sees it as providing an external image of what is within us, he does not, with one exception, imagistically reinsert the artifact into the human interior, or speak of the object as though it had living matter in it. The exceptional instance is of course the compass which he presents not as an instance of an artifact that we make, but as the artifactual reflex of the mind itself. In its capacity for creation, he writes in *De mente,* the human brain is "a living measure" [*illam mensuram esse vivam*], measuring itself through itself, a "living pair of compasses [*circinus vivus*] measuring by itself."[25]

Leonardo da Vinci, whose notebooks contain many sketches of the compasses that he himself reinvented by perfecting the hinge, also positions them within the human interior, as in that most famous of Leonardo's drawings: the man centered in his circle, his arms at full extension, his fingertips just barely touching the perimeter as though with a single atom of contact; his legs poised on the arc below; his outstretched limbs thus miming the work of the compass that made the circle that in turn contains him. Less familiar but equally moving is Leonardo's drawing of a pair of compasses (figures 4, 5), at work and fully splayed, inserted within a half-hemisphere that, though perhaps only a richly articulated geometric figure, bears a great deal of resemblance to the brain that contains Donne's migrating cross.

Limbs and brain become the home of the compass, but so, too, does that part of the body most associated with the formation of language. The passage about the appearance of the Holy Ghost was artificially truncated when introduced earlier, and actually reads as follows:

> Every good person in the Congregation . . . feeles *This Spirit of the Lord, this Holy Ghost* as he is *this cloven tongue,* that sets one stemme in his ear, and the other in his heart, one stemme in his faith, and the other in his manners, one stemme in his present obedience, and another in his perserverance, one to rectifie him in the errours of life, another to establish him in the agonies of death; For the holy Ghost, as he is a *Cloven tongue,* opens as a Compasse, that reaches over all our Map, over all our World, from our East to our West, from our birth to our death, from our cradle to our grave, and directs us for all things, to all persons, in all places, and at all times; *The*

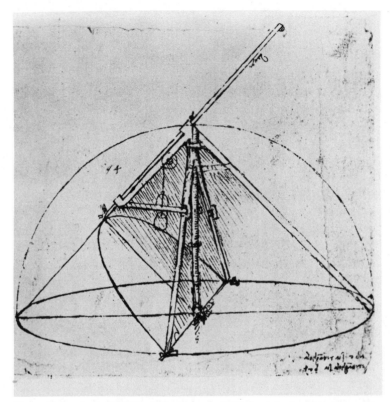

Fig. 4. Leonardo da Vinci, Parabolic Compass. Il Codice Atlantico, fol. 394, recto-a. Biblioteca Ambrosiana, Milan.

Comforter, which is the Holy Ghost, whom the Father will send in my Name, he shall teach you all things.

John Donne continually takes an inventory of the body—tongue, heart, arms, legs, eyes, and brain—and finds the often graphically described tissue coinhabited by towns, books, nouns, names, narratives, cross, lens, and compass, as well as many other constructions such as beehives, a garden, and even an entire farm. The inventory includes

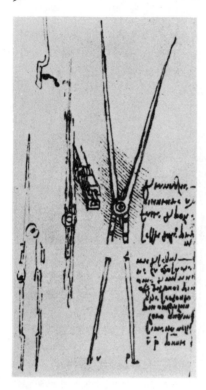

Fig. 5. Leonardo da Vinci, Measuring Instrument, Compass. Il Codice Atlantico, fol. 375, recto-a. Biblioteca Ambrosiana, Milan.

both verbal and material artifacts, and if my description has been moving unapologetically between the two, it does so because Donne keeps reminding us that things like pages and books are at once language and matter, a continuity he often explicitly illustrates, as he did a moment ago in his transition from tongue to compass. Even, finally, in instances where the object does not, like a book or the compasses, overtly span the two realms, every material object in Donne, because it bears in its outline the evidence of inventive intelligence, the record of the human capacity for invention, is itself soaked in language, as can be seen by turning for a moment to that most language-soaked of all Donne's artifacts, the bell in *Devotions Upon Emergent Occasions*.

Every world, wrote James Scully in 1974, has its own omnipresent background sound, calling attention to the analogy between crickets in Connecticut and gunfire in Chile.[26] For Donne, the omnipresent sound was the knelling of the bells of St. Gregory's.[27] The knelling of the bell, the bell itself, and indeed at moments even the steeple are collapsed into a single phenomenon, so that it comes to be not the sound alone which arcs down into the room where he lies sick but the material object. Inevitably, the bell makes its way not just into the room, but into the intimate vicinity of the body, for he recalls that bells were once enfolded into the garments worn by ancient priests (104). Soon it enters inside the body of another man and then brushes along the outside of Donne's body: another man's illness "may lie in his bowels, as gold in a mine, and be of no use to him; but this bell, that tells me of his affliction, digs out and applies that gold to me" (109). It is thus progressively interiorized and, in its final arc through his room, is absorbed into Donne's veins where it will throb as his own pulse (114). But when it enters there, what will enter there will be language as well as object. Already an indistinguishable merging of matter and sound, the bell has over the course of the meditation gradually absorbed layer upon layer of language into its surface, like a sequence of successive glazes, fragments of verbal history from Antwerp, Constantinople, or Roan (102) now themselves overlaid with ghostly narratives from neighboring monasteries (103), these voices in turn merging with God's voice ("He speaks to me aloud from that steeple; he whispers to me at these curtains" [107]), until the bell is so heavy with language that it comes to seem a materialized representation of the principle of intelligibility itself. It is appropriate that this many-, many-page-long meditation should come to be so known in the world by not even one sentence, but by one part of one sentence in which the bell is so generously legible that it preempts the question that might be asked of it: "therefore never send to know for whom the bell tolls; it tolls for thee" (109).

Finally, these objects are for Donne the locus of human volition, thus themselves becoming the agent of a revised materialism centered in a noncontingent body. Donne has, in part because of Coleridge's rhapsodic descriptions,[28] long been recognized as a poet of the will. Though this identification is in some way deeply accurate, it is in other ways wholly askew because the naked will ordinarily entails an array of associations—a heightened sense of the separation between male and female, or of the categories of action and inaction—from which Donne (the poet of equity and reciprocity as Helen Gardner once called him)[29] could not be more distant. It is not clear how one would even go about talking of the nature of "action" with a poet who is so invested, who locates such monumental consequences, in lying or half-sitting, facing west or facing east, issues of weight distribution, posture, and what is, within perception, called "proprioception" or, more to the point, the sheer "neuronal conviction" of being alive.[30]

Yet Donne *is* willful, and Coleridge was, of course, talking about the moral will, will as the exercise of one's power not over other persons but over one's own resources and, in particular, one's own body. His preoccupation with the voluntary, the consentual, is visible in almost every sphere of his writing. He defends suicide in *Biathanatos*, for example, not to endorse or encourage it, but to reinterpret the state of being alive as something one does with one's own volition: free to kill oneself, one's breath becomes one's own. By the same logic, he repeatedly contemplates and defends the possibility of a woman's infidelity, despite his obvious preoccupation with constancy. The act of making love is consentual ("let me," "license me"); but so, too, the act of refraining from making love with others is done by one's own consent rather than by laws, codes, conventions, or oaths that preempt her volition and thus prevent her from being the author of her own constancy.[31] So, finally, in his contemplation of and conversations with God, Donne, the undiscouraged consentualist, conceives of himself as in some sense free to negotiate his own fate. Speak to God, he tells his congregation, simultaneously with "prayer and praise": "Prayer is as our petition, but Praise is as our Evidence." God proceeds by precedent, and to praise him for a past generosity will provide him with a map for his present disposition.[32] He is drawn to passages about negotiation in both the Old and the New Testament, moments such as that when Jacob (Genesis 32:26) refuses to let God go until he has secured a blessing for him;[33] and the single sentence in the entire scriptures to which he is most drawn is that spoken by Jesus, "Into thy hands, Oh my God, I commend my spirit," a sentence that he returns to many times in his writings and that he explicates in the next-to-the-last paragraph of his final sermon. By those words Jesus brilliantly revises his own death: he "delivers that soul (which was never out of his Father's hands), by a *new way*, a voluntary emission of it into his Father's hands."[34] Donne ends by speaking of one's own death as a contract.

In the context of this absorption with contract and consent, Donne's horror of disease becomes fully intelligible, for (despite the apparently consentual language: one "contracts" the flu; one "catches" a cold) the nonconsentual nature of disease is not simply one of its many attributes, but is, in some fundamental sense, what it is. Thus in Hippocrates' treatises on epidemic, case study after case study opens with a sentence in which the person is described as "seized" by one of the symptoms: "Pythion, who lived by the temple of Earth, was seized with trembling which began in the hands,"[35] "Hermocrates, who lay sick by the new wall, was seized with fever,"[36] "The man lying sick in the garden of Delearces . . ."[37] and so the case studies continue. The opening sentence on Galen's treatise *On the Natural Faculties* identifies us with our capacity for volition: disease is later defined as the negation of that given,[38] and the symptoms are again described in language of preempted consent: the stomach is "oppressed by the quantity of its content . . . seized with diarrhea." Renaissance medical texts, too, use the language of military incursion or, as with Galen and Hippocrates, criminal trespass: thus Paré speaks of those with the plague as "molested with a desire to vomit,"[39] (as the seventeenth-century French physician Lazarus Riverius describes the blood disease purpura as generating "black and blew marks" that "possess whole members . . ."[40] Donne conceives of the body as the space of culture and tends never to refer to it as "Nature" unless it has been taken away by disease: "Nature," he writes in *Devotions*, "will not admit preventions, nor anticipations, nor obligations upon her, for they are precontracts, and she will be left to her liberty" (123).

Medical science, religion, and lyric poetry animate the body, deliberately enter it, and in doing so revise it to be volitional. Bell, lens, book, page are the repository of the peculiarly human in part because they are themselves the outcome of conscious intention. Nicholas of Cusa, who within the church governance of the papacy was himself a consentualist,[41] identified artifacts as the site of the consentual: when a person (idiot, layman, citizen) makes a wooden spoon, the person has invented an object without precedent or model: hence it becomes the manifestation of the voluntaristic, the capacity to operate outside contingency and accident.[42] Donne's formulations are similar, if not so elegant. Both verbal and material objects are connected to the volitional: the written word, says Donne, is a manifestation of the will;[43] and it is again on this basis that he distinguishes between the artifactual and the natural, writing in *Biathanatos* that fires and tapers extend our power of vision better than the moon because they are not natural: "they are more domestique, and obedient to us . . . they are our creatures."[44] Thus the inlaying of nouns, and names, and pages is a reinteriorization of the volitional.

Finally, the inlaying of artifacts into the human interior may seem to entail a *deanimation* of that interior, and indeed there is a limited sense in which this is so, for Donne's era stands on the verge of the recognition that disease comes about by the agency of other life forms, and there *is* within consentual materialism an attempt to narrow the category of "the acceptably alive" to "the exclusively human." Donne's designation of artifacts as "our creatures" entails an implicit background phrase "as opposed to other creatures" which will not be interiorized, which will in fact be shut out. Thus Donne's own lifetime is framed on one side by the sixteenth-century physician Hieronymus Fracastorius whose theory of fomites is seen as a precocious anticipation of the "bacterial theory of disease"[45] and on the other side by Athanasius Kircher's mid-seventeenth-century discovery of "innumerable animated worms" or "innumerable and invisible corpuscula."[46] Even within literary representations of disease one sees this same framing. Thus both within Boccaccio's account of the plague and Defoe's there is a sudden astonished recognition that the cats, dogs, and other creatures are dying:[47] there is no suggestion that these animals themselves are at fault, yet there is in that silence what could be called a kind of "cross-species suspicion" that what is happening has something to do with animal life.

Donne's retraction of life is usually *only* a retraction of *other* forms of life, and there is an emphasis on heightened sentience—even, as in the sermons, on reanimation. Occasionally, there is a retraction of the specifically human, as when in his elegy on Lady Markham he conceives of her dead body not as subject to decay but as clay turning to porcelain. More typically, Donne not only avoids but actively argues against that position, as when in his 1622 Lenten sermon on the scriptural text "Jesus Wept," he imagines that Jesus could have looked at the four-day rotting corpse of Lazarus and said, "There is no such matter, he doth not stink," but says instead, He is rotting, there is a stench, but yet he is my friend ("but though he do, my friend shall not lack my help").[48] This, finally, is Donne's most characteristic reflex, to bring forward the human hand at moments of both desire and repulsion; to say, but yet he is my friend. Poetry shares this with religion and medicine in what Donne, using the language of "Sweetest love, I do not goe," would have identified as the shared project of keeping one another alive.

NOTES

My special thanks to Annabel Patterson for so wisely guessing the pleasure I would take in thinking about Donne's materialism, and to Margreta de Grazia for many generous and spirited conversations along the way.

I am grateful to the Biblioteca Ambrosiana, the Louvre, and Windsor Castle for permission to reproduce the Leonardo studies.

1. John Donne, Preached at St. Paul's, Easter, 1625, *The Sermons of John Donne*, ed. and introd. George R. Potter and Evelyn M. Simpson (Berkeley and Los Angeles: University of California Press, 1962), 6:265–66.

2. John Donne, "Paradox xi: That the Gifts of the Body are Better than those of the Minde," in *The Complete Poetry and Selected Prose of John Donne*, ed. and introd. Charles M. Coffin (New York: Modern Library, 1952), 288.

3. Donne, Preached to the King, White-Hall, First Sunday of Lent (February 11, 1626/27), *Sermons* (1954), 7:362.

4. "The Extasie" as well as all other poems cited in this essay are quoted from Charles M. Coffin's *The Complete Poetry and Selected Prose of John Donne.* Line numbers where relevant will be cited parenthetically in the text.

5. John Donne, "Meditation viii," *Devotions Upon Emergent Occasions: Together with Death's Duel* (Ann Arbor: University of Michigan Press, 1959), 116. All references to *Devotions* as well as to "Death's Duel" are to this edition; page numbers will be cited parenthetically in the text.

6. Donne, "To Mr. T. W. (Thomas Woodward)," in Coffin, *Complete Poetry and Prose*, 134.

Although many gendered attributes of the body absorb Donne's attention, the fragility of the body, its susceptibility to disease or injury, cuts below the contours of gender. Donne's own astonishing alertness to disease has caused some to see him as hypochondriacal, but that alertness comes to seem not only intelligible but also inevitable in the context of the intimate details of his day-by-day life, as well as overarching historical events (the sequence of plagues, for example, in 1592–94, 1603–5, 1625). By the time he was nine years old, three young sisters were dead. By four, his father had died; by the time he was sixteen, his stepfather was dead as well (see Robert Cecil Bald, *John Donne: A Life* [London: Oxford University Press, 1970], 35, 37, 38, 537). Because his stepfather was a physician—formerly, in fact, the president of the Royal College of Physicians—Donne grew up in the neighborhood of St. Bartholomew's Hospital (Bald, 37, 38). Between the age of seventeen when Ann More married him and thirty-three when she died, she was pregnant twelve times, or one hundred and eight months of her short adult life; and Donne, as R. C. Bald notices, repeatedly in his letters alludes to his household of young children as a "hospital" (156, 279, 324). Given his absorption with, and tireless stand against, disease, it is utterly remarkable that fate should have made Donne part of the "counterfactual" mission to the Continent to try to stop, before it started, the Thirty Years War, an event that has been called "the greatest epidemiological experiment" known to man because of the extremity of disease caused by the constant exchange of infection among small bands of people on the move (Hans Zinsser, *Rats, Lice, and History* [Boston: Little, Brown, and Co., 1935], chap. 15). Bald's biography is superb throughout but his sustained re-creation of this Continental mission is a masterpiece (338–65).

7. Don Cameron Allen, "John Donne's Knowledge of Renaissance Medicine," *Journal of English and Germanic Philology* 42 (July 1943):322–42.

8. Paul Valéry, "Note et Digression," in *Les Divers Essais sur Léonard de Vinci* (Paris: Éditions de La N.R.F., 1938), 30–31. The translation follows, with slight modifications, that of Malcolm Cowley and James R. Lawler in *Léonardo, Poe, Mallarmé*, Bollingen Series 45 (Princeton: Princeton University Press, 1972).

9. Donne, Preached at St. Paul's, Whitsunday, 1627, *Sermons* (1954), 7:435.

10. Donne, "Expostulation xix," *Devotions*, 124. Italics added.

11. The long-standing critical sense that there are "things in Donne's words" is perhaps most beautifully and succinctly expressed by John Carey who writes, "Words are packed into the poems like boulders, and the voice clambers over them. . . . The verse form is made to seem the wrong size" (*John Donne: Life, Mind and Art* [New York: Oxford University Press, 1981], 117).

The formulation brings together the two very different ways in which the "materiality" of Donne's language has traditionally been acknowledged in the criticism. The first is the sense that there is *too much*, or there are *too many*, of whatever is inside the lines. This insistent attention to "volume" or "space" could only occur if the interior is felt to have "mass" or palpable objecthood, even if the content is otherwise understood as mental or abstract in character. As persistent, for example, as the critical attention to Donne's "wit" has been the attention to the plurality, plenitude, or overfullness of that wit—the sense that his ingenuity takes up space and presses against the language that seeks to contain it. *The Guardian's* 1713 phrase, "*Redundancy* of Wit," resurfaces in Moses Browne's 1750 paraphrase of Dryden's claim that Donne "'had *more* Wit than is to be found in *all* our other Poets put together,'" and again in Thomas Gray's 1752 description of his school as "*full* of conceit," Thomas Birch's 1752 claim that his poetry shows "a *prodigious fund* of genius," James Granger's 1769 "*prodigious richness* of fancy," as well as Robert Anderson's 1793 reliance on the repeated words "prodigious" and "abound." The principle of plenitude probably achieves its climax in Coleridge's celebration of Donne's "*squandering* golden hecatombs on a fetisch," "fearless of an *immense surplus* to pay all lawful debts," the "*purse-proud opulence*" of innate power," and the "*almost boundless* stores of a *capacious* memory" (each of the cited critical commentaries is reprinted in *John Donne: The Critical Heritage*, ed. A. J. Smith [London:

Routledge & Kegan Paul, 1985], 185, 203, 209, 210, 239, 257, 267, 268, 275, italics added throughout). The mental acquires the status of the material by the continual resort to this quantifying language.

Donne's mimesis of materiality is registered in a second critical reflex: the invocation of material objects themselves—often, as in the case of Carey's "boulders," objects whose obdurate objecthood (weight or mass or hard tactile surface) is pronounced. Behind Carey's boulders stands a tradition of stone. Thomas Warton, for example, wrote in 1781 that Donne's "asperities were such as wanted and would bear the chisel" (in Smith, 245), as Coleridge later wrote in his Notebooks, "By successive Chipping the rude Block becomes an Apollo or a Venus" (reprinted in Smith, 276), and the anonymous writer for the 1823 *Retrospective Review* described the Satires as "unhewn stones that have just been blasted from their native quarry . . . they must have come upon the readers . . . with the force and effect of the same stones flung from the hand of a giant" (reprinted in *Discussions of John Donne*, ed. Frank Kermode [Boston: D. C. Heath, 1962], 15).

As Coleridge's own image of the translation of stone into human form indicates, the central material object in Donne's writing is not stone but the weighted human body, the alive body: "sinews even in thy milk," "things in thy words." Thus Don Cameron Allen observes that, for all Donne's interest in cosmology, astronomy, and other external sciences, he was "much more interested in the intrinsic agonies of his own viscera" ("John Donne's Knowledge of Renaissance Medicine," 322), and for Carey, too, to return to our starting point, it is not finally boulders, but the space-taking human body, that fills the lines: "Donne, cajoling, demanding, enunciating, occupies so much of the foreground that we only occasionally catch a glimpse, over his shoulder or under his arm, of some anonymous figure at whom the flow of language is being directed" (118, and see his brilliant chap. 5, "Bodies").

The two forms of saluting Donne's materiality—the registration of plenitude and mass—have frequently converged in a single location, as in Thomas Carew's famous lines about the bending of our "stubborn language" ("made only fit / With her tough-thick-rib'd hoopes to gird about / Thy Giant phansie, which had prov'd too stout / For their soft melting Phrases" [reprinted in Kermode, 3]) and in Samuel Johnson's descriptions of "the mass of materials" and "copiousness of sentiment" in Donne's writing (reprinted in Smith, 219).

12. Letter from Donne to Mathew (August 1619), *Tobie Mathew Collection*, 336, cited in Bald, *John Donne: A Life*, 359.

13. Letter from Donne to Buckingham (September 13, 1621), *Cabala: sive Scrinia Sacra*, 314, cited in ibid., 375.

14. Donne, Preached at St. Paul's, Easter Day, 1630, *Sermons* (1962), 9:197.

15. Leo Steinberg, *The Sexuality of Christ in Renaissance Art and in Modern Oblivion* (New York: Pantheon, 1983), 82.

16. See "Holy Sonnet xi," "The Litanie," stanza 5, and especially Donne's beautiful modulation of body and garment in *Devotions* (63, 66, 85, 94) which climaxes in his imagining that the person whose funeral bell now rings may have been an artificer, a coatmaker, who, having disappeared from the world, ceases to be sought by those needing new garments (116). The coalescing of physical terrain and cloth appears in poems such as "Satyre II," lines 87, 103, 104.

17. Lewis Mumford, *Technics and Civilization*, 2d ed. (New York: Harcourt, Brace & Co., 1963), 125.

18. Donne, Preached at St. Paul's, Christmas 1621, *Sermons* (1957), 3:365.

19. Because Donne in this elegy coaxes his mistress to undress, the poem turns at its midpoint on the difference between the clothed and unclothed body; but the force of the poem arises in part from its refusal to permit the distinction between "dress and nakedness" to open out into an opposition between "culture and physical body." There is instead only "culture and culture," for the poem moves from the "external culture" (girdle, breastplate, busk, gown, and coronet) of her outward dress to the "internal culture" (mines of precious stones, empires, pictures, and mystic books) interior to her body. The Renaissance reflex of absorbing cultural objects into the bodily interior has perhaps its single most breathtaking expression in Titania's description of the mother of the changeling boy in *A Midsummer Night's Dream:* the two women sit gossiping by the sea in the "spiced Indian air" of evening, and watch the sails of the ships grow "big-bellied" in the wind; then the votress, herself pregnant with the changeling boy, gets up and "with pretty and with swimming gait," imitates the ships by moving across the sand to gather rich trifles for Titania (2.1). Here, as in Donne, the interiorization of the artifactual is motivated in part by the recognition of the body's acute natural fragility: "But she, being mortal, of that boy did die."

20. Ralph H. Major, ed., Introduction to Leonardo Botallo's *Commentarioli duo*, in *Classic Descriptions of Disease: with Biographical Sketches of the Authors*, 3d ed. (Springfield, Ill.: Charles C. Thomas, 1945), 616.

21. Major, Introduction to Nicholas Tulp's *Observationes Medicae*, in *Classic Descriptions of Disease*, 141.

22. We today generally assume that the body should be thought of "as a whole" rather than as "parts," since the latter seems to imply an aggressive, if only mentally executed, dismemberment. While this reflex is generously motivated, it may also be a luxury of our relative immunity to disease. In the Renaissance, "part" and "whole" appear to have very different values: the naming of body parts often seems to be performed as a stay against disease which works to "spoil" part after part and eventually to take over the whole body, subverting the capacity to differentiate among parts: "As long," Donne writes, "as a man is alive, if there appear any offence in his breath, the physician will assigne it to some *one* corrupt *place*, his *lungs*, or *teeth*, or *stomach*, and thereupon apply convenient remedy thereunto. But if he be dead, and putrefied, no man askes *from whence that ill aire and offence comes*, because it proceeds from thy whole carcasse" (Preached at St. Paul's, Christmas 1621, *Sermons* 3:364).

Throughout Renaissance medical treatises there recurs what could be called the "trope of the entire body," which signals the moment when the physicians have lost, the disease has won, the attempt to "track" the disease is no longer possible, it being everywhere. Boccaccio, following the course of plague boils from their starting place in armpit or groin, says at last they *"came indifferently in every part* of the body" (1353, *Decameron*, "To the Ladies," reprinted in Major, *Classic Descriptions of Disease*, 81); Kircher, tracking the plague pustules as they spread to all parts from the heart, writes that "the patient has lost his strength, and can not fight," the poison "conquers *the entire body*" (1680, *Natürliche und Medicinalische*, 39, reprinted in Major, *Classic Descriptions of Disease*, 85); as Paré also abandons the attempt to track the "rageing matter" as it flies from part to part finally "infecting the heart, and *so the whole body*" (1644, *The Workes of that Famous Chirurgion Ambrose Parey*, chap. 22, reprinted in Major, *Classic Descriptions of Disease*, 88).

These descriptions recur equally in diseases other than bubonic plague, whether typhus, sweating sickness, scarlet fever, or syphilis. The slow, confident, enumeration of parts is followed by a sudden rapidity of naming as the lesion, carbuncle, or pain "flies" from part to part (see in Major, John Caius, 205; Johannis de Vigo, 26; Jacques de Béthencourt, 37) which is then in turn followed by the final collapse into the idiom "the whole body." The three steps may occur over the course of an entire chapter, or instead in a more contracted grammatical space, as when Daniel Sennert, writing of scarlet fever in 1641, tells within a single sentence the narrative of "a certain boy from Breslau" and moves through feet, legs, scrotum, abdomen, face, knees, lungs, throat, whole body, and death (*De febribus libri* 4, 178, reprinted in Major, *Classic Descriptions of Disease,* 193).

The whole-body trope is not limited to Renaissance medical texts. Dangerous diseases in the twentieth century also elicit from us a ritual recitation of body parts (cancer of the breast, cancer of the lungs, cancer of the throat, of the mouth, of the prostate, of the pancreas, of the brain, of the liver, of the skin, of the cervix) and the spread to the whole body, even when submerged in a verb like "metastasize," reenacts the "flying from part to part" language of the earlier centuries. AIDS has reoccasioned this same rapid reanatomization of the body: over the course of several years, our collective attention has moved relentlessly from body part to body part—genitals, anus, blood veins, lungs, saliva, skin, brain, chapped lips, and finally, even tears. The disease, as Donne would have understood with such acuity, has worked to empty each "body part" of its cultural content, "spoiled" it, making it for a time apprehensible to others only as a "pestaduct," a site of contagion, hence fear and revulsion. Donne and his counterparts in other centuries work against disease by making the body, even when sick or hurt, the home of narratives and inlaid poetry.

23. See *Bibliotheca Palatina: Katalog zur Ausstellung, 8 Juli bis 2 November 1986, Heiliggeistkirche Heidelberg,* ed. Elmar Mittler, with Vera Trost, Markus Weis (Heidelberg: Universität Heidelberg, 1986).

24. Letter to Bishop Laud from Donne (April 1627) citing Cusanus's 1461 critique of the Koran, *Cribratio Alchorani,* quoted by Bald, *John Donne: A Life,* 493.

25. The Latin in this passage is quoted by Pauline Moffitt Watts in her *Nicolaus Cusanus: A Fifteenth-Century Vision of Man,* Studies in the History of Christian Thought (Leiden: E. G. Brill, 1982), 30:148. The English translation combines that given by Watts and that given in the full 1650 English translation

of *Idiota de mente* available in the W.P.A.'s *Occasional Papers,* introd. W. R. Dennes, Reprint Series no. 19 (San Francisco: California State Library, 1940), 55. Very few of Cusanus's many writings are available in English other than in excerpted form. I am very indebted to Pauline Watt's remarkably lucid and expansive account of those writings, especially *Idiota de mente, Idiota de sapientia, De visione Dei, De coniecturis, De beryllo,* and *De ludo globi.* Donne's own restless display of ingenuity is illuminated by Cusanus's conflation of creation and measurement: Donne invents to take the mind's measure, make visible its capaciousness. Leonardo's mathematical drawings appear, according to Umberto Cisotti, to have been "inspired" by Cusanus's *De geometricis transmutationibus* ("Die Mathematik von Leonardo da Vinci," in *Leonardo Da Vinci: Das Lebensbild eines Genies* [Wiesbaden: Emil Vollmer Verlag, 1955], 202).

26. Letter from Scully in Santiago, privately circulated, Storrs, Conn., 1974.

27. Bald, *John Donne: A Life,* 453.

28. Coleridge, in Smith, *John Donne: The Critical Heritage,* esp. 268.

29. Helen Gardner, "The Argument about 'The Ecstasy,'" in *Essential Articles for the Study of John Donne's Poetry,* ed. John R. Roberts (Sussex: Harvester Press, 1975), 252, 256, 257. Gardner's emphasis on reciprocity and equity is called into question by the contemporary critical argument that Donne wrote for a male audience: see, for example, Arthur F. Marotti's consistently interesting but not always convincing study, *John Donne, Coterie Poet* (Madison: University of Wisconsin Press, 1986), which suggests that Donne is more interested in being overheard by men then heard by women. But Donne has, by many women, long been felt to speak directly to them, whether indulgently or in high good spirits. It is a tribute to Donne that, even at a time when there were few women in the profession of literary criticism, the best and strongest—Helen Gardner, Evelyn Simpson, Barbara Hardy, Rosemond Tuve, Marjorie Nicolson, Kathleen Tillotson, among others—again and again turned to work with him.

30. This phrase is Michael Ignatieff's and was used in a discussion of the writings of Oliver Sacks.

31. "Plaies some soft boy with thee," Donne asks in "Sapho to Philaenis," as he imagines his beloved "More" eliciting love from "all men" (ll. 31, 62); see also his description of "the doctrine that denies Freewill" (l. 48) in "To Mrs. M. H. [Magdalen Herbert]."

32. Donne, Preached at St. Paul's, n.d., *Sermons* (1962), 5:272; see also *Sermons* 3:358.

33. Donne, *Devotions*, 93.

34. Donne, "Death's Duel," 189.

35. Hippocrates, "Epidemic III," in *Hippocrates*, vol. 1, trans. W. H. S. Jones, Loeb Classical Library (Cambridge: Harvard University Press, 1923), case 1, 219.

36. Ibid., case 2, 219.

37. Ibid., case 3, 223.

38. Galen, *On the Natural Faculties*, trans. A. J. Brock, Loeb Classical Library (Cambridge: Harvard University Press, 1916), 197, 247–49.

39. Paré, in Major, *Classic Descriptions of Disease*, 90.

40. Lazarus Riverius, *The Practice of Physick, in Seventeen several Books* (1668), 613, reprinted in Major, *Classic Descriptions of Disease*, 516.

41. See John Patrick Dolan's description of the attempt to "democratize and federalize" the Church through the conciliar theory in his Introduction to *Unity and Reform: Selected Writings of Nicholas de Cusa* (South Bend, Ind.: University of Notre Dame Press, 1962), 23–25.

42. Nicolaus Cusanus, *De Mente*, in Watts, *Nicolaus Cusanus*, 134. Cusanus's notion that the "volitional" is carried in the act of "creation" reemerges in his writings from the 1440s through the 1460s; see Watts, 187, 205, 211.

43. Donne, Preached at St. Paul's, Christmas 1621, *Sermons* 3:358.

44. John Donne, *Biathanatos: Reproduced from the First Edition*, introd. J. W. Hebel (New York: Facsimile Text Society, 1930), 156. Toward the end of *Devotions*, Donne begins to speak of what he understood to be his contract at the time he agreed to take on a body. This astonishing discussion takes place through an interiorized artifact, in this case the "entire farm" glancingly referred to at an earlier moment.

45. Major, Introduction to Hieronymus Fracastorius, in *Classic Descriptions of Disease*, 37.

46. Athanasius Kircher, *Scrutinium physico-medicum Contagiosae Luis, quae Pestis dicitur* (1658), 140, reprinted in Major, *Classic Descriptions of Disease*, 10, 11.

47. Boccaccio, in Major, *Classic Descriptions of Disease*, 81; and Daniel Defoe, *A Journal of the Plague Year* (1665), reprinted in Major, 93.

48. Donne, Preached at White-Hall, First Friday of Lent, 1622/23. *Sermon* (1959), 4:334.

 *Frances Ferguson*

Malthus, Godwin, Wordsworth, and the Spirit of Solitude

At the end of the eighteenth century in England, the population debate that had been in progress for more than fifty years took a curious turn.[1] The debate in its early stages had proceeded as part of eighteenth-century England's efforts to assess itself in relation to the ancients. Populousness was taken for a sign of national success and good government. The received wisdom was that modern states produced smaller populations than ancient ones had, and that this population decrease betokened a larger pattern of decline.[2] Thus, when Thomas Malthus, in his *On the Principle of Population* of 1798,[3] predicted that populations could well increase faster than food supplies, he was considerably revaluing a topic that had long been invested with a sense of crisis. This perspective appeared compelling, however, not because there were in 1798 too many people in the world—not even Malthus claimed that the world was over-populated at the time he wrote. Rather, as I will argue, Malthus's *Essay*, instead of being a response to the pressure of too many bodies, registers the felt pressure of too many consciousnesses, and his specter of over-population represents what might be called a Romantic political economy, much as the sense of psychic crowding that William Wordsworth's descriptions of London in book 7 of *The Prelude* represents a Romantic poetic consciousness. For Malthus and Wordsworth both, a Romantic consciousness emerges in reaction to the proliferation of other consciousnesses, or rather to the claims of other consciousnesses—for example, women's—on the individual. Solitude comes to be cultivated as a space for consciousness in which the individual is not answerable to others, and the waste landscape becomes the site of value because one can make it a peopled solitude, anthropomorphizing rocks and stones and trees, without encountering the pressures of a competing consciousness.

Insofar as this observation constitutes a critique of Malthus and

Wordsworth, and in particular a feminist critique, it may be said to have been anticipated by Germaine Greer in her recent *Sex and Destiny: The Politics of Human Fertility*. There Greer writes about population to suggest that the problem is not that there are too many people but rather that too many people believe that the world is overpopulated. Concluding the book with a passionate plea that the so-called developed nations not export their beliefs about population control, she calls for a reexamination of the allocation of resources. "If," she writes,

> we in the West think that only our kind of life is worth living, then clearly the numbers that the earth supports will have to be substantially reduced. The world could become a vast luxury hotel, complete with recreational space for us to hunt and ski and mountaineer in, but it must not be forgotten that our luxurious lifestyle demands the services of a huge number of helots, who cannot be paid so much that they can afford rooms in the hotel for themselves.[4]

Greer thus maintains that Western capitalism offers a most efficient variety of enslavement for the majority of the world's population and that Western views on the desirability of birth control translate into our commitment to cash in other people's necessities for our luxuries, viewing other people's lives as expendable, and seeing them as superfluities, just so much waste.

Overpopulation, from her standpoint, is a myth conceived in apology for the fact that Westerners are more concerned with a certain luxurious life-style than with the lives of other people. No one, she claims with some justice, knows "how many people the earth can support," and consequently no one knows if the earth is now overpopulated. Although she immediately affirms that "it is quite probable that the world is overpopulated and has been so for some time" (490), she moves from a hopeful discussion of redistributing the earth's resources to produce food for the many instead of luxuries—and even luxurious food—for the few to a vision of Western decline and fall. Like many of the eighteenth-century writers on population, she sees luxury as tending toward depopulation and the weakening of a society. And less interested in resource management than in the intrinsically moral aspects of the issue, she sketches with a certain relish an apocalyptic future in which Western nations are done in by the very luxury that they love:

> Rather than being afraid of the powerless [she writes], let us be afraid of the powerful, the rich sterile nations, who, whether they be of the Eastern or Western variety, have no stake in the future.
>
> (492)

Greer's defense of the reproductive practices of Third World nations thus does not merely claim that the "powerless" ought to be allowed what is very nearly the only power they have—the power to reproduce; she inverts the values that she sees in developed societies in her prediction of who will prevail. The populous powerless will live, the sterile rich will die. Thus she ultimately recapitulates the narrative of scarcity that has animated the discussions of population for the last two and one-half centuries. While first appearing to say that the rich nations should not impose their reproductive practices on poor nations so that all can live, she finally re-creates a world in which scarcity pits rich and poor against one another—but the difference between our present and her future is not that all will live but that the roles of living and dying will be reassigned.

Greer raises the issue of out-and-out scarcity to debunk it, suggesting that we probably have enough food to support a big population if we live lower on the food chain, but then she moves not just to an argument that we need to reallocate resources but well past that to the argument that we need to eliminate rich people and rich nations. She thus restages the Malthusian battle for resources, suggesting once again the appeal of the scarcity argument from the time of its initial appearance in the eighteenth century in the work of James Steuart and, later, Malthus. The argument about scarcity, that is, emerges not just as an attempt to fit numbers of persons to quantities of resources; it also, and more importantly, is a very satisfactory mode of pitting groups of persons against one another, indeed of pitting one idea of what a person is against others. What is problematic about Greer's work—at least from a contemporary feminist standpoint—is that she relegates consciousness and individual freedom to the realm of luxury. Essentially advocating an agrarian system so "natural" or nontechnological as to involve all-consuming labor to produce subsistence living, Greer would eliminate the waste that she takes consciousness to be. This would of course produce equality—even though it would involve everyone's being universally enthralled to the production of mere sustenance, and Greer thus has no patience with accounts of women's acceding to consciousness in a way that might threaten Malthus.

The eighteenth-century debate about population likewise tended to emphasize the fitting of labor and resources rather than the relationship between population size and individualism. Thus writers on population, looking around them and seeing work to be done and land to be improved, had first made the claim that the world was not overpopulated but the reverse. The land needed improvement, and people were therefore needed to improve it. Robert Wallace, in his *Dissertation on the Numbers of Mankind* of 1753, said that no state could "be said to be populous, where there are great tracts of land uncultivated"[5] and went on to offer plans for promoting agricultural industry in Scotland. Writers on population frequently cited Montesquieu's *Persian Letters* to the effect that "there were fifty times in the world as many people in the days of Julius Caesar, the first Roman emperor, as are in it at present"; they might demur, with Wallace that this was "certainly too high a proportion" (35), but they seldom differed with the basic premise that ancient nations had had more substantial populations than modern nations did. Godwin, writing in response to Malthus in 1820, stated categorically that "we live, as I have often had occasion to regret, in an unpeopled world."[6] Claiming that the world was empty rather than full, he indignantly wrote that "it is in this wreck of a world, almost as desolate as if a comet from the orbit of Saturn had come too near us, that Mr. Malthus issues his solemn denunciations, warning us on no consideration to increase the numbers of mankind" (486).

Population counts, these writers claimed, were more than a matter of neutral numbers. Those convinced that the modern world was "unpeopled," "dispeopled," or "waste," saw the superior populousness of ancient nations as yet another argument for the superiority of ancient governments over modern ones. As Wallace remarked in a footnote,

> The question concerning the number of mankind in ancient and modern times, under ancient or modern governments, is not to be considered as a matter of mere curiosity, but of the greatest importance; since it must be a strong presumption in favour of the customs or policy of any government, if, *ceteris paribus,* it is able to raise up and maintain a greater number of people.
>
> (14)

A good government, many writers argued, was a government that made people happy, and happy people tended to reproduce themselves (14).[7]

These claims were easy to affirm—and equally easy to deny, because they were based on the flimsiest of data, including the various conflicting figures that ancient historians had offered about the numbers of soldiers whom various nations had sent to battle, along with modern census tables in a bewildering variety of arrangements. The debate about population proceeded as a series of conjectural histories with more powerful information about the symbolic value of population than about the actual numbers of human beings alive at any given time. The persistent and pervasive assumption was that populousness was a positive value, and that one could indicate the virtuousness of any cause by establishing a causal connection between it and an ample population—or the viciousness of anything that seemed to impede the growth of population. Thus Benjamin Franklin boasted of extraordinary American fertility rates and stated that the people of America multiplied "by procreation, so as to 'double their numbers every twenty years,'" a claim William Godwin quotes in *Of Population;* "'if in Europe,'" Franklin wrote, "'they have but four births to a marriage, we may here [in America] reckon eight'" (126–27). Godwin, reading Franklin's claims with a jaundiced eye, found them less useful for establishing reliable information about the American population than about Franklin, whom he judged to have been always "eminently an American patriot," eager "to exalt the importance and the glory of his country"

(127). Similarly, Wallace provided less information about population than about his views on Catholicism when he maintained that the number of persons who had become priests and nuns "may justly be accounted one of the causes of the *scarcity* [emphasis mine] of people in all the countries under the pope's dominion" (88).

Given the pervasiveness of the assumptions that populousness in and of itself betokened happiness and civic virtue and that modern nations—particularly England—were woefully depopulated, Malthus's account of the inevitability of overpopulation in England was alarming not just because it constituted a dire prediction but also because it located danger in a hitherto unanticipated quarter. The production of people that had seemed desirable came to appear hazardous at best. Moreover, Malthus's mathematical ratios enabled him to make projections of population and food supplies that were both necessarily true because they were the result of an abstract technology for producing numbers and conveniently removed from any actual numbers of persons or quantities of farm produce. Because it is indisputable that a geometric progression quickly overtakes an arithmetic progression, the only matter in doubt is whether the increase in agricultural production and the increase in population are appropriately tied to these respective ratios. And although Malthus's entire treatise revolves around the actuarial terror that the inexorable operation of these ratios is supposed to inspire, the treatise itself calls for the abrogation of this mathematical principle of population increase. Could the geometric progression not be altered, there would be no point in writing the *Essay,* which does not merely lament the fate of the earth but also proposes strategies that would avert the onward march of the geometric ratio.

The dispute between Malthus and an opponent like Godwin thus first comes down to the question of how to fit people to resources. Malthus, despite the fact that he writes to discourage population increase, figures reproduction as a mathematical process, the inevitable and essentially unvarying production of numbers from ratios of other numbers. Against this vision of the immortality of a mathematical body that replicates itself of necessity, Godwin sets one that argues the power of consciousness to intervene. Yet the power of consciousness is framed as much in terms of the weakness of the biological body as in terms of the force of human thought. Godwin would save humans from the inexorable operation of Malthus's immortal mathematical body by attributing to them a time-limited biological body, where individual foresight both imposes constraints on reproduction and appropriates the accidents of mortality to its own purposes.

Godwin thus maintains that population, insofar as it is a problem, is one that corrects itself. In example, he points to Sweden as a country about which "we have something approaching to authentic information" and firmly states "that if there has been any actual increase, it at least amounts to comparatively very little" (196). Malthus arrives at a terrifying account of population expansion, Godwin holds, by assigning to individuals a reproductive power in society that they could have only if humans were both immortal and so thoroughly incapable of reflecting on their circumstances that they never curtailed the size of their families (207-8). Malthus uses a mathematical language of stability to maintain that food is subject to increase according to an arithmetic progression, that population is subject to increase in geometric progression, and that the "passion between the sexes" is "in algebraic language," a "given quantity" (52). The mind-limited body that Godwin imagines, however, checks population increase, so that the birthrate is only high in countries like the United States which are societies that are "incomplete." While it obviously cannot forestall the possibility of future crop failure and scarcity, mortality, and so forth, it continually changes what Godwin, in scathing quotation of Malthus's language of mathematical function, calls their "values."

The question of freedom—as the freedom at least to plan—thus intrudes itself into even the actuarial debate in which Malthus and Godwin are engaged. The argument for connecting numbers with liberty and individual consciousness had been advanced by David Hume in 1751, in his essay "Of the Populousness of Ancient Nations." Hume, specifically, addressing himself to the issue of the relationship between ancient nations and modern ones, argued against what he saw as the cant of believing that the world was in decline, in numbers of people and in government (esp. 443). He wonders if it is "certain, that antiq-uity was so much more populous, as is pretended" (383). And his doubt specifically attaches to Rome and the institution of slavery. Without leaping to condemn slavery as morally reprehensible, Hume performs an economic analysis of it. Since, he reasons, it must have been more expensive to rear children in the city, where domestic slaves were most in demand, Roman slaveholders must have discouraged their slaves from procreating—to the point of establishing separate living quarters for men and women and forbidding their intercourse. Just as few cattle are bred "in all populous, rich, industrious provinces" (388), where "provisions, lodging, attendance, [and] labour" are all dear (388), so economic disincentives work to check the increase in the number of children born to domestic slaves. Thus Hume refutes the claim of the supposed fertility of Roman slaves, concluding that "The human spe-cies would perish in those places where it ought to encrease the fastest; and a perpetual recruit be wanted from the poorer and more desert provinces" (388). And he proceeds to argue that slavery and warfare were related ways of reducing ancient populations. In his account, slavery is a way of reading some people out of the count of repro-ducible persons, and warfare is a way of subtracting, since it eliminates some persons altogether (in killing them) and keeps others from repro-ducing (in consigning them to slavery). Observing that the ancient republics were almost perpetually at war with one another out of "their love of liberty" (400), Hume later remarks that "these people [the ancients] were extremely fond of liberty; but seem not to have understood it very well" (403). The ancient nations' imperfect under-standing of liberty involves, of course, their commitment to their liberty as opposed to—and at the expense of—the liberty of others. Being dead means having no consciousness, and being a slave also turns out to mean having no consciousness, in that one is never at liberty to act on one's consciousness; and having no consciousness turns out to be the most effective check to reproduction. You must be a person to be allowed to reproduce, and liberty is the power not only to count but to have one's reproductive capacity counted in the ratios of population increase.

On Hume's account, material conditions determine fertility only insofar as they overlap with slavery or freedom. To be a slave is to have no choice but to attend to—or have someone else attend to—your market value, the cost effectiveness of your production. Malthus and Godwin, taking up the issue of freedom and slavery, continually argue about what condition approaches slavery most nearly—the restraint that keeps someone from procreating out of an anticipatory fear of possible future dearth or the production of individuals who might be free only to starve.

Malthus and Godwin disagree, then, on whether or not there is a dearth of resources to support human life, on whether or not population should be checked, and on how effective individual decisions about procreation would be in limiting the size of a population. They agree, however, on one thing—that present governmental arrangements tend toward slavery rather than freedom. This agreement, of course, dissolves as soon as they begin to specify the features of government that are problematic. For Malthus sees government as delusive when it acts to disguise what he everywhere forbiddingly calls the operation of "Necessity"; Godwin, on the other hand, sees it as preventing the kind of equality and improvement among individuals that would bring an end to want. Thus Malthus denounces the Poor Laws because they encourage a false security in offering people like tenant farmers the illusion that they can be protected against want. Should crops fail, the small farmer with more family than food can know that society intervenes to distance him and his family from starvation. Yet, Malthus argues, the Poor Laws, in appearing to distance the laboring classes from unexpected sufferings, in fact institutionalize the sufferings of the poor by luring them into a false happiness that makes them think themselves free to procreate, to produce more persons like themselves with whom they will have to share their portions.

Thus Malthus very sternly declares that "A labourer who marries without being about to support a family may in some respects be considered as an enemy to all his fellow-labourers" (40). This language would seem particularly melodramatic if it did not read the English Poor Laws as a way of reversing the drive toward independence that

Malthus has seen civilization promoting. The insurance provided by parish aid, in his account, turns out not really to be protection against hardship that can be figured in terms of money or even food; rather, it offers the only kind of insurance that he sees society able to pro-vide—the security of the slave, the human whose need causes him, as in ancient nations, to cashier his independence.[8] Early in the *Essay* Malthus describes the progress of civilization toward increasingly efficient ways of supplying food and resources to people. And while it might seem to be a merely economic account of the transition from societies that supply their wants through hunting and herding to those that do so through agriculture and manufactures, the progress that he sees coincides with a decrease in slavery or virtual slavery, the property that people have in other people and their labor.

> The North American Indians, considered as a people, cannot justly be called free and equal. In all the accounts we have of them, and, indeed, of most other savage nations, the women are represented as more completely in a state of slavery to the men than the poor are to the rich in civilized countries. One half the nation appears to act as Helots to the other half, and the misery that checks population falls chiefly, as it always must do, upon that part whose condition is lowest in the scale of society.
>
> (27)

Women and children suffer, he says, as the women, "condemned as they are to the inconveniences and hardships of frequent change of place and to the constant and unremitting drudgery of preparing every thing for the reception of their tyrannic lords" (27–28), cannot give the "necessary attention" to their labor-intensive infants. Moreover, even though one of the two cardinal points of the *Essay* is that the attrac-tion between the sexes is constant, he cites reports "that the passion between the sexes is less ardent among the North American Indians than among any other race of men" (27), as if to suggest that an ex-treme enough system of inequality begins to affect even the most basic and constant biological forces. The attraction between the sexes fails in the inexorable course it earlier apparently had, and consciousness in the form of unhappiness interferes with biological function.

The march of progress in Malthus's catalog of social organizations and the allocation of peoples and foodstuffs is one in which labor has constantly increasing returns and people impinge upon people to a lesser extent. Thus herding represents an improvement over hunting. "The women lived in greater ease than among nations of hunters" (29), and the men, united in groups that magnified their individual strength, "felt, probably, few fears about providing for a family" (29). This happiness, however, bred both contentment and children, which forced the tribe into migration and war in its search for food supplies. These were "bold and improvident Barbarians" (30), for whom the response to scarcity was the sacrifice of the many to the conquest of "an Alaric, an Attila, or a Zingis Khan" (30) and the exercise of "a power even, if distressed, of selling their children as slaves" (30).

Malthus's analysis of how early societies fit people to resources has thus far concentrated on how an individual's liberty has historically been the luxury that could be converted into necessities. Faced with starvation, earlier men could sell themselves or their children. The question of how many people the earth will support changes, he suggests, when it is a question of how many free people it will support. And Malthus's survey of civilizations clearly moves beyond the question of the mere satisfaction of food and the attraction between the sexes when he begins his account of an eighteenth-century man of marriageable age:

A man of liberal education, but with an income only just sufficient to enable him to associate in the rank of gentlemen, must feel absolutely certain that if he marries and has a family he shall be obliged, if he mixes at all in society, to rank himself with moderate farmers and the lower class of tradesmen. The woman that a man of education would naturally make the object of his choice would be one brought up in the same tastes and sentiments with himself and used to the familiar intercourse of a society totally different from that to which she must be reduced by marriage. Two or three steps of descent in society, particularly at this round of the ladder, where education ends and ignorance begins, will not be considered by the generality of people as a fancied and chimerical, but a real and essential evil.

(34)

Famine, plagues, and death in combat have all appeared as serious but conveniently remote perils of ancient forms of civilization in Malthus's conjectural history, but the thought of a woman unhappily married beneath her station also counts as "a real and essential evil." While the women of the hunting and herding societies had their misery reserved for them, it was rendered as a misery occasioned by excessive labor and inadequate visibility: they were always in danger of being absorbed into the production of the tyrant or the warrior hero. The woman who might be a suitable match for our young man of liberal education, however, is more visible than her predecessors precisely because she does not labor, because her produce is happiness or misery unmediated by any gainful employment. The very palpability of this imaginary woman's possible unhappiness suggests that she has a consciousness that counts, but the "idea of grief" that comes to Malthus as he contemplates her is the most effective prophylactic in the *Essay*. As marriage here, as elsewhere in the eighteenth and early nineteenth centuries, always stands for marriage-and-children, the young man who woos and wins her must be prepared to provide for several mouths if he is to ward off this unhappiness. And miserable as the single life may be, Malthus clearly paints it as preferable to acting on the attraction between the sexes so that one must confront the misery of scarcity not in the world but in the household.

The central fact about this example of misery is that it has nothing at all to do with the kind of misery involved in the prospect of imminent starvation. There is no way of remedying it by economizing on groceries or learning to eat lower on the food chain. And it epitomizes all that Greer loathes in its abject inability to see food and the attraction between the sexes as the only two simple and irreducible needs that are both necessary and sufficient for life. What is particularly important is that Malthus stages it as the only account in his brief history of world civilization that attributes a consciousness to a woman, the only one, that is, that recognizes that it might matter to anyone how a woman might feel about her lot in life. The passage, of course, registers its plangency mainly in terms that sound like "I hate it when women cry," but it also suggests how the account of sustenance begins

to shift if we are talking about creating a space for more than one consciousness, about whether there is room for two in these resources.

Godwin, of course, opposes the Malthusian model because he sees
it as setting off a false alarm—seeing scarcity where there is none—and
because he views it as a way of consolidating and exacerbating all that
is wrong with English government and property law. Malthus would,
he claims, derive property rights from the geometric ratio, would, that
is, protect property against people—or against all but previously prop-
ertied people. In giving individuals priority to property, Godwin's
Enquiry concerning Political Justice (first edition 1793, third edition
1798)[9] and his *Of Population* (of 1820) articulate the most forceful argument against the Malthusian account of the pressure of population.
Yet the irony is that Godwin in the later work begins to outdo Malthus
as a calculator as he projects the possibility of realigning the relationships between food, human sustenance, and human labor. The earth can
be improved to provide sustenance for more people—machines will
bring "something like a final close to the necessity of manual labour"
(503) as plows are "turned into a field . . . [to] perform [their] office without the need of superintendence" (503). And people can be improved to
need less sustenance or to find it in its most abundant forms: "no good
reason can be assigned, why that which produces animal nourishment,
must have previously passed though a process of animal or vegetable
life" (500).

The argument that Godwin makes is one that makes infinite population increase look possible on the basis of increasingly efficient tech-
nologies for fitting people to resources. But if he presents it as possible,
his *Enquiry concerning Political Justice* had suggested that it is anything
but desirable. Yet while Godwin claims that the free human consciousness can alter even the material conditions of the world (look at recent
advances in chemistry, he says), the consciousness of other people
appears to him an even more dramatic form of slavery than it did to
Malthus. For Godwin describes a society that would be composed
directly out of individuals—that is, without any institutional mediation through government. He can thus speak of population as suscep-
tible to infinite increase so long as society is merely the individual

magnified, but the possibility of more than one person leads to the specter of inequality, and the idea of inequality leads to the ideas of imprisonment and slavery. "All formal repetition of other men's ideas," he writes in *Political Justice*, "seems to be a scheme for imprisoning . . . the operations of our own mind" (2:504). The institution of marriage is a monopoly whereby a man maintains exclusive property in a wife. Thus common labor and cohabitation are undesirable, because society must be formed from individuals who are unconstrained by the influence of others. That is, this wreck of a world could contain more and more people, but they must never be in the same room, as the presence of more than one individual always threatens to produce the coerciveness that government embodies for Godwin. And Godwin finally concludes his defense of consciousness in *Of Population* with an argument for its restriction, for the kind of slavery that domesticity offers: a man's "children and his wife are pledges he gives to the public for his good behavior [he writes]; they are his securities, that he will truly enter into the feeling of a common interest" (586).

In Godwin's account, the self is spread thin, particularly given the fact that his commitment to anarchy means that every reflecting individual is required to have a social policy. If human beings by dint of reflection are supposed to adjust to fluctuations in population to produce children as necessary, how will each individual know whether the society, like that of the United States, is complete or incomplete? Against Malthus's anticipatory dread of the unhappiness of a woman who has married beneath her, Godwin sets the model of a self that must expand infinitely to become identical with the full population of the society while also remaining untouched by the presence of other consciousnesses.

Malthus can, then, admit—and forestall—the consciousness of the unhappy woman, so long as it is the *idea* of the unhappy woman; Godwin can introduce a wife and family as an individual's pledge to society, so long as society does not include any possibility of one consciousness being contaminated by the operation of other consciousnesses. And, as David Ferry has observed, Wordsworth learns from his love of nature a love of man that is a love of the *idea* of man—and that is, in turn, again a love of nature.[10] But if Wordsworth continually seeks out landscapes that are conspicuously "unimproved" (or undoes their improvements and manufactures so as to present them as unimproved), this solitary nature on which he will not tolerate previous marks keeps producing shadows of other people despite—or perhaps because of—his best efforts to suppress them.

Let "Lines written a few miles above Tintern Abbey, on revisiting the banks of the Wye during a tour, July 13, 1798"[11] stand as an example of the negotiations between the individual, nature, and society in Romantic poetry. As has long and frequently been observed, the poem initially appears to be a locodescriptive poem, "a summons to self-consciousness"[12] in Geoffrey Hartman's phrase, in which the poet is alone with the landscape. Seeing the same landscape twice on occasions separated by five years is like taking one's blood pressure at intervals: it enables Wordsworth to see which way he's going, to get his spiritual bearings.

Moreover, seeming to tell over to himself the story of his memory of the place and his present sense of it, he makes himself both teller and listener to this story that is so slight as to have almost no plot at all—just the merest "the place is much as I remember it." And the movement of description proceeds to link up the various elements of the landscape as if to say that their connection does not involve their encroachment upon one another; in fact, things in this natural scene are scarcely allowed to be what they are, in the effort to ward off the possibility of one thing impinging on another; the "orchard-tufts" "lose themselves" "Among the woods and copses," and the "hedge-rows" are "hardly hedge-rows."

Now, on one level Wordsworth is approvingly noting that the human intervention in the landscape blends in. The agricultural improvements, the orchard-tufts and hedge-rows, do not "disturb/The wild green landscape." The only element that appears to exert any force on the landscape is that of the

> . . . steep and lofty cliffs,
> Which on a wild secluded scene impress

Thoughts of more deep seclusion; and connect
The landscape with the quiet of the sky.

And even though the pressure of the cliffs' intrusion palpably frames
the landscape (so that one knows what Wordsworth means), the co-
nundrum built into this landscape, this scene, is that one never quite
knows when it is a landscape. How can the orchard-tufts and the
hedge-rows not be part of the landscape, how can the cliffs not exactly
count in the scene?

The point of all the exactitude of Wordsworth's description is that
they do count—but not because they came together. Instead, the mention of signs of cultivation and the surmise about gypsies or a hermit
function to indicate that they, too, have been subsumed in the landscape—not primarily, however, through natural agency but instead
through the poet's molding of the scene. The ultimate mark of his
seclusion, that is, is not that there are not any traces of other people
in the scene; he instead lays claim to seclusion by presenting himself as
the only one who views the scene in this particular way. He is the only
one who is humanizing nature by seeing at this angle the human elements in it naturalized.

It would be possible to see this pattern, with some recent critics,[13]
as involving a politically reactionary stance. Wordsworth, in this view,
sacrifices the reality of other people to an archaic vision of the land
that continues his privilege and other people's suffering. And Wordsworth's account of how "These forms of beauty" have sustained him in
the "din / Of towns and cities" might well be read as simply a statement of how an aesthetic memory can be used as a defensive weapon,
a kind of shield to ward off a consciousness of the existence of other
people. Yet a difficulty with that reading emerges when we remember—
and when Wordsworth remembers—that Dorothy is there.

Or is she? One argument that has been advanced by some critics is
that she only appears to be there and functions as a kind of optical illusion that enables Wordsworth to end by talking to someone other
than himself. On this account, Dorothy appears as a function of the
territorial imperialism of Wordsworth's ego, which incorporates people

and things as it pleases. She is, then, not an independent consciousness but merely an epiphenomenon of his. But that model doesn't quite conform to the poem's odd premise—which is that Wordsworth must retreat into the landscape so that he can produce a sense of self, since he doesn't have enough selfhood for one person, much less two. Rather, that moment of remembering that Dorothy came with him is the unraveling of the imposition of solitude on the scene, the moment in which he implicitly backtracks from the reading of agricultural improvements, the marks of other people, as wasteland. It is his acknowledgment that the waste is always improved, that the self is already socialized.

But if Wordsworth appears more resigned to the existence of another consciousness than Malthus or Godwin, discovering that the self already is another instead of warily anticipating a possible encroachment, "Tintern Abbey" curiously insists that the presence of other people—even Dorothy—always appears as a kind of accident to the individual consciousness. The anthropomorphism that enables him to read the landscape as if it were a self that could endow him with a self effects its own curbs on the numbers of consciousness that can become visible. Malthus fears a reproachful consciousness of the unhappy woman at variance with his imaginary young man; Godwin shrinks from any contact between consciousnesses that might differ as he postulates the expansion of the individual into an identity with society, and Wordsworth defines a scene as wild, random, to proceed to make it yield meaning to and for his determining consciousness—only to have to rehabilitate the accident of another person's existence by imagining that she sees what he sees. The individual consciousness reading the landscape, that is, unlike the United States in Godwin's description, always takes itself to be complete.

NOTES

1. My thinking on this subject has been particularly inspired by H. J. Habakkuk, *Population Growth and Economic Development since 1750* (Leicester:

Leicester University Press, 1971), which presents an especially thoughtful analysis of the economic conditions of population growth in the later eighteenth century in Britain, and by Catherine Gallagher, "The Body versus the Social Body in the Works of Thomas Malthus and Henry Mayhew," *Representations* 14:83–106, an essay that insightfully locates a shift from a labor-theory account of the value of the individual body to an exchange-theory account.

2. David Hume provides a particularly clear account of these assumptions in "Of the Populousness of Ancient Nations," *Essays Moral, Political, and Literary,* ed. T. H. Green and T. H. Grose (London: Longmans, Green, 1898), 1:381–443. All references to this essay are to this edition; page numbers are cited parenthetically in the text.

3. Thomas Robert Malthus, *An Essay on the Principle of Population,* ed. Philip Appleman (New York: Norton, 1976). All references to the work are to this edition; page numbers are cited parenthetically in the text.

4. Germaine Greer, *Sex and Destiny: The Politics of Human Fertility* (New York: Harper & Row, 1984), 489. All subsequent page references are cited parenthetically in the text.

5. Robert Wallace, *Dissertation on the Numbers of Mankind in Ancient and Modern Times* (Edinburgh: Archibald Constable, 1809), 121.

6. William Godwin, *Of Population: An Enquiry concerning the Power of Increase in the Numbers of Mankind, Being an Answer to Mr. Malthus's Essay on That Subject* (London: Longman, Hurst, Ree, Orme and Brown, 1820), 485. All references to the work are to this edition; page numbers are cited parenthetically in the text.

7. See also Malthus, *Essay,* 46.

8. Cf. Wallace, *Dissertation,* 90.

9. William Godwin, *Enquiry concerning Political Justice and Its Influence on Morals and Happiness,* facsimile of 3d ed., ed. F. E. L. Priestley (Toronto: University of Toronto Press, 1969). All references to the work are to this edition; page numbers are cited parenthetically in the text.

10. David Ferry, *The Limits of Mortality: An Essay on Wordsworth's Major Poems* (Middletown, Conn.: Wesleyan University Press, 1959), 104–5.

11. William Wordsworth and Samuel Taylor Coleridge, *Lyrical Ballads: A Text of the 1798 edition with the additional 1800 poems and the Prefaces,* ed. R. L. Brett and A. R. Jones (London: Methuen, 1963), 111.

12. Geoffrey H. Hartman, *Wordsworth's Poetry 1787–1814* (New Haven: Yale University Press, 1971), 29.

13. See particularly Jerome J. McGann, *The Romantic Ideology: A Critical Investigation* (Chicago: University of Chicago Press, 1983), 81–92, and passim. An interesting example of this general view also appears in David Aers, "Wordsworth's Model of Man in 'The Prelude,'" in *Romanticism and Ideology: Studies in English Writing 1765–1830,* ed. David Aers, Jonathan Cook, and David Punter (Boston: Routledge & Kegan Paul, 1981).

 *Jerome Christensen*

Setting Byron Straight:
Class, Sexuality, and the Poet

> Boldly conjuring up a scene of moral devastation, he requires you to
> regard it as you would the phaenomena, which denote some former
> war of elements—some past convulsion of nature, mysterious, and
> unknown. The sombre graces of his manner, the dark energies of his
> pen, render the spell powerful; and he is obeyed.
>
> —Review of Lord Byron's *Giaour* in the *Critical Review*

> . . . be assured that whatever you do comes so distorted through the
> prism of prattling ignorance & the fogs of the Jura that it will re-
> quire some efforts of credible eye witnesses to put it into the straight
> line of truth & reason.
>
> —John Cam Hobhouse to Lord Byron

I

Early in her *Vindication of the Rights of Women* Mary Wollstonecraft undertakes to account for the historical fact of male dominance
without invoking principles that would implicitly legitimate it. She
concedes the "natural superiority" of men but urges that the only "solid
basis on which the superiority of the sex can be built" is "bodily
strength."[1] She then tactically subdivides strength between a biological
peculiarity which has enabled the male to enforce his dominance and an
attribute of a plastic, "human" body which has been constituted in a disciplined, rational way rather than inherited in any old way. Strength
remains the criterion of sexual difference, but what had been a *cause* of
historical domination has become an *effect* of disciplined exercise.
Nietzsche would later aphorize, "Only that which has no history is
definable."[2] Wollstonecraft defines precisely to void the historical, a category which includes both an "arbitrary" quality called strength and the
social class to which that quality properly belongs, the aristocracy. In

opposition to the "brutal force that has hitherto governed the world" for the sensual benefit of a "male aristocracy," Wollstonecraft proposes a benign, universally human hygiene of self-improving "exercise."[3]

In its awkward deviations and undisciplined repetitions, Wollstone-craft's text charts its failure to emancipate its "Reason" from spasms of aggressiveness. A particularly sensational eruption occurs near the end of *Vindication*, where Wollstonecraft recklessly charges that the "causes of female weakness branch out of one grand cause—want of chastity in men." She continues:

> This intemperance, so prevalent, depraves the appetite to such a degree, that a wanton stimulus is necessary to rouse it; but the parental design of Nature is forgotten, and the mere person, and that for a moment, alone engrosses the thoughts. So voluptuous, indeed, often grows the lustful prowler, that he refines on female softness. Something more soft than women is then sought for; till, in Italy and Portugal, men attend the levees of equivocal beings, to sigh for more than female languor.[4]

Politics has been fully sexualized. Antiaristocratic animus transmutes into homophobic fantasy.

This configuration of a "fastidious sensualist" sighing for a languor-ous equivocal being might be named a Scene of Fascination to distin-guish it from Harold Bloom's famous "Scene of Instruction." If for Bloom the "ultimate" Scene of Instruction is described by Raphael in book 5 of *Paradise Lost*,[5] the pattern for the scene of fascination is that where, transfixed, Satan gazes at the nakedly veiled Eve, tempted to become the tempter.[6] No doubt Wollstonecraft has Milton in mind; but a nearer and more highly charged referent is the famous set piece from *Reflections on the Revolution in France* where Burke, mixing Lu-ciferian and Evenic motifs, nostalgically recalls the royal levee where he had last seen "the queen of France, then the dauphiness, at Versailles; and surely never lighted on this orb, which she hardly seemed to touch, a more delightful vision. I saw her just above the horizon, decorating and cheering the elevated sphere she just began to move in,—glittering like the morning-star, full of life, and splendor, and joy."[7] Against Burke's best intentions, Wollstonecraft would happily appropriate this

charming epiphany as an instance of her paradigm, perhaps concate-
nating it with the earlier, soft-core depiction of the queen's hairbreadth
escape from rape and death, and with the moment when Burke, sicken-
ing with the pleasure of having his queen and beating her too, falls into
misogynist rant against "the abused shape of the vilest of women."[8]

Examples of the scene of fascination could be multiplied. Cowper's
itinerant Kate, whose gaudy distress briefly arrests the flow of sentiment in the first book of *The Task,* has been crazed by loss, but she is
marked as equivocal and rendered fascinating to the reader, who inhabits the spectral perspective of her dead husband, by an attachment
to her ribbons that is greater than her instinct for survival. Cowper's
Kate spawns Wordsworth's female vagrants and particularly Margaret,
who, impatiently drooping toward organic oblivion, is the object of
the Pedlar's feelingful attention in "The Ruined Cottage." This poem
is unmatched in its archaeology of the odd lot of hieroglyphic objects
and inscriptions—a spider's web, a shard of pottery, "dull red stains"—
that are infused with value by their synthesis in the figure of a seated,
melancholy woman—the equivocal being over which the sentimental
traveler can sigh and which he can sorrowfully exploit as the nexus of
various literary, political, and economic themes.

The supply of Romantic scenes of fascination is indefinite.[9] There
is, however, a problem of gender in my examples. Although I have accused Wollstonecraft of homophobia, the levees I have mentioned all
gender the equivocal being as female. In point of fact, Wollstonecraft's
readers would have understood the implicit referent behind "lustful
prowler" to be William Beckford, author of *Vathek* and notorious
pederast, who fled to Portugal and Italy in large part to escape the kind
of persecution that Wollstonecraft echoes. Yet my liberties with gender merely follow the lead of Wollstonecraft herself, who refers only
to a "more than female languour." "More than female"—it does not,
finally, make any difference if the being rendered equivocal is a boy
dressed up as a girl or a girl dressed up as a boy, or a girl or a boy
dressed up beyond reason. It is the "more than" that signifies, attracts,
fascinates—attracts as the fascination of signification.

We can get an idea of the historical moment here by recalling Fou-

cault's observation that "the first figure to be invested by the deployment of sexuality, one of the first to be 'sexualized,' was the 'idle'
woman. She inhabited the outer edge of the 'world,' in which she had
to appear as a value, and of the family, where she was assigned a new
destiny."[10] The idleness of the woman, that which frees her from
ascriptive ties and burdens her with the social destiny of being "more
than female," is the corollary of political economy's valorization of the
classically condemned concept of luxury. As Hume observed, "Luxury
is a word of an uncertain signification."[11] Luxuries as commodities are
similarly equivocal—and essential for that very reason. Political economy is a system wherein what has been indicted as dangerous or sinful
under a previous regime is put to work as an agent of systemic elaboration. Economically vital, the idle woman in Humean, liberal discourse
also has a privileged political status: idle woman replaces idle aristo-
crat; female as equivoque (object as subject, consuming and consumed)
displaces the noble as ambivalent (sovereign deed, violent expenditure
without reserve). The narcissistic moment of fascination functions as
a pivot on which politics swings into economics, class into gender,
subject into object. In a spectacular and powerful redoubling of bad
faith, the necessity for that moment which is, conceptually and historically, the precondition for political economy coming to know itself,
is blamed on the "natural" perversity of woman, which it is the part
of enlightenment both to deplore and to gratify. As Wollstonecraft's
example shows, resistance to that assignment to the equivocal that is
made in the names of woman and enlightenment collaborates with the
overall project of political economy. The vindication of one group,
such as woman, from assignment to the drawer labeled "a fanciful kind
of *half* being"[12] entraps other interstitial figures, such as the outrageous
Beckford, thereby extending the "outer edge of the 'world'" to include
new margins and markets, like Italy and Portugal.[13] By letting the
gender lapse, Wollstonecraft stretches eighteenth-century political
economy and the achievement of the eighteenth-century man of letters as far as they will go: gone is the luxury as object, as woman, or
even as boy. The equivocal being is merely the commodified sign in all
its potential to allure as more than female, more than person, more

than thing, and to affiliate men and women under the rubric "human"
as clients of the commercial economy. The sign takes up the slack in
the "more than" and regulates it according to an economy that orients
all the "less than" that is desire.

II

Both in what she affirms and in what she denies Wollstonecraft contributes to that discursive practice in which, as Theodor Adorno writes,
"the network of the whole is drawn ever tighter, modelled after the act
of exchange. It leaves the individual consciousness less and less room
for evasion, preforms it more and more thoroughly, cuts it off *a priori*
as it were from the possibility of differencing itself as all difference
degenerates to a nuance in the monotony of supply."[14] The categories
with which Wollstonecraft engages gender and class difference are
strength and mobility: aristocratic strength becomes male mobility. By
no accident those are the historically sanctioned terms for characteriz-
ing the figure, event, and text called Lord Byron. The text of Lord
Byron is the test of difference in the Romantic period—whether it
need be straightened out and adjusted to the network of exchange or
whether by some evasion it can separate itself from that very code by
which it becomes recognizable.

Here is a scene of fascination framed by Byron in a letter from
Greece to his former traveling companion John Cam Hobhouse:

> At Vostitza I found my dearly-beloved Eustathius—ready to follow me not
> only to England, but to Terra Incognita, if so be my compass pointed that
> way. . . . The next morning I found the dear soul upon horseback clothed
> very sprucely in Greek Garments, with those ambrosial curls hanging
> down his amiable back, and to my utter astonishment and the great abomi-
> nation of Fletcher, a *parasol* in his hand to save his complexion from the
> heat.—However in spite of the *Parasol* on we travelled very much enam-
> oured, as it should seem, till we got to Patras, where Strané received us into
> his new house where I now scribble.[15]

However enamored, this lord, unlike Wollstonecraft's more scrupulous voluptuary, displays a rather breezy detachment. Although there can be little doubt that Byron's first genital intimacy with boys occurred during his first trip to Greece, and probably with Eustathius, this moment seems no more unmediated than any other. Indeed, the tableau is *about* mediation. The gaze is mediated by its doubling between the abominated expression of Fletcher and the quizzical esteem of Byron. The lyrical freeze frame concatenates with additional moments and even, as the epistolary format implies, other minds. The gaze is subordinated to an exchange, and the exchange is ultimately referred to a moment of production, "I now scribble."

What is being produced? First, a discourse of what has come to be called "liberation"—a liberation that runs the scale between sex and politics and that combines in supposedly mutual benefit both agent and object. The tag "Greek love" does not euphemize this bond. Lord Byron learned his homosexuality from books—old books. One of the most impressionable students of the classics the English public schools have ever formed, Byron invested sexual desire only in Greek boys. For Byron "Greek love" means love of Greeks.[16]

The liberation of homosexual desire only becomes possible after desire has been sexualized, which in turn, as Foucault has argued, depends on the hypothesis of repression. Generalized, the repressive hypothesis permits the fluent translation of the domain of sexuality into nationality. Only the repression of the Greek by the Turk allows for the possibility of his liberation; it renders him an equivocal being and makes him interesting. For Byron the Turkish occupation of Greek soil is homologous with the parasol covering Eustathius's fair skin. The sexual body of the boy is produced as the effect of that which covers and corrects it. Byron desires the boy only insofar as the body is repressed—he desires "him" as sign.[17]

Let me be precise here. The convergence of a certain discourse of golden-age innocence and truth with the ocular evidence of a repression by the despotic Turk *constitutes* Byron's homosexuality. Evidence of repression orients and organizes his inchoate political and erotic impulses, which then become *homosexual,* retrospectively. For us, not for him. Byron never intimated that he had been a homosexual before leaving England, nor even after he had indulged with Greek boys did he suggest that he had left something undone in his relations with John Edleston, the Cambridge choir boy toward whom he frankly acknowledged a love "violent, although pure" (*BLJ* 8:24).[18] Greek love could not be practiced with English lads. Moreover, the love of the sentimental liberator can never confess to its violence and so can never be pure.

The repressive hypothesis is well meaning; it gives Byron a purpose, some good work to do. He will liberate himself; he will liberate the Greek—or, as Jerome J. McGann puts it, neatly hybridizing the "isms" natural supernatural and Oriental: Byron becomes "obsessed with the idea of renewal of human culture in the west at a moment of its deepest darkness. This means for Byron the renewal of the value of the individual person, and the renewal of Greece as an independent political entity."[19] But this is surely a misrecognition. Lord Byron believed in no such thing as "human culture," nor did he cherish the idea of a transhistorical individual whose value fluctuated like the funds. He did, at times, however, project a *specific* form of renewal or liberation, as in this note to *Childe Harold* II: "The English have at last compassionated their Negroes, and under a less bigoted government may probably one day release their Catholic brethren; but the interposition of foreigners alone can emancipate the Greeks, who, otherwise appear to have as small a chance of redemption from the Turks, as the Jews have from mankind in general" (*CPW* 2:202).[20]

Lord Byron's messianism is less Christological than feudal. He imagines the redeemed purity of the Greek as the gift of a chivalrous knight, who magnanimously presents the repressed with *their* emancipation as a corollary of the revival of *his* mythic past. Subjected to the repressive hypothesis, difference (historical, geographical, subjective) is thematized as the consequence of a lost or stolen original purity, which the sentimental liberator will profess to *return* to the Greek, but which he is actually *donating for the first time.* Eustathius and the Greeks are engendered by the dream of their emancipation—a story that produces their bygone freedom as the alibi for the representational practice of the liberator, in the same way as the pure white body of the boy is the alibi for the parasol — for the signifier that constitutes him as a sign and shadows him forth as an object of desire. Byron can imagine freeing the Greeks, but he cannot imagine the Greeks free:

> The Greeks will never be independent; they will never be sovereigns as heretofore, and God forbid they ever should! but they may be subjects without being slaves. Our colonies are not independent, but they are free and industrious, and such may Greece be hereafter.
>
> (*CPW* 2:201)[21]

It is a telling coincidence that Byron scribbles his Greek love at "Patras," for the colonization that Byron calls freedom is a form of patronage. That Byron's relations with boys were established along lines of patronage has not gone unnoticed,[22] but the sentimental structure of such relationships has. Its flavor can be sampled in the 1807 letter to Elizabeth Pigott in which Byron writes of the "*Chaos of hope & Sorrow*" into which he has been thrown by his separation from John Edleston, described as his "protege," who is committed to entering a "mercantile house in Town" on Lord Byron's interest. The dismal denouement of this relationship (during his voyage Byron was doubly shocked by the news that the urbanized Edleston had been accused of "indecency" and that soon after he had died of consumption) was partially the result of the misprision attendant on the attempt to maintain patronage as a mediatory fiction between men of different social classes and between a schoolboy world of "violent, although pure" love and the tranquil gloom of a countinghouse. Once the doomed Edleston (who, in the iconography of nineteenth-century medievalism, played Lady of Shalott to Lord Byron's Lancelot) left the safety of Cambridge, he and Byron ceased to meet. So distant did they become that Edleston's revival of the fiction of patronage in response to Byron's crass misreading of an earlier appeal seems embarrassingly abject: "At present I must beg leave to repeat that [it] is only the favor of your Lordship's *personal* Influence and Patronage [not money] which I humbly presumed in my last as well as now,—to request."[23]

The transactions with Edleston are an extreme example of a characteristic mode in Byron: the structure and ethos of patronage, usually bedecked in the finery of chivalric *noblesse*, were invoked to reconstruct and normalize contacts with men and women that were in their happening invisible, fluid, even anarchic. By "invisible, fluid, even anarchic," I mean what Lord Byron's crony Scrope Berdmore Davies meant when, upon departing from a stay at Newstead Abbey, he jotted the note, "This whole week passed in a delirium of sensuality."[24] Davies, like Byron, has impressive claims to authority on such matters, having spent his schooldays at Eton, where as a Kings Scholar he was housed with roughly fifty other lads in a dormitory room where, as his biographer describes it, "between the hours of 8 o'clock at night, when they were locked in, and 7 o'clock the next morning when they were released by the Head Master's servant the boys were left totally to their own devices."[25] We have no way of knowing what those devices were. No doubt there was "cruel bullying and sexual malpractices," but the "total lack of privacy" for the individual had the consequence of conferring privacy or, better, complete invisibility on the dreamlike, delirial world of boys, each and all with their peculiar devices. If this world can be described as the "other face of the 18th century, the face unglimpsed in Jane Austen's novels, brutal, filthy, and corrupt," it can only be once the eighteenth century has been given a recognizable face by such writers as Austen.[26] Only then, in a self-consciously *nineteenth* century, could this region of delirium, unreadable according to the Malthusian and Benthamite schemata, be given the physiognomy of the other, corrupt and brutal, in order that it could be redeemed for the future by Christian muscle and chivalric myth.

Hours of Idleness, Byron's first book of poems, situates itself at the divide (called the "Rubicon" in the Preface) between minority and legal maturity and eagerly contributes to the general cultural project of recasting the invisible world of dirty little boys in terms of the regulative format of chivalric romance. The cultural plot is expounded with intelligence and wit by Mark Girouard in the *Return to Camelot*.[27] But Girouard does not observe what "Lord Byron Minor" failed to see: that not only was the consequence of seeing, remembering, schooldays their annihilation, but also this medievalist strategy was so readily available because it repeated with remarkable fidelity the monarchic attempt to control the bullyings and sexual malpractices among the nobility that was the policy behind the royal institution of tournaments and heraldic codes in the thirteenth century (henceforth the nobles' devices would never be totally their own).[28] It would be some time before Lord Byron would come to understand nostalgia as a form of suicide.[29]

Lord Byron's attempts both to memorialize the delirial world of his youth and to contain similar possibilities in the present are epitomized by his relations with Nicolo Giraud, singled out among the "sylphs" with whom Byron "rioted" at the Capuchin monastery at Athens. "I am his 'Padrone' and his 'amico,'" Byron writes, "and the Lord knows what besides" (*BLJ* 2:12). About Giraud we know little more than what Byron tells us, but the switching between "Padrone" and "amico" is wholly characteristic of Byron, who in his first public appearance as poet split his poetic persona between Julius Caesar and William Cowper, as well as between the reluctant commander of "To the Earl of Dorset" and the stripling friend of "To the Earl of Clare." This oscillation would remain a constant threat to the stability of the Byronic poetic subject (see, for example, the wavering between a jolly democracy and a melancholy despotism in the opening of *The Corsair*), until in *Don Juan* the undecidable priority between "Padrone" and "Amico" becomes the whirligig on which character and narrator ride in outlandish parody of chivalrization and its discontents.

For the roving Lord of 1810, however, who is unconnected by anything but debts to the world of men in which he has, despite himself, grown up, freeing the Greeks is a profession of sorts. So is writing about it. The pursuit of boys may satisfy diverse aims, but "the end of all scribblement is to amuse" (*BLJ* 2:20). And if it is arguably the case that Byron could not have coitus with any boys while Hobhouse, an "enemy to fine feelings & sentimental friendships" (*BLJ* 2:155), was around, it is certainly true that Byron could not write to Hobhouse with Hobhouse around. The departure of Hobhouse is ultimately less important for allowing Byron to have the experience than it is for

for enabling Byron to represent the experience, tantalizingly, for an audience of intimate male friends.

In his book *Byron and Greek Love*, Louis Crompton sets Byron's Eastern journey against the background of a Cambridge circle (which included Byron, Hobhouse, and Charles Skinner Matthews) knit by what he calls a "homosexual bond." "In a sense," Crompton observes, "the three share what would today be called a gay identity, based on common interests and a sense of alienation from a society they must protect themselves from by a special 'mysterious' style and mutually understood codes."[30] Crompton refers to an exchange between Byron and Matthews on the eve of the former's embarkation with Hobhouse for the East. Byron writes,

> I take up the pen which our friend has for a moment laid down merely to express a vain wish that you were with us in this delectable region, as I do not think Georgia itself can emulate in capabilities or incitements to the "Plen. and optabil.—Coit." the ports of Falmouth & parts adjacent—We are surrounded by Hyacinths & other flowers of the most fragrant [na]ture, & I have some intention of culling a handsome Bouquet to compare with the exotics I hope to meet in Asia.
>
> (*BLJ* 1:206–7)

Matthews replies by congratulating Lord Byron "on the splendid success of your first efforts in *the mysterious*, that style in which more is meant than meets the Eye." He goes on to encourage Byron in his "Botanical pursuits" and decrees "that everyone who professes *ma methode* do spell the term which designates his calling with an *e* at the end of it—*methodiste*, not method*ist*, and pronounce the word in the French fashion. Every one's taste must revolt at confounding ourselves with that sect of horrible, snivelling, fanatics."[31] Though barely utterable, the code is easily deciphered: "Hyacinths" are boys; the Latin abbreviation "Plen. and optabil.—Coit." is from *The Satyricon* and refers to "full and to-be-wished-for intercourse."[32]

Rather than the formation of a gay sense of identity in response to real or imagined persecution, this bit of correspondence describes the deliberate formation of a *literary* sense of identity, a shared sense of what Matthews calls a profession. The profession is formed by the positing of a particular kind of sexual experience as that which, because it cannot meet the eye, underwrites everything that can. Of greater importance than the wished-for coitus is the idea of it. Rendered jokingly as the pursuit of a natural history of all beautiful boys, that idea makes possible both the ritual exchange of pens between Hobhouse and Byron, anticipating their literary collaborations, and the economical style of the "mysterious," which forecasts the darkly implicative portrayal of a character who unites "the eager curiosity of youth with the fastidiousness of a sated libertine" that was to be the first literary fruit of Byron's pilgrimage.[33] The linkage of the mysterious style with the broodings of the Byronic hero connect it to the gothic motif of the "unspeakable," which, as Eve Kosofsky Sedgwick has incisively remarked, was in the Romantic period "a near-impenetrable shibboleth for a particular conjunction of class and male sexuality."[34] In *this* context the mysterious style, if almost unutterable, is most significant as that which is highly writable. It has all the conspicuous visibility and fluent transmissibility of a code, which here operates not primarily to hide something but as a kind of trademark to identify an association of senders and receivers. The "mysterious style" enables a profession; it is what Defoe, speaking of brewers, Swift, speaking of stockjobbers, Coleridge, speaking of contemporary critics, or Byron, speaking of publishers, would describe as the cant of the trade.[35] Its jargon artificially creates the body of traders, establishing the line between inside and outside, forming the basis for and boundaries of association. Their "mysterious style" binds these three Cambridge students together in what is a professional organization that *elects* not to speak its name.

The jargon of homosexuality expresses what Jacques Lacan calls a "formal fixation, which introduces a certain rupture of level, a certain discord between man's organization and his *Umwelt*, which is the very condition that extends indefinitely his world and his power."[36] In the case of these men, the jargon of homosexuality produces a specific kind of paranoiac knowledge in the service of a distinctive literary identity. The extension of world proceeds imperially according to the metonymic association of subjects: boys, Greek boys, Greeks, the Orient.

Although it may be appealing to regard this as the sort of project in which the poet carries with him relationship and love, K. J. Dover's distinction between "legitimate" and "illegitimate" eros shames such vanity. Among the ancient Greeks, according to Dover, the legitimacy that was conferred on a philanthropic relationship between an *erastes* and his youthful *eromenos* was sharply contrasted with "gross misbehaviour for monetary payment [which] is the act of a hubristes and uneducated man."[37] Although there is no evidence that Lord Byron, "Padrone and amico," was ever so vulgar as to offer money directly for sex, Nicolo Giraud, Eustathius's replacement in Byron's affections, was employed as "dragoman and Major Domo" (*BLJ* 2:29), a position that almost certainly entailed payment in love *and* money. But more important than specific acts of monetary payment is the imperial conception of a tour that would induce Byron to describe himself as a very Caesar of sexuality (*BLJ* 2:14). That hubristic orientation is first established by the jocular denomination of boys as "Hyacinths & other flowers." Botany is not just a convenient metaphor; it is the privileged metaphor for the instrumentality of metaphor—for the way natural bodies can, à la Rousseau in *The Reveries,* at once be "loved" and regarded as specimens, can be cathected, collected, and then inserted into books which, like Hobhouse's memoires and *Childe Harold,* are then sold as commodities on the open market (Byron speaks of his Greek boys as his "antiques" [*BLJ* 2:29]). The process by which a formal fixation underwrites both a literary identity and a hubristic extension of cognitive and rhetorical power would seem to vindicate Wollstonecraft's vision of "bodies of men who must necessarily be made foolish or vicious by the very constitution of their profession."[38]

The jargon of homosexuality furnishes not only a subject but also a way to write about it. Professing homosexuality, Matthews decrees, means professing *ma methode,* which in turn entails adopting a certain style—epitomized by the addition of an *e* to "method." The *e* is the letter of affection and affect, both the sign and the act of male bonding. In its capacity to charm, Matthews's *e* resembles the "naked letter" of romance with which, according to Richard Hurd, Gothic poets enchanted their

readers or, closer to home, the *a* with which Jacques Derrida neolo-
gized *"differance,"* at once volatilizing the text of Western metaphysics
and spellbinding a generation of literary critics.[39] But *differance* is not
methode. By Frenching and feminizing English method, Matthews's
supplemental letter merely translates it into a new, fetching, but altogether functional uniform. Unnaked, the letter is a device by which
romantic force can be made recognizable and put to work as the no-
nonsense instrument of interest. In the moment of its institution, the
code, ostensibly meaningful, masking from all but initiates the existence of forbidden sexual desires, is rendered as the meaningfulness *of*
the ostensible, the letter that invites but does not require decoding, like
a style. Following Matthews, we may hazard the neoclassical maxim
that for these men homosexuality is nature methodized. Having said
that, however, the revision naturally follows that for these writers
homosexuality is style methodized.

The *e* that translates method into *methode* does not defend against
the threat of homophobic persecution; it is the mark of distinction, of
self-classification. The project of comparing Hyacinths means inventing a *class* of equivocal beings—half boys, half flowers. Whatever sexual
anxiety percolates through the suavity of Matthews's *methode* is indistinguishable from a class anxiety—the anxiety of sharing pens with a
lord and of setting the terms for a new professional writing class,
which must, by hook or by crook, be segregated from an emergent,
methodistical working class.[40] Aimed at establishing an airtight sexual,
social, and cultural identity, Matthews's *methode* owes its energy to a
fear of confoundment.

Matthews's *e* serves the same function as Eustathius's parasol—as
ornament and protection. A lure, it is also the prop of an equivocal
being. If it is the profession of a postmethodist style of sexuality and
of writing that affiliates Matthews and Lord Byron (the *e* by which
Byron affects to archaize his Child*e* Harold is the most flagrant example of his collaboration), it is also Matthews's reliance on method that
dramatizes their difference, which hangs on the constitutive imitabil-
ity of *methode.* As in the paradigmatic case of the heraldic device, the
very mark of self-distinction is the instrument for appropriation by

the other: in methodically identifying itself, the self formulates the terms of its replication and estrangement. As Adorno has argued, "Identification has its social model in exchange and exchange would be nothing without it."[41] Unlike Matthews, however, Lord Byron's strength distances him from any single style, even the Byronic.[42] What makes the difference between Lord Byron, a clubfooted young man who swims from Sestos to Abydos and lives to write about it, and the stay-at-home Matthews, who was drowned in the weeds while bathing in the Cam, is Lord Byron's radical openness to the kind of confoundment that frightens his friend. Matthews's brief life uncannily illustrates the ill-fated career of those Burkean monsters, "men of theory."[43]

It may seem cruel to vindicate Lord Byron's difference by blaming Matthews for drowning, but as his letters show, Matthews, like Keats, understood the profession of literature as a life of allegory—and Romantic careers, like Romantic poems, prove allegory's cruelty. Within the Byron circle, swimming prowess was a crucial test of strength—and for Byron, on occasion, an easy legitimation of mastery. Here is Lord Byron to Hobhouse rating his "sylphs": "I have as usual swum across the Piraeus, the Signore Nicolo also laved, but he makes as bad a hand in the water as L'Abbe Hyacinth at Falmouth . . ." (*BLJ* 2:14). The most complex site for the allegorization of swimming, however—and one which disturbed Byron's customary sense of superiority—involves his relations with Shelley. One extract from an extraordinary lettter:

He [Shelley] was once with me in a Gale of Wind in a small boat right under the rocks between Meillerie & St. Gingo—we were five in the boat—a servant—two boatmen—& ourselves. The Sail was mismanaged & the boat was filling fast—he can't swim.—I stripped off my coat—made him strip off his—& take hold of an oar—telling him that I thought (being myself an expert swimmer) I could save him if he would not struggle when I took hold of him . . . —we were then about a hundred yards from shore—and the boat in peril.—He answered me with the greatest coolness—"that he had no notion of being saved—& that I would have enough to do to save myself, and begged not to trouble me".—Luckily the boat righted. . . . And yet the same Shelley who was as cool as it was possible to be in such circumstances—(of which I am no judge myself as the chance of swimming naturally gives

self-possession when near shore) certainly had the fit of phantasy which
P[olidori] describes.

(BLJ 6:126)

Shelley, as Byron implicitly acknowledges, lays incontestable claim to
the position of sovereignty which, I have argued, Byron assumes vis-à-
vis Matthews. In one inspired gesture Shelley rejects both the interposition of Byron's body and the imperative of survival. In this context,
or, rather, at this moment, Shelley exposes swimming prowess as a
reification of strength, a mere matter of expertise acquired through
Wollstonecraftian exercise, aimed at defending against chance, and
devoted to the proprietarial conservation of a self anxiously possessed.
The Byronic position, as Shelley shows and the vicissitudes of the
Byronic text prove, need not and finally cannot be occupied solely by
Byron. Circumstances, like luck, change.

III

Although Byron's "sexualization" coincided with his orientation
toward Greece, the debates about his sexuality began a little later,
when Lady Byron began to solicit medical and legal opinions in order
to legitimate her desertion of her husband soon after the birth of their
daughter in 1815. The ensemble of those debates comprises what has
come to be called the Separation Controversy. Here are a couple of
Lady Byron's more controversial remarks:

> In his endeavours to corrupt my mind he has sought to make me smile first
> at Vice. . . . There is *no* Vice with which he has not endeavoured in this
> manner to familiarize me—attributing the condemnation of such practices
> merely to the manners of different Countries, & seeking either to ridicule
> or reason me out of *all* principle.

And again,

> He laboured to convince me that Right & Wrong were merely Conven-
> tional, & varying with Locality & other circumstances—he clothed these

sentiments in the most seductive language—appealing both to the Heart
and Imagination. I must have been bewildered had I not firmly & simply
believed in one Immutable Standard.[44]

Now, suppose we buy Lady Byron's story. We still need to ask exactly what was going on. If Lady Byron was being subjected to persua-
sion, to what and how was she being persuaded? Crompton maintains
that her hints refer to an exchange about Lord Byron's bisexuality.[45]
Even if that were true, even if we suspected there were nothing more
behind Byron's sweet talk, we could not ignore the fact that that truth
came dressed as a discourse about relativism. The pious Lady Byron
Wollstonecraftily claims to have clung to an immutable standard of
right and wrong in determined resistance to Byron's insidious doctrine
that an act condemned in one place can be perfectly okay when performed in another.[46] Her story does not, however, account for Lady
Byron's fear of being bewildered, which is quite a different thing from
being induced to believe in relativism. The notion that good and evil
are conventional does not in and of itself lead to confusion about the
conventions appropriate here and now, let alone force someone to
abandon a cherished belief.

Indeed, it is fair to ask whether there really is any difference of opinion between Lady Byron and her husband, for there is an apparent
symmetry between his thesis that all behavior is subject to convention
and her recourse to a standard that, however single and immutable, is
based only in her belief. Convention, as recent theorists such as Stan-
ley Fish have seductively argued, is the "Standard" that allows for com-
parisons and conversions among diverse systems of belief. There is no
real difference between the absolutism of the Lady and the relativism
of the Lord: both are universalists; the only operational distinction is
whether that universal is something imperiously transcendent like the
Bible or something more ingratiatingly conditional like gold or language. One consequence of this symmetry is to make Lady Byron's
resistance look pretty foolish—she really had nothing to fear.

But that symmetry also has the consequence of making Lord Byron
look far less unconventional. Byron may be arguing for the morality

of bisexuality, but bisexuality has been sublimated into a feature of a broader economy: it has been coded as a neat illustration of exchange value. In some places and some times I like to do things to boys: I pay them in piasters: and in some times and some places I like to do things to women: I pay them in pounds sterling (or titles). The differences can be measured and adjusted: I always know what I am doing, whom I am doing it to, where I am doing it, and, most importantly, what it costs.⁴⁷ Moreover, piasters can be translated into pounds—I can use my Master Card to avoid any confoundment. Having been abstracted into exchange value, the content of the experience hardly makes any difference at all—or makes a difference only insofar as it, too, is marketable as "risky" or "safe." Bisexualizing renders all sexual beings and sexual experiences equivocal. What makes sexuality pleasurable and incipiently perverse, something like stockjobbing, is toying with the differential, pumping the margin.

Insofar as the difference between Lady and Lord Byron comes to a contest between a humorless piety and a cheerfully repressive desublimation, we know that the clout of history backs up Byron and Master Card, and we may take whatever comfort we choose. But, it must be remembered, both Lady Byron's puritanism *and* Lord Byron's relativism are narrative reconstructions by Lady Byron, comprising both method and *methode.* "Lord Byron," she mysteriously attested, "has never *expressly* declared himself guilty of any *specific* crime—but his insinuations to that effect have been much more convincing than the most direct assertion." Doris Langley Moore acidly comments that it is "marvellously typical of Lady Byron to be more convinced by insinuations rather than by direct assertion."⁴⁸ Typical of Lady Byron but also marvelously typical of every reader of Byron. Scott, for example, gave considerable credit to Byron's insinuative powers when, in 1818, he attempted to account for his popularity: "But it was not merely to the novelty of an author speaking in his own person, and in a tone which arrogated a contempt of all the ordinary pursuits of life, that *Childe Harold* owed its extensive popularity: these formed but the point or sharp edge of the wedge by which the work was enabled to insinuate its way into that venerable block, the British public."⁴⁹ Lady

Byron's remarks, then, identify her as just another suggestive reader of her husband, typically entranced by Byron's insinuations. Entranced up to a point, that is: Lady Byron comes to complain bitterly of Byron's practice of making "*Romance*... the colouring and the mask of vice." Of course, no more than Byron does Lady Byron come to the point and say what the hidden vice is. She bases her critique on the vice of concealing vice, which is nothing more than the betrayal of interest. An axiom for all second-generation Romantics: romance begins to fail and romancers begin to be disgusting when they seem interested, methodical, when romance degenerates into labored arguments about relativism.

Lady Byron's version of Byron is completely conventional. She never says anything about Byron's plots that is any different from what you could find scattered through the reviews of *Childe Harold* and the Oriental tales. In fact, Lady Byron's decisive break with her husband coincided with a general turn against Byron by the reviews, which crystallized with the publication of *Parisina*. Both sets of objections can be reduced to two heads: (1) moral: Byron's attempt, as the *Eclectic* says, to "inculcate the dangerous error that vice does not degrade the mind";[50] and (2) aesthetic: Byron propagates that error under the guise of exotic motifs which in their repetition have become odious. As the *Critical Review* patiently explains in its 1816 review of *Hebrew Melodies,*

> The truth is, that an individual who publishes so much and so repeatedly, ought to have a larger stock of true poetical feeling than is possessed by the author of these melodies. It is not mere fervor of mind, nor energy of expression (with both of which his Lordship is eminently gifted) that will always satisfy; they cease to produce any effect after a time, and the author who has nothing more to offer, must after that time, be contented with a certain though gradual oblivion.[51]

The terms of censure simply reverse the earlier terms of praise. Initially, the reviews had acknowledged that intriguing postures and characters made Byron's style recognizable; and they observed (or effused) that the exaggerated disparity between superficial Oriental color and deep Oriental sin made his poems alluring. Like Napoleon, Lord

Byron's success has become the very basis for his failure.[52] But that is not the whole of the indictment. Frequently, moral and aesthetic condemnation is backed up, however reluctantly, by an appeal to the market, as when the *Eclectic* clucks that the public is "apt to mistake the recurrence of obvious traits of style . . . for the sameness of impoverished genius, and to grow, in consequence, fastidious, and at length unjust, towards the productions of their favourite."[53] In its neat inversion of Wollstonecraft's fantasy of the sensual male who, become a "fastidious sensualist, . . . then makes the contagion which his unnatural state spread, the instrument of his tyranny" [sic],[54] the *Eclectic* dramatizes the reversibility of the cultural scene of fascination remarked on above: Wollstonecraft's "luxurious monster" has subjugated readers to a sensuality that, grown monstrous itself, turns to tyrannize over its creator—and, consequently, Lord Byron becomes the first, worst victim of that "moral disease" called "Byronomania."[55]

Whatever the merits of Lady Byron's distaste, in Regency England there was, as the Regent himself would prove, at least one substantial difference between buying a book and entering wedlock: marriage could not be dissolved by a change of opinion nor desertion justified by fastidiousness. Lady Byron could not legitimize her flight by appealing to canons of taste or even to common sense. Hence there were *two* decisive moments in her separation: first, rejection and flight; second, legal absolution of that revulsion from the imputation of an unjust fastidiousness. The second, revisionary moment occurred when Lady Byron returned to London to consult with her attorney Dr. Lushington. A confession was made that convinced the outraged Lushington to decree that the separation was irrevocable. It was exactly at that point, where the intimacy of the bedroom yielded to the privilege of attorney and client, that Lady Byron's fastidiousness became underwritten by the law. And it is that confidential moment which has aroused the most debate among Byron's biographers. What awful secret did Lady Byron tell? Speculation first produced the rumor of a murder; it then hunted out incest; it has since settled comfortably on the suspicion of homosexuality. None of those explanations, as G. Wilson Knight was the first to show, is satisfactory. Lord Byron had claimed and Lady Byron had corroborated that he had never "done an act *that would bring me under the power of the law* . . . at least on this side of the water"—a disclaimer that covers both domestic half-incest and foreign "intercourse-to-the-full."[56] It was to bring Lord Byron under the power of the law that Lady Byron appealed to Lushington; and to bring Byron under the law was to move beyond insinuation and the exotic; it required that Lady Bryon establish a privileged relationship to him, prove that she had been the victim of an act that was not only criminal but unique in its "indelicacy."

G. Wilson Knight has provocatively conjectured that the monstrous secret with which Lady Byron turned her attorney's heart to stone was that Byron had buggered her, an act both illegal and vile.[57] Doris Langley Moore indignantly challenged both Knight's documentary evidence and, more fiercely, its psychological and physiological verisimilitude. For Lady Byron to make such a shocking charge, says Moore, would involve either one of two equally impossible assumptions: that she was ignorant of what was being done to her at the time or, worse, that she had at first been responsive and only later changed her mind.[58] The options are good ones; it was imprudent of Moore to rule them out. The latter has more psychological plausibility—it corresponds to the shape of the reader response to Byron's "fervor" as it is rehearsed again and again in the reviews. Yet if a change of mind may actually have brought about Lady Byron's disgust, it can hardly be adduced as evidence, when the nature and naturalness of changes of mind, of opinion, and of aim are precisely at stake. Although Lady Byron might in fact have pleasurably acquiesced, for her to confess before the law that she had knowingly done so and *then* changed her mind (on the basis of what act if not the most unnatural that the law recognizes?), could only weaken her case by making it appear a matter of taste. And there is no accounting for taste. A physiological blindness that is completely caught up in erotic oblivion is necessary to hide (in a strong sense, to *be*) the trauma of an unequivocal and unforgivable transgression of the law, which later can be recovered and healed/punished.[59] Knight may be wrong in that there is no convincing evidence that Byron actually buggered his wife. But, pace Moore, making sense of the separation requires the positing of an extraordinary, literally unimaginable confoundment.

I claim no privileged knowledge about whether such a mistake by Lady Byron could actually be made, whether out of ignorance, abandonment, or a truly religious abstraction. But I do insist that to bring Lord Byron before the law such a mistake—a dangerous error—must be theoretically possible. When Lady Byron takes Byron before Lushington she endeavors to establish a privileged relationship with her husband in order to justify a separation in law. Hence she has to prove or posit a relation that is something other than the inferential connection available to any reader of him. She requires a direct assertion—brute Byron. She does not produce testimony of the surrender of her single immutable standard to the license of relativism, of her normative heterosexuality to the depravity of bisexuality: Byronic relativism is not licentious; Byronic bisexuality is rather fastidiously normative. She produces instead the direct assertion of confoundment: confoundment in the act, confoundment in the telling, confoundment between the telling and the act—exactly that bewilderment which, like Matthews, it has been the aim of her method to ward off. This primordial and perdurable bewilderment (it ramifies through all the commentary) is not vice without the mask of romance but romance without the alibi of vice, direct assertion without the excuse of interest or inadvertence. The confusion that Lady Byron and her attorney must posit and produce as the only way to single out Byron does not refer to any express or specific act of violation but presents the liquifying, nihilative ambivalence that is the experience of the sacred. Or the experience of the "naked letter" of romance. Byronic bewilderment is romance pure and violent.

Let me align the parallels. To accomplish a legal separation from her husband, Lady Byron needs to separate her relation to him, heretofore based on inference, from the public's—to divulge something she knows about him that the common reader does not. That knowledge erupts, in camera, as a moment of categorical bewilderment, which violently marks off Lord Byron's difference from everyone else: from the camps of East and West, past and present, boy and girl, pro and con, fore and aft. The direct assertion of Byron is a radical "mark of separation"—a mark, as Lord Lushington attests, that spread with unnerving velocity and vigor, like contaminating impiety or infectious laughter, through what, after the separation, has become the Byronomanic text: "I return you Lord Byron's letter with the inclosures & entirely agree with you in thinking any reply *to him* useless. Indeed the danger of misrepresentation is so great, that it is scarcely possible to make any communication by letter or otherwise without almost a certainty of perversion."[60] This "mark of separation," a term which I borrow from Edward Young[61] and which I want to link with the insupportable dazzle that fronts the naked letter of romance, is Byron's genius—or, if you prefer, his lordship, his sovereignty, or his quintessentially aristocratic style. Any of those concepts can be deployed in lip service to whatever law of context is locally in force, but the ideal for the critic who wants to establish an uncommon intimacy with Lord Byron is to approximate that "irregularity without a concept"[62] that is Byron's strength, his mark of separation.

The path branches here. One fork leads to the consideration of the more general context in which Byron's lordship first erupts, of how his mark of separation exposes the social and political disarticulations that made his genius possible by making it easier for him to become a great poet than a mediocre one—or, worse, a responsible member of the House of Lords. We would begin with an investigation of the way the fiasco that followed the publication of Lord Byron's insouciant *Hours of Idleness* destroyed Byron's prudential strategy for navigating from the delirial realm of Harrow and Cambridge into the professionalized culture represented by Henry Brougham and the *Edinburgh Review.*

Alternatively, to persuade that Byron is a poetic as well as an erotic revolutionary requires that these moments of confoundment be textualized, which could best be accomplished by abandoning Lady Byron's gothic readings of Byron for the more serviceable comments of the workaday reviewers themselves. A crossing would be made by engaging more directly the first, psychologically plausible moment in the sequence of separation. If accounting for the revisionary moment has led, willy-nilly, to lurid conjectures about cataclysmic events, addressing the triggering moment would entail some mitigation, would require asking whether or not Lady Byron rejected her lord, husband,

and poet in response to some nuance in the monotony of supply—and then to ask just what that nuance might have been, how it could be so effectively different from the mere division of parts that makes supply possible at all. Attention to the issues of gender in the Oriental tales and to the way the Oriental tales are themselves engendered would recover those poetic events in which nuances in the monotony of supply became, to everyone's surprise, differences indigestible according to the dominant canons of taste. These spasms of rejection are moments of change; these convulsions are paradigm shifts or parodies thereof—which, a narrative of Byron's career would discover, come to much the same thing. But either path stretches beyond the horizon. I shall conclude here and now by directly asserting that rendering an account of Byron's genius will mean a history of his random acts of violence and love, his random acts of writing.

NOTES

1. Mary Wollstonecraft, *A Vindication of the Rights of Women* (London: Dent, 1929), 44.

2. Friedrich Nietzsche, *On the Genealogy of Morals,* trans. Walter Kaufmann (New York: Random House, 1969), 80.

3. Wollstonecraft, *Vindication,* 42, 97, 47–50, passim. Wollstonecraft's usage of "exercise" shows her conformity with the enlightenment project of transforming the notion of exercise as deployment into exercise as training. This project ranges over mental and physical culture. Its itinerary extends from *Spectator* No. 94, where Addison endeavors "to show how those parts of life which are exercised in study, reading, and the pursuits of life are long but not tedious," through Lord B's self-congratulation for the "innocent exercises" he has given Pamela's wit, to Thomas Reid, the philosopher of common sense, who, in a particularly Wollstonecraftian moment, exclaimed that the "extent of human power is perfectly suited to the state of man, as a state of improvement and discipline. By the proper exercise of this gift of God, human nature, in individuals and societies, may be exalted to a high degree of dignity and felicity, and the earth become a paradise" (Thomas Reid, *Philosophical Works,* 2 vols.

[Hildesheim: Georg Olms Verlagsbuchhandlung, 1967], 2:530). In his great sports romance "The Fight," William Hazlitt endorses a regimen similar to Reid's: "The whole art of training . . . consists in two things, exercise and abstinence, abstinence and exercise, repeated alternately and without end" (*Selected Writings*, ed. Ronald Blythe [Harmondsworth: Penguin, 1970], 82). Writing and prizefighting converge in the second-generation romantics. Byron had a keen interest in pugilistic training. In the 1830 introduction to *Lady of the Lake*, Walter Scott conspicuously lamented that during his early poetic prominence he had been more like "the champion of pugilism" than "the champion of chivalry." For a discussion of David Hume's strategic redefinition of power in terms of exercise and of his illustration of it in light of the privileged topos of the miser (cf., for example, canto 12 of Byron's *Don Juan*), see Jerome Christensen, *Practicing Enlightenment: Hume and the Formation of a Literary Career* (Madison: University of Wisconsin Press, 1987), 69–76. The most thorough and complex historiographic meditation on the virtue of exercise appears in Edward Gibbon's deeply ambivalent description of "The State of Germany till the Invasion of the Barbarians," chap. 9 of *The Decline and Fall of the Roman Empire*.

4. Wollstonecraft, *Vindication*, 152.

5. Harold Bloom, *A Map of Misreading* (New York: Oxford University Press, 1975), 37.

6. In *The Bride of Abydos*, the Oriental tale most devoted to the dynamics of fascination. Byron gives this account of Eve's daughter, Zuleika:

Fair—as the first that fell of womankind—
   When on that dread yet lovely serpent smiling,
Whose image then was stamped upon her mind—
   But once beguiled—and ever more beguiling.

If the Byronic interpretation were applied to the initial scene in Eden, one would need to drop the "then" to account for Satan's initial fascination. Satan is charmed by the smile of the serpent he is to become. (The verse is quoted from *Byron: The Complete Poetical Works*, ed. Jerome J. McGann, 4 vols. [Oxford: Clarendon Press, 1980–86], 1:1:158–61. Subsequent references to *CPW* will be made by volume, canto [when appropriate], and line in the text.)

7. Edmund Burke, *Reflections on the Revolution in France* (Penguin: Harmondsworth, 1969), 169.

8. Ibid., 165.

9. Another example that falls in the line of Crazy Kate and Margaret is the anecdote that Scott tells in the introduction to *Guy Mannering* of his "solemn remembrance of a woman *of more than female* height, dressed in a long red cloak," who became the prototype for Meg Merrilees (my emphasis). As a group such scenes belong under Geoffrey H. Hartman's category "Eastering," a regressive countermovement back along the path of westering enlightenment. See Geoffrey H. Hartman, "Blake and the Progress of Poesy," in *Beyond Formalism: Literary Essays, 1958–1970,* (New Haven: Yale University Press, 1970), 199–200.

10. Michel Foucault, *The History of Sexuality.* Vol. 1: *An Introduction,* trans. Robert Hurley (New York: Pantheon, 1978), 121.

11. David Hume, "Of Refinement in the Arts," *Essays Moral, Political, and Literary* (1777: rept., Indianapolis: LibertyClassics, 1985), 268. For a useful history of the concept of luxury in Western thought, see Alan J. Sekora, *Luxury: The Concept in Western Thought, Eden to Smollett* (Baltimore: Johns Hopkins University Press, 1977), 23–131.

12. Wollstonecraft, *Vindication,* 44. For another, more spectacular example of this classificatory strategy—the attempt by David Hume, in the name of enlightenment, to contain Rousseau by labeling him as a chimerical "imaginary being"—see Christensen, *Practicing Enlightenment,* 251–55.

13. A classical move. In *Greek Homosexuality* (New York: Random House, 1978), K. J. Dover quotes from the peroration of Aiskhine's *Prosecution of Timarkhos* (346 B.C.) the prescription: "Tell those who are hunters of such young men as are easily caught to turn to foreign visitors or resident foreigners, so that they may not be denied the pursuit of their inclinations and you (*sc.* the people of Athens) may come to no harm" (31). In the eighteenth century this regulated, if not calculated, displacement of perverse desire is parasitic on the hysterical language of taint and contagion. Again, Wollstonecraft ably synthesizes a variety of motifs: "The indolent puppet of a court first becomes a luxurious monster . . . and then makes the contagion which his unnatural state spread, the instrument of tyranny" (*Vindication,* 22). Catherine Clément's account of the dynamics of this systemic strategy is compelling:

> The imaginary groups thus defined have only a fictive independence. . . . [As Lévi-Strauss says,] "Their peripheral position in relation to a local system

does not prevent their being an integral part of the total system in the same way that this local system is." They provide, somehow, the guarantee that locks the symbolic systems in, taking up the slack that can exist between them, carrying out, in the Imaginary, roles of extras, figures that are *impossible at the present time* (Hélène Cixous and Catherine Clément, *The Newly Born Woman*, trans. Betsy Wing [Minneapolis: University of Minnesota Press, 1986], 8–9).

14. Theodor W. Adorno, *Prisms*, trans. Samuel and Shierry Weber (Cambridge: MIT Press, 1981), 21.

15. *Byron's Letters and Journals*, ed. Leslie A. Marchand, 12 vols. (Cambridge: Harvard University Press, 1973–82), 2:66. Subsequent references to *BLJ* will be indicated by volume and page number in the text.

16. Byron's romantic classicism was not, of course, his own invention; it has a pedigree that extends backward to the Jacobins and refracts through Napoleon. The Napoleonic career was always before Byron, whose own politico-sexual itinerary could be described as a mock-Bonapartism. See, for example, Lord Byron's attempt to resolve disputes among his tenants on his return from the East: "But I shall not interfere further (than like Buonaparte) by diminishing Mr. B's *kingdom*, and erecting part of it into a *principality* for Field Marshal Fletcher!" (*BLJ* 2:52).

17. Besides Foucault, my analysis heavily depends on Jean Baudrillard's *For a Critique of the Political Economy of the Sign*, trans. Mark Poster (Minneapolis: Telos Press, 1981), esp. chap. 3, "Fetishism and Ideology."

18. In denying that Lord Byron was initiated into homosexuality before departing from England, I am rejecting Louis Crompton's revisionary reading of the texts surrounding the supposed advances made to Byron by Lord Grey de Ruthyn, tenant of Newstead Abbey, during Byron's visit with Grey in 1804. Differing from Byron's biographers Leslie A. Marchand and Doris Langley Moore, Crompton argues that the available evidence supports the inference that some sexual contact occurred (*Byron and Greek Love: Homophobia in 19th-Century England* [Berkeley: University of California Press, 1985], 81–85). The strong evidence of repulsion disables Crompton's case, though it is not, I would argue, repulsion toward homoerotic contact. Byron was disgusted not by the sexual nature of Grey's advances but by the advancing nature of Grey's sexuality. In the same letter to his mother in which Byron mysteriously refers to Grey as his "inveterate enemy," he boasts, "But however the way to *riches*

to *Greatness* lies before me, I can, I will cut myself a path through the world or perish in the attempt. others have begun life with nothing and ended Greatly. And shall I who have a competent if not a large fortune, remain idle, No, I will carve myself the passage to Grandeur, but never with Dishonour" (*BLJ* 2:49 [sic]). All other evidence of Byron's relations with boys shows him in the active role. To imagine him in the pathic with the tenant of his ancestral home is to promote an incredible aberration—particularly in one who is strongly afflicted with status anxiety and who takes his erotic patterns from the Greeks. My reservations are similar, though less strenuous in regard to Cecil Y. Lang's claim that there was a sexual liaison between Byron and the Ali Pacha on Byron's trip East (see "Narcissus Jilted: Byron, *Don Juan*, and the Biographical Imperative," *Historical Studies and Literary Criticism*, ed. Jerome J. McGann [Madison: University of Wisconsin Press, 1985], 143-79). Lang's ingenuity, which promises to disseminate the Byronic text in a radical and exciting way, tempts belief. Unfortunately that ingenuity is yoked to the quaint thesis that the biographical method is not, as Brooks and Warren once taught, irrelevant to interpretation. Who out there is arguing? But there is more than one biographical method, and, like Crompton's, Lang's reduces to decoding: he wants to use facts to get through the poetry to *the* fact (what the Ali Pacha actually did to Lord Byron, how *Don Juan* would really have ended). It is not the seductiveness of the Ali Pacha I deny—he could be politically and sexually accommodated to the interpositional model of Greek love described in notes 19 and 20 below. If Byron did have sexual relations with Ali Pacha, he did it for love of the Greeks. Regardless, I reject the sentimental commitment to the liberation of the referent that Lang's argument entails—Lang's insistence that "it" all comes down to one thing in the end. On the investment in the ethical distinction between active and pathic roles among the ancient Greeks, see Dover, *Greek Homosexuality*, passim.

19. Jerome J. McGann, *The Beauty of Inflections: Literary Investigations in Historical Method and Theory* (Oxford: Clarendon Press, 1985), 260. Cf. Maurice Godelier's comment that "the image of Asia stagnating for millennia in an unfinished transition from classless to class society, from barbarism to civilisation, has not stood up to the finding of archaeology and history in the East and the New World. . . . What was born in Greece was not civilisation but the West, a particular form of civilisation which was finally to dominate it while

all the while pretending to be its symbol" ("The Concept of the 'Asiatic Mode of Production' and Marxist Models of Social Evolution," in Anthony Giddens, *A Contemporary Critique of Historical Materialism* [Berkeley and Los Angeles: University of California Press, 1981], 87). Cf. the review of *Childe Harold's Pilgrimage* in the *Monthly Review* of May 1812, which after quoting Byron's patronizing remarks about the Greeks' need for interposition, observes that "perhaps [Lord Byron] rather under-rates the value of the co-operation of the natives, which would certainly be essential on such an occasion" (*Romantics Reviewed*, ed. Donald A. Reiman [New York: Garland, 1972], B:4:1734).

20. Sexualized, Byron's notion of the "interposition" of himself between the aggressor Turk and victimized Greek, giving and receiving, would be diagnosed as bivalently sadomasochistic, especially if contrasted with the strikingly similar, overtly sexual gesture of liberation proposed by Lytton Strachey who, when asked at the 1916 inquiry into his claims to be a conscientious objector, "What would you do if you saw a German soldier attempting to rape your sister?" replied, "I should try and interpose my own body" (Michael Holroyd, *Lytton Strachey: A Critical Biography*, 2 vols. [New York: Holt, Rinehart & Winston, 1967–68], 2:179). Both Strachey's known homosexual preference and the incest taboo restrict the function of "interpose" to the provision of a masochistic buffer rather than a sadomasochistic hinge.

21. Byron's liberation of Eustathius amounted to a substitution of a "green shade" for "that effeminate parasol"–a change in inflection but no reconstitution of the boy's sign-value (*BLJ* 2:7). Not that the change in inflection, accent, or color is insignificant. Neil Hertz addresses the element of hysteria in the debates regarding the proper shape of the ideologically charged Phrygian cap, which veered between a drooping, emasculated/ing, Asiatic, Medusa-like model and the more than Roman cone shape (Neil Hertz, *The End of the Line* [New York: Columbia University Press, 1985], 179–91). Although there is, I think, a fair analogy between parasol/shade and droopy cap/cone cap, it would be too farfetched to mention were it not that the two articles of clothing are linked in one of the most influential colonialist fantasies in the English language, *Robinson Crusoe*. An account of the political, economic, racial, and sexual themes invested in Crusoe's goatskin parasol and cap is given in Derek Walcott's brilliant *tour de force Pantomime*, staged in New York City, 1986–87.

22. See Doris Langley Moore, *Lord Byron: Accounts Rendered* (London: John

Murray, 1974), 89, and Crompton, *Byron and Greek Love*, 152.

23. Moore, *Lord Byron*, 90.

24. T. A. J. Burnett, *The Rise and Fall of a Regency Dandy: The Life and Times of Scrope Berdmore Davies* (London: John Murray, 1981), 36.

25. Ibid., 14.

26. Ibid. Because the "face unglimpsed" is no face at all, perhaps it would be more accurate to note that in *Northanger Abbey*, for example, Austen gives a face to the other side of the eighteenth century and "romantically" names it "Gothic." Both the countenancing of the other as Gothic and the denial that Gothic plots bear any relation to actual circumstances are part and parcel of the near-hysterical denial by Henry Tilney, Catherine Morland's patron, that there could be anything unglimpsed in a society so elaborately contrived for the ends of surveillance as contemporary England: "Does our education prepare us for such atrocities? Do our laws connive at them? Could they be perpetrated without being known, in a country like this, where social and literary intercourse is on such a footing; where every man is surrounded by a neighbourhood of voluntary spies, and where roads and newspapers lay every thing open?" (chap. 24).

27. Mark Girouard, *The Return to Camelot: Chivalry and the English Gentleman* (New Haven: Yale University Press, 1981), 163–76. Girouard's history could be read as an extended commentary on Scott's account in the General Preface to the Waverley Novels of the schoolboy "bicker" in which neighborhood brawled with neighborhood and class battled class in a brutal melee on the streets of Edinburgh, until, magically, "a lady of distinction presented a handsome set of colours," eradicating peculiar devices by chivalrizing one and all. Scott's recollection, offered with an aplomb that almost disarms criticism, not only craftily deploys all the motifs and devices we have been addressing, but is characteristically self-conscious about the social and political implications of their deployment.

28. Maurice Keen, *Chivalry* (New Haven: Yale University Press, 1984), 86–90, 125–34.

29. Cf. Girouard's account of the humiliating failure of the Eglinton Tournament in 1839 (*Return to Camelot*, 87–110).

30. Crompton, *Byron and Greek Love*, 129. In his usage Crompton does not clearly distinguish between the terms "homosexual" and "gay." John Boswell

incisively frames the terminological issue in his *Christianity, Social Tolerance, and Homosexuality* (Chicago: University of Chicago Press, 1980), where he defines "homosexuality" as comprising "all sexual phenomena between persons of the same gender, whether the result of conscious preference, subliminal desire, or circumstantial exigency," and "gay" as referring to "persons who are conscious of erotic inclination toward their own gender as a distinguishing characteristic or, loosely, to things associated with such people" (44). Although Boswell is clearer, his definitions increase rather than diminish the ambiguity. "Gay" by this definition is a trope; it need not be sexual at all. Its relation to homosexuality is fundamentally contingent. For an admirable, historically nuanced discussion of the variations in homosexual identity that were constructed in the nineteenth century, see Jeffrey Weeks, *Sex, Politics and Society: The Regulation of Sexuality since 1800* (London: Longman, 1981), 108–17.

31. Crompton, *Byron and Greek Love*, 127–29.

32. Crompton mentions that the code was first deciphered by Gilbert Highet in 1957 at the request of Leslie A. Marchand (128). That it remained mysterious for so long has more to say about the decline of classical education than it does about the inherent difficulty of the code.

33. But not the only fruit. In a later letter Byron jokingly promised a treatise on sodomy (*BLJ* 1:208). During the journey the friends hatched the project of launching a literary journal to be called the *Bagatelle* (allowing glimpses of the cat in the bag?). The Wollstonecraftian characterization of Childe Harold appears in George Ellis's review for the *Quarterly* in March 1812 (*Romantics Reviewed*, B:5:1991).

34. Eve Kosofsky Sedgwick, *Between Men: English Literature and Male Homosocial Desire* (New York: Columbia University Press, 1985), 95.

35. For Defoe on jargon, see *The Complete English Tradesman in Familiar Letters*, 2 vols. (1727; rept. New York: Augustus Kelley, 1969), 1:26–34; for Swift, *Examiner* (November 2, 1710), *The Works of Jonathan Swift*, ed. Thomas Roscoe, 6 vols. (New York: O'Shea, 1865), 3:454; for Coleridge, see *Biographia Literaria*, ed. James Engell and W. Jackson Bate, vol. 7 of *The Collected Works of Samuel Taylor Coleridge*, gen. ed. Kathleen Coburn, 2 vols. (Princeton: Princeton University Press, 1983), 1:60–67 and 2:109–10. Here is a frustrated Lord Byron addressing his publisher John Murray: "Indeed you are altogether so abstruse and undecided lately—that I suppose you mean me to write—'John Murray

Esqre. a *Mystery* a composition which would not displease the Clergy nor the trade.–" (*BLJ* 9:168).

36. Jacques Lacan, "Aggressivity in Psychoanalysis," in *Ecrits: A Selection,* trans. Alan Sheridan (New York: Norton, 1977), 17.

37. Dover, *Greek Homosexuality,* 47.

38. Wollstonecraft, *Vindication,* 21.

39. Richard Hurd, *Letters on Chivalry and Romance* (1762; rept. Los Angeles: Augustan Reprint Society, 1963), 113. Jacques Derrida, "Differance," in *Speech and Phenomena: And Other Essays on Husserl's Theory of Signs,* trans. David B. Allison (Evanston: Northwestern University Press, 1973), 129–60.

40. On the definition "of a culturally defined elite" according to a code that expresses the sense of distance which separated gentlemen from those who were not gentlemen in eighteenth- and nineteenth-century England, see J. C. D. Clark, *English Society 1688–1832* (Cambridge University Press, 1985), 103–5.

On the varieties of methodist associations with political and religious ferment, which extended from radical revivalism to reactive quietism to what Cobbett described as the corporatism of a "new bureaucracy, composed of 'the most busy and persevering set of men on earth,'" see E. P. Thompson, *The Making of the English Working Class* (New York: Vintage, 1963), 350–400. For another example of the use of neologism as a homosocial device, see Coleridge's promotion of his coinage "aspheterized" to his pantisocratic comrade Robert Southey in 1794 (*The Letters of Samuel Taylor Coleridge,* ed. Earl Leslie Griggs, 6 vols. [Oxford: Clarendon Press, 1956–71], 1:84). Scott makes the connection between slang, methodism, prurience, and a corruptiveness that hovers between the political and the sexual in his contemptuous dismissal of Thomas Moore's early, pseudonymous erotic poetry: "In fact, it is not passages of ludicrous indelicacy that corrupt the manners of a people–it is the sonnets which a prurient genius like Master Little sings *virginibus puerisque*–it is the sentimental slang, half lewd, half methodistic, that debauches the understanding, inflames the sleeping Passions, and prepares the reader to give way as soon as the tempter appears" (J. G. Lockhart, *Memoirs of Sir Walter Scott,* 5 vols. [London: Macmillan, 1900], 1:431). It is not possible to disentangle these various connotations and alliances here. It is worth noting, however, that not only can Matthews's fate be interpreted (see below) as a judgment on such debauchery, but Byron also depicts just such a victim of "sentimental slang, half lewd, half methodistic" in the tragicomic figure of Tom the highwayman, who is fatally wounded by Juan at the beginning of canto 11 of *Don Juan.*

41. Theodor W. Adorno, *Negative Dialectics,* trans. E. B. Ashton (New York: Seabury Press, 1969), 146; trans. amended by David Held, *Introduction to Critical Theory: Horkheimer to Habermas* (Berkeley and Los Angeles: University of California Press, 1980), 220.

42. "I think they must own that I have more *styles* than one" (*BLJ* 8:155).

43. Applied to the Jacobins by Burke, *Reflections,* 128. Note that Matthews, who perversely substituted French verbal formulas and legalistic prescriptions for the good, old English method of experience, who was a homosexual (and therefore only theoretically a man), and who was a homosexual only in theory (he never practiced what he professed), was nicknamed "citoyen Matthews" by Byron and Hobhouse. If the illustration is uncanny, it is because it releases something hidden in Burke's own text: the homoerotic subtext and pretext of *Reflections*—entitled *A Philosophical Enquiry into Our Ideas of the Sublime and the Beautiful*—it stands in the unnatural relation to its successor of a theory that dictates ensuing practice.

44. Crompton, *Byron and Greek Love,* 215–16.

45. Ibid., 216.

46. "[U]nless [women's] morals be fixed on the same immutable principles as man" (*Vindication,* 11).

47. On Lord Byron's economizing in the East, see his letter to his mother of November 12, 1809, where commenting on the substitution of love for "sequins," he exclaims, "It is astonishing how far money goes in this country" (*BLJ* 1:230; see also the postscript, 231). Crompton's enlightened endorsement of Lord Byron's bisexuality involves some fudging of sexual power relationships. In the case of Byron's homosexual liaisons, this entails some sentimentality about boy love, which takes the form of the pathos of the pederast (and, of course, the Orientalist): "In our day and age we speak of the sexual exploitation of the young. This may occur, but in such affairs it is often the emotional vulnerability of the older male that makes him most open to exploitation, as Byron's later attachment to Lukas Chalandurtsanos was to demonstrate" (*Byron and Greek Love,* 238). Crompton not only overlooks the dominant lesson of Dover's *Greek Homosexuality,* that what is exploitation in our day was also regarded as potentially exploitative in the Western pattern of a homosexual

culture, but he also misses the Wollstonecraftian implications of the textbook example of the scene of fascination that emerges in Byron's "Last Words," his penetratingly self-pitying late poem to Lukas:

> What are to me those honours or renown
>   Past or to come, a new-born people's cry[?]
> Albeit for such I could despise a crown
>   Of aught save laurel, or for such could die;
> I am the fool of passion—and a frown
>   Of thine to me is as an Adder's eye
> To the poor bird whose pinion fluttering down
>   Wafts unto death the breast it bore so high—
> Such is this maddening fascination grown,
>   So strong thy Magic—or so weak am I.
>
>   (quoted in Crompton, 327)

48. Moore, *Lord Byron*, 444.

49. Unsigned review from the *Quarterly Review*, issued in September 1818; quoted in *Byron: The Critical Heritage*, ed. Andrew Rutherford (New York: Barnes & Noble, 1970), 140. Cf. the *Antijacobin* on *The Giaour*, which is perhaps even closer to Annabella's predicament: "When, however, Lord Byron advances any paradoxical position, he clothes it in such pleasing strains, that we are almost seduced to admit the justice of his reasoning by the fascination of his language" (*Romantics Reviewed*, B:1:33).

50. *Eclectic Review* (November 1813: reviewing *The Giaour*); *Romantics Reviewed*, B:2:715. In its review of *The Giaour* the *Christian Observer*, also nervous, "beseeched" Lord Byron "not to add himself to the infamous catalogue of those who have endeavoured to make vice reputable, who have ruined their country by overthrowing its altars and expelling its gods" (November 1813; *Romantics Reviewed*, B:2:574).

51. *Romantics Reviewed*, B:2:647.

52. See Peter Paret's discussion of the way Napoleonic "institutional and tactical modernization spread to armies far beyond France," contributing to the decline of Napoleon's absolute superiority in "Napoleon and the Revolution in War," *Makers of Modern Strategy from Machiavelli to the Nuclear Age*, ed. Peter Paret (Princeton: Princeton University Press, 1986), 134–36.

53. March 1816 review of *The Siege of Corinth* and *Parisina* (*Romantics Reviewed*, B:2:733).

54. Wollstonecraft, *Vindication*, 22.

55. *The Knight Errant*, 1817 review of *Manfred* (*Romantics Reviewed*, B:3:1223).

56. Moore. *Lord Byron*, 444–45.

57. G. Wilson Knight, *Lord Byron's Marriage: The Evidence of Asterisks* (New York: Macmillan, 1957), 247.

58. Moore, *Lord Byron*, 447. A conversation with Annabel Patterson helped me think through the relative merits of Moore's objections.

59. Byron prescribed a romantic regimen of oblivion: "It seems strange; a true voluptuary will never abandon his mind to the grossness of reality. It is by exalting the earthly, the material, the *physique* of our pleasures, by veiling those ideas, by forgetting them altogether, or at least, never naming them hardly to one's self, that we can prevent them from disgusting" (*BLJ* 3:239). Lady Byron's fall from the voluptuary's special grace shows how fragile such exaltation can be.

60. Malcolm Elwin, *Lord Byron's Wife* (New York: Harcourt Brace & World, 1963), 457.

61. Edward Young, "Conjectures on Original Composition" (1759), in *The Great Critics*, ed. James Harry Smith and Edd Winfield Parks (New York: Norton, 1932), 419.

62. Gillian Rose's description of the project of Gilles Deleuze in *Dialectic of Nihilism: Post-Structuralism and the Law* (Oxford: Basil Blackwell, 1984), 2. Cf. George Bataille's exaltation of "the image of terrestrial love without condition, erection without escape and without rule, scandal, and terror" ("The Solar Anus," *Visions of Excess: Selected Writings, 1927–1939*, trans. Allan Stoekl et. al. [Minneapolis: University of Minnesota Press, 1985], 8–9).

Carroll Smith-Rosenberg

Domesticating "Virtue"

COQUETTES AND REVOLUTIONARIES
IN YOUNG AMERICA

Passion corrupting virtue, libertines destroying happiness, independence misused, seduction, betrayal and death.

This is a summary not of the torrid plots of afternoon soap operas or harlequin romances, but rather of the themes that obsessed America's first novelists, in the years following the American Revolution. Written as our national identity and modern class structure first took shape, America's earliest best-sellers—*Charlotte Temple, The Coquette, Ormond*—were filled with scenes of fortune-hunting rakes and army officers, of young girls in flight from patriarchal homes, of unwed mothers and dying prostitutes.[1] Since popular fiction both reflects and shapes the world that reads it, the new American nation and the new middle class were formed at least in part by these lurid tales.

Historians, however, have rarely examined them. Melodramatic romances seemed to say little about the critical events of the early national period: the emergence of a capitalist class structure, the evolution of class identities, the ideological battle between classical republicanism and the rhetoric of economic and political laissez-faire.[2] Nor have historians been alone in their compartmentalized vision. The political debates of the new nation held little interest for literary scholars exploring the origins of the American novel.[3] But does only the coincidence of chronology connect these two genres? Or can we hear behind fantastical plots about virtue endangered and independence abused echoes of another quite different discourse, that of republican political theory? The vocabulary found in both genres is remarkably similar. In both corruption undermines "independence"; the vicious, nonproductive elegance of the aristocracy threatens "virtue"; reason and restraint serve the common good while passion promotes self-interest and civic disorder. Do the novels of the middle class and the political rhetoric of the middle class address the same social and political dilemmas?

To answer that question requires a radical repositioning of the novel of seduction and of republican political rhetoric. We must learn to read both as central components of the ideology and discourses of the emergent middle class. Sexual and domestic, political and economic discourses wove in and out of one another as that radically new and protean class sought to construct an identity inclusive enough to encompass its divergent, often warring, components. Repositioning the political and the sexual, we will reread the body. No longer will it appear simply as a repository of the erotic and the reproductive, a psychic entity confined to social margins and domestic space. As a physical text written and read within a political context, it assumes new dimensions. A representation of the civic individual, associated with themes of autonomy or aggression, it becomes a legitimate figure in the public arena. To reread the body in this way forces a second critical recognition—that the body's physical integrity constitutes as significant a material vehicle for symbolic representation as the body's evocative sensuality. After all, feminists have long argued that who controls the body is as important a question to ask as what excites the body—and that the first question must be understood in political, not erotic, terms.[4]

Let me rephrase this argument in the analytic language of the historian. Republican ideology cannot be studied in isolation from an analysis of middle-class discourse and identity formation, any more than middle-class discourse and identity can be understood isolated from the ways gender and sexuality were conceptualized and constructed—or gender and sexuality isolated from class and ideology. We cannot fully understand the construction of a new sexual and domestic female in America between the 1780s and the 1830s unless we view it against the constantly changing construction of the male citizen—from the opening shots of the American Revolution, until he emerged as both "the common political man" and "the self-made economic man" of Jacksonian America. The political body is always gendered just as the gendering of the body is always political—and relational.[5] The genders exist in conceptual opposition and in intimate social interaction. Whig theorists and republican mothers belonged to the same class, read in front of the same fires, often from the same texts.[6] The fundamental contradictions that characterize the developing civic and class ideologies of these years can be more fully understood if we examine them as shared texts which middle-class women and men understood and used in subtly different ways.

But we must beware of flipping backward through our texts. Too often we have read the class identities and the sexual attitudes of the Enlightenment conditioned by Victorian texts, permitting the dark hues of the later period to color our perceptions of the more ebullient and explorative eighteenth century. Sexual and class identities were more hesitant and ambivalent in the years when both were just taking form. The rigidities of the later period—and its new potentials for subversion and revolt—cannot be projected backward. To understand the women and men of the new class and the new nation we must, rather, trace the way they formed their ideologies out of the heritage of earlier eighteenth-century discourses and in interaction with the material practices of their own time. Affected by radical reworkings of those material practices—the rise of commercial economy and the commercial city, technological innovation, political revolution—they perceived those reworkings with minds conditioned by conceptual systems and values formed in interaction with older material and discursive practices. This heritage of words simultaneously blinded and directed them. As J. G. A. Pocock suggests, "men cannot do what they have no means of saying they have done and what they do must in part be what they can say and conceive that it is."[7] To read the texts and discourses of the new class our focus must simultaneously bridge material reality and its representation, link the past, as embedded in language and literary forms, with the present, caught at that moment when language intersects the material to produce perception.

We must also link the voices of the varied speakers—and the silences of the listeners. M. M. Bakhtin argues that a cacophony of social dialects representing different classes, ethnicities, generations, professions—and, I would add, genders—characterizes every heterogeneous society, a cacophony reproduced differently within the consciousness of each individual speaker in that society.[8] Power runs through this cacophony. The language of the economically and politically dominant will struggle to deny the legitimacy of more marginal social discourses, yet influences flow in both directions. Nor will the marginal ever be silenced. Rather, different social groups and subgroups will continually challenge each other's perceptions, conceptual systems, even the literal meanings of their words. Especially during periods of radical social change, this constant flow of conflicting meanings assumes an almost electrical urgency, like flashes of light refracting through a prism.[9] In this way, language re-presents social experience.

To elucidate the discordance inherent in the discourses of the new nation and the new class, to trace the complex and inharmonious interaction of the new gender, class, and political identities, let us examine the process by which the new capitalism complicated classical republicanism's linking of "virtue," "independence," "liberty," and "happiness." Such an examination is complicated by the fact that both American middle-class identity and ideology and republican political discourse in England and America were extremely protean entities. Throughout the eighteenth century, new speakers and new ideological dialects repeatedly transformed classical republicanism. Merchants in London and Philadelphia created the dialect of commercial republicanism; the artisans of London and New York constructed the dialogue of radical republicanism; women across a broad social and economic spectrum rewrote these varied male texts. By the century's end, the lexicon of republicanism had fragmented.[10]

To illustrate this point let us examine the transformation of the twin pillars of republican ideology, "virtue" and "independence."[11] Classical republicanism had identified the virtuous citizen as the free man who valued his liberty above all and who devoted himself to serving the common good. His ability to do both depended on an economic independence rooted in unalienated and unalienable property—literally, in the gentry's real estates secured by entail and primogeniture. Classical republicanism counterpoised the "virtuous" landed gentry to the "corrupt" new men of paper and place—the new capitalism's stock jobbers, government bureaucrats, and army officers. These men, the gentry argued, lived in a passionate and venal world driven by fantasy and credit, obsessed with stocks, speculation, and debt. Lacking landed independence, their interests, votes and pens were easily bought.

The man of trade occupied a more ambivalent position within classical-republican discourse. The value of the gentry's land, the source of the gentry's political independence, depended on trade, and hence on the actions of traders and on events occurring in London and in ports around the world. Their independence thus circumscribed by men and processes beyond their control or ken, the gentry responded with nervous suspicion. Trade, they wrote each other, was productive, linked to England's and their own prosperity. But trade also "introduces luxury . . . and extinguishes virtue." It depended on credit which hung upon opinion and the passions of hope and fear. It was cathected with desire. It might seduce independent men away from the simple ways of their fathers. It could entrap them in an endless web of debt and ruin.[12]

Creatures of trade and credit, middle-class men defended against this association of themselves with the corrupt world of fantasy and passion by redefining both "virtue" and "independence." In the commercial-republican lexicon, "independence" was rooted in productive labor and self-reliance. Talent, frugality, and application epitomized the new "virtue" and warded off the indulgences of luxury and indebtedness which the gentry had accused trade of eliciting. Traders were productive members of society, they argued. But were the gentry? Indeed, the new middle class began to take the offensive by reversing the symbols of corruption, proposing that the status of the gentry, like that of the aristocracy (the figure of corruption all republicans defined themselves against) depended on land inherited irrespective of talent or industry, and that the gentry, in common with the aristocracy, occupied political places secured not by productive labor but by family privilege. Challenges to patriarchy followed challenges to landed wealth, though the new bourgeois men spoke for the independence of sons far more than for the rights of wives and daughters. They also altered the meaning of "liberty." To the gentry it had meant the citizen's right to be actively involved in making and executing decisions in the public realm. The new commercial men, like Locke, saw liberty, rooted in the social contract, as the free man's right to secure his private property from the incursions of a potentially dangerous state. Inverting the gentry's understanding, they now claimed liberty as all men's right, not one class's privilege.[13]

The ways the men of the new middle class constructed the middle-class woman further complicated their inheritance of the political assumptions of the British gentry, not only because middle-class women occupied an ambiguous place within the economy and ideology of their class but, more importantly, because the middle-class men's construction of gender repeatedly contradicted the middle-class men's transformation of the male republican discourse.

To illustrate this point let me return to the word "virtue." Classical republicanism masculinized and gentrified virtue, rooting it in military service and landholding. In constructing their new class identity, middle-class men fused a republican understanding of civic virtue with more private and moral understandings garnered from evangelical religious texts.[14] In doing so they began to associate the virtue of their class not only with the frugality of middle-class men but also with the sexual propriety of middle-class women. Elite men within the new middle class, urban merchants and their professional coterie, then further complicated the sexually proper woman's relation to virtue by requiring her to embody their class in a second and equally significant way. The elite woman's personal elegance, in clothing and in speech, and her familiarity with things cultural were to represent middle-class men's own economic security and cultural superiority to all other classes. Yet their construction of the elegant woman as the sign of class warred with their earlier association of class with virtuous male frugality, and so a fundamental flaw emerged in middle-class men's symbolic representation of their class.

Shifting definitions of "independence," the material underpinning of both the gentry's and the middle-class's understanding of "virtue," further compromised the middle-class woman's symbolic qualifications. Classical republicanism had rooted virtue in the independence created by unalienable land, and thus denied women access to civic virtue. Commercial men had transposed the gentry's landed independence into the independence of productive industry. This shift in the grounding of independence occurred at the very moment when economic change and bourgeois ideology deprived the middle-class woman, and married women of all classes, of the opportunity to labor productively and to support themselves independently. Having required the bourgeois woman to be both elegant and nonproductive, how could the bourgeois man ever trust her virtue or rest securely in the symbols of his class?

These ideological ambiguities and contradictions only multiplied as middle-class men displaced onto middle-class women criticisms the gentry had leveled against them. As the gentry had accused middle-class men of venality and extravagance, so middle-class men, depicting themselves, as we have seen, as hardworking and frugal, harangued middle-class women for alleged extravagances in dress and household management. More seriously, the gentry had denied that commercial men, living in the fantastical, passionate, and unreal world of paper money, stocks, and credit, could achieve civic virtue. How significant, then, that throughout the eighteenth and nineteenth centuries middle-class men endlessly accused bourgeois women of being untrustworthy and incapable of virtue because they lived in another fantastical, passionate, and unreal world of paper—the world of the novel and the romance?[15]

The proliferation of popular literature, the explosive second paper revolution, gave both middle-class women and men ample opportunity to explore, defend, and re-form these contradictions and displacements. Although bourgeois men had inscribed a male text of class onto bourgeois women, bourgeois women did not always read that text as their men intended. Rather, bourgeois women, increasingly empowered by the printing press and the emergence of a commercial market for popular literature, began to produce their own texts of civic and class identity, texts that differed significantly from male inscriptions.

The novel is a particularly useful genre for historians in search of this discursive interchange. Not only was and is the novel considered a particularly female genre (romantic, fantastical, domestic, sexual, often written by women), more than most other literary and professional genres, but it also captures those dynamic moments of social change when disparate groups, battling for hegemony, form and reform language. "The novelistic word," Bakhtin tells us, "registers with extreme subtlety the nicest shifts and oscillations of the social atmosphere. . . . Each character's speech possesses its own belief system. . . . It . . . also refract[s] authorial intentions and consequently . . . constitute[s] a second language for the author."[16] The diversity of characters, the novel's reliance upon conflict and change for the development of plot and character, permit both the overt and covert expression of contradictions and conflicts inherent in the ideologies and discourses of the times. The evocative nature of the novel intensifies its ability to enact social conflict. While the hegemonic genres of a culture—sermons, for example, advice books, even political rhetoric—warn against danger and seek to repress ambiguities, the novel (and this was particularly true of the eighteenth-century novel of seduction) plays upon dangerous desires. Its melodramatic trials of a woman's virtue call forth its readers' repressed desires, permitting those desires to be vicariously enjoyed and as vicariously punished. While ultimately affirming the permissible, it makes us familiar with the forbidden. It is the novel, therefore, that most fully represents the conflicts and contradications of its time.

To explore this aspect of the novel, let us examine America's first bestseller, Hannah Foster's *The Coquette; or the History of Eliza Wharton. A Novel Founded on Fact. By a Lady of Massachusetts,* originally published in 1797 and repeatedly republished through the 1870s.[17] At first reading, *The Coquette* appears a melodramatic representation of the values of commercial republicanism. Eliza Wharton, a young and virtuous woman, has just ventured into the eighteenth-century marriage market. The daughter of a respected minister who, dependent on a salary, has left her little capital inheritance, Eliza plays the role of a venture capitalist. As such, she confronts the same dilemmas a young merchant faces in the confusing economic markets of the late eighteenth century: how to credit financial and moral worth in a world of words and fancy; whether to trust traditional community wisdom or, depending on her own judgment, to risk all for possible great gains. It is in the language of commercial metaphor that Foster has Eliza present herself to us and evaluate her chances. "Fortune," Eliza tells her friend and confidante, Lucy Freeman, "has not been very liberal of her gifts to me; but I presume on a large stock in the bank of friendship, which, united with health and innocence, give me some pleasing anticipation of future felicity." Freeman responds in kind: "I shall be extremely anxious to hear the process and progress of this business" (9, 27).

The plot revolves around the choice Eliza must make between two suitors. One, the Reverend Mr. Boyer, as a minister, represents simultaneously the authoritative voice of social norms and the hard-working, honest, professional middle class. Offering Eliza a life of respectable dignity and service to the community, he is rational, honorable, and prudent. His words harmonize with communal wisdom. The second suitor, Major Sanford, is a rake, corrupt and deceitful. He assumes the airs of the very wealthy and the distinction of a military title—both highly suspect within either classical or commercial-republican ideology. Worse yet, having wasted his fortune, he pretends to a station he has no right to claim. (This is symbolized by his mortgaged estate. An encumbered estate is an anathema to all forms of republicanism, a paper mortgage masking the reality of an empty purse.) He refuses honest employment as beneath the dignity of a "gentleman and a man of pleasure," preferring to prostitute himself to a marriage of convenience. With double deceit, he holds out to Eliza the temptations of a gay life and marriage although he cannot afford the one and does not intend the other. He compounds his sins by encouraging her resistance to the constraints of domesticity. Asserting her independence, Eliza sets out on her own to evaluate the worth of these two men. Swayed by fancy and ambition, scornful of her family's advice, Eliza judges wrongly and falls.

Read as a celebration of the values of commercial republicanism, this is just the novel we would expect to find written in the New England of the 1790s. But such a reading is too simple. *The Coquette* painstakingly and persistently complicates what should be clear-cut.

First, Eliza is not a heroine like Pamela or Clarissa, virtuous to the core. Rather, as Cathy Davidson argues in her fine study of early American literature, *The Revolution and the Word*, Eliza fuses talent and virtues with serious moral failings. Even more remarkably, her failings and her fall endear her to her friends within the novel and to her readers outside. Second, the novel persistently leads the reader to resist the prudent marriage and to root for the rake. Third, the moral spokeswomen of the novel end by warning the heroine that male ministerial texts can be as misleading and dangerous as women's romances and novels. Finally, *The Coquette* is not simply a fiction, but, as Davidson details, a rewriting of an earlier, male-authored historical text, the popular reporting of the scandalous death of Elizabeth Whitman (xi).

Elizabeth Whitman, a respected daughter of New England's professional middle class, related to Jonathan Edwards, cousin of Aaron Burr, daughter of a highly respected Hartford minister, herself a frequently published poet and friend of the Hartford Wits, died, alone, under an assumed name in a Massachusetts inn, having given birth to an illegitimate child. Newspapers and sermons thundered against her criminal sexuality as they speculated about the name of her seducer. The men's reading of the event emphasized women's social and sexual vulnerability: woman's passion, uncontrollable when enflamed by novel and romance reading, easily overcame women's fragile hold on virtue (xi).

Hannah Foster's *Coquette* offers us a different narrative. Eliza Wharton's downfall, Foster tells us, was not lust but the desire for independence coupled with the wish to rise socially. As such she represented those within the emergent middle class, who, rejecting traditional norms, anxiously embraced individualism, risk, and the new capitalism.

To be appreciated fully, *The Coquette* must be read as a gendered misprisioning of the political and economic discourses of its time. Just as the capitalist revolution problematizes "independence" and "virtue" as understood within classical republicanism, so *The Coquette* underscores the ways concepts of female "independence" and "individualism" further complicated the republican lexicon. The book's opening sentence alerts the reader to the significance of this issue. "An unusual sensation possesses my breast," Eliza writes her friend, Freeman, "a sensation which I once thought could never pervade it on any occasion whatever. It is *pleasure,* pleasure, my dear Lucy, on leaving my paternal roof. Could you have believed that the darling child of an indulgent and dearly-beloved mother would feel a gleam of joy at leaving her? But it is so" (5). Two events, Eliza continues, have freed her: the death of her father and the death of the man her father had chosen as her husband, another minister, whom she did not love. While both patriarchal figures lived, Eliza had exhibited behavior appropriate to her class and gender. "Both nature and education had instilled into my mind an implicit obedience to the will and desires of my parents. To them, of course, I sacrificed my fancy in the affair, determined that my reason should concur with theirs, and on that to risk my future happiness" (5).

To read these statements in a political context, let us start by juxtaposing Eliza's comment, "determined that my reason should concur with theirs, and on that to risk my future happiness," to one drawn from that primer of American republican rhetoric, the Declaration of Independence. Here we find "certain inalienable rights" listed, "among these, life, liberty and the pursuit of happiness." *The Coquette* begins by telling us that the heroine, as a virtuous daughter, has resigned her *liberty* of choice and her pursuit of *happiness* in deference to parental wishes; she has agreed, that is, to link happiness to the sacrifice, not the assertion, of liberty. This pious sacrifice is then contrasted to the pleasure she now reports experiencing at resuming her lost independence, pleasure, a word that she twice repeats, and that Hannah Foster italicizes. Circumstances reversing her position, Eliza now associates liberty with pleasure—and with her ability to pursue happiness on her own.

The Declaration of Independence tells us that liberty and the pursuit of happiness are unalienable rights. Numerous other republican texts warn Americans that to relinquish them will endanger virtue. But the Declaration also insists that a passion for liberty be balanced by prudence. "Prudence, indeed, will dictate that Governments long established should not be changed for light and transient causes." But

Eliza's very first sentence signals a subtle shift away from the hegemonical Declaration of Independence, a shift that challenges the traditional relation among pleasure, happiness, and prudence. Eliza has called pleasure an "unusual" emotion, especially when associated with independence and liberty. To most eighteenth-century republicans, it was both an unusual and a dangerous emotion. Popular version of moral philosophy, especially that most common to Puritan New England, pitted pleasure against both happiness and prudence.[18] For them, "happiness" signified contentment with one's place in life, "the attainment of what is considered good."[19] It was subservient to, indeed rooted in, social norms. "Pleasure," in contrast, implied delight in the sensations; it hinted at passion—an association reinforced when Eliza represents her pleasure in a physical, indeed, a sensual vocabulary. Pleasure, invoked by her newfound independence, she tells Freeman, "possesses my breast." It illuminates her with "a gleam of joy." When independence is absent in this text, so is sensuality. In acquiescing to her parent's will, Eliza tells Freeman, she had "sacrificed my fancy." "My heart" was not "engaged." "I never felt the passion of love." Eliza, in short, has invested her female independence and liberty of choice with desire. And with an equally dangerous emotion—individualism. Pleasure, especially in Eliza's usage, presumes individuals capable of fancying and privileging their own desires, of acting independent of society's approval in order to secure them. Eliza significantly ends her letter by underscoring this note of individualism. "This letter," she confesses to Lucy, "is all an Egotism" (5–6). What a significant beginning for a novel written in the shadow of the American Revolution!

Throughout the novel, Eliza Wharton will insist that pleasure can legitimately be wedded to a desire for independence and liberty, that marriage without such a "wedding" will destroy happiness.[20] Her family and friends will tell her virtue and happiness are tied to prudence and a socially appropriate marriage, that pleasure and fancy will endanger both. Throughout, Eliza will insist on her right as an independent woman to pursue happiness guided by her own standards.

The following interchange between Eliza and the proper and prosperously married Ann *Richman* schematically presents the conflict.

Eliza, rejecting Richman's advice to cut short her newfound liberty and marry the minister, replies: "I hope my friends will never again interpose in my concerns of that nature. A melancholy event has lately extricated me from those shackles which parental authority had imposed on my mind. Let me, then, enjoy that freedom which I so highly prize. Let me have opportunity, unbiased by opinion, to gratify my natural disposition in a participation of those pleasures which youth and innocence afford." Richman's response warns Eliza against conflating independence and pleasure, a conflation which Richman links to scenes of fashionable dissipation. "Of such pleasures, no one, my dear, would wish to deprive you," Richman insists, "but beware, Eliza! Though strewed with flowers, when contemplated by your lively imagination, it is, after all, a slippery, thorny path. The round of fashionable dissipation is dangerous. A phantom is often pursued, which leaves its deluded votary the real form of wretchedness" (13).

The disruption of the easy relations between happiness and virtue which Eliza's desire for pleasure and independence affected underscores a second disjuncture which greatly troubled the eighteenth century, that between perception and reality. The eighteenth century desired mimesis and despaired of achieving it. They feared that fancy and passion, tied to individualism and to the twin paper revolutions of credit and printing, would disrupt the ability of words and the imagination to represent material reality. Reality would become a chimera, especially for the innocent and the inexperienced, especially, that is, for women and the young. In the particular dialogue just cited, for example, Eliza insists that female independence is not only legitimate and pleasurable but a real option. The married and thus mature and experienced Richman dismisses Eliza's words as immaterial, "phantoms" obscuring the bodily reality of "slippery, thorny paths," and the "real form of wretchedness" which female independence, fused with female pleasure, will bring. Eliza alarms rather than persuades the reader by her willful and defiant response: "I despise those contracted ideas which confine virtue to a cell" (13).

Here, then, is the dilemma Foster presents. Independence endangers at the same time as it gives pleasure; domestic restraints destroy pleasure and liberty at the same time as they guarantee virtue and economic security. At all the key points in the novel two critical disjunctures appear. The imagination and the passions threaten to distort perception; virtue, independence, liberty, and happiness are divided against themselves. Eliza would like to unite all. Her virtuous advisers tell her this is no longer possible. Take the correspondence between Eliza and Freeman in which Eliza contrasts social independence (which she depicts in corporeal and fanciful terms) to marriage and public service (which she associates with the loss of economic independence, social liberty—and pleasure). "My sanguine imagination paints, in alluring colors, the charms of youth and freedom, regulated by virtue and innocence," Eliza writes Freeman, "Of these I wish to partake." She tells of her fears of the stuffy minister who wants to carry her off to the wilderness of New Hampshire. "I recoil at the thought of immediately forming a connection which must confine me to the duties of domestic life, and make me dependent for happiness, perhaps, too, for subsistence, upon a class of people [the minister's parishioners] who will claim the right to scrutinize every part of my conduct, and, by censuring those foibles which I am conscious of not having prudence to avoid, may render me completely miserable." She then asserts her right to make her own decision. "You must either quit the subject, or leave me to the exercise of my free will" (29–30). Lucy Freeman, whose role in the novel is to express republican ideals, snaps back. Eliza's words and fancy have obscured Eliza's perceptions of reality.

Freeman's heated response underscores the opposition between pleasure and happiness, women and liberty, female independence and female virtue. "You are indeed very tenacious of your freedom, as you call it; but that is a play on words. A man of Mr. Boyer's honor and sense will never abridge any privileges which virtue can claim" (30–31). Indeed, liberty or "freedom" for women is so inconceivable to Freeman that it exists only "as a play on words." She replaces "freedom" with female "virtue" which can only claim privileges from a posture of dependence. And privilege, other republican texts tell us, is dangerous, tied to corruption, as in the unearned privileges of birth, which commercial republicanism scorns.[21]

If women's relation to liberty and freedom underscores the complexities and uncertainties of those words, women's relation to economic independence does the same. Indeed *The Coquette* quite pointedly spells out the ways women's relation to independence limits their
right to liberty—and predetermines the boundaries of their happiness.
The same characters that tell Eliza that her independence/freedom is
a play on words, Freeman, Richman, and the Reverend Mr. Boyer,
warn her that middle-class women lack the financial resources to support an independent social role. (Eliza stretches the limits of her mother's income when visiting Freeman in Boston and must compromise
her independence by accepting presents [73].) Freeman and Richman
warn her not to overstep her class in her ambition to make a fashionable show. A minister is just the right husband for her. "His situation
in life," the prudent Freeman advises," is . . . as elevated as you have a
right to claim. Forgive my plainness, Eliza. . . . I know your ambition
is to make a distinguished figure in the first class of polished society,
to shine in the gay circle of fashionable amusements, and to bear off
the palm amidst the votaries of pleasure" (27).

It is Eliza's twin desires for the pleasures of social independence and
social eminence that attract her to the rake, Major Sanford. When Mr.
Boyer finally rejects Eliza, it is not her loss of chastity that motivates
the minister, but her independence coupled with her extravagance in
dress and her desire to rise above her father's social station. And, significantly, it is at this point that Boyer enters into a debate about the
contested meanings of the word "virtue," defining it as far more than
sexual propriety. In a letter to his friend and colleague, the Reverend
Mr. T. Selby, Boyer writes, "I would not be understood to impeach
Miss Wharton's virtue; I mean her chastity. Virtue in the common
acceptation of the term, as applied to the sex, is confined to that particular, you know. But in my view, this is of little importance, where all
other virtues are wanting!" (78).

Boyer's denunciation of Eliza's assertion of social independence un-
supported by economic independence is the turning point in the
novel. Once the minister has rejected her as an appropriate wife for his
class, no other man proposes. Eliza's passion for liberty and social

independence has reached imprudent limits. It has propelled her into the classless state of the spinster, with only marginal rights to the economic resources of any man. Her independence has cost her what it at first promised: pleasure, happiness, free access to the world outside the home. It will ultimately cost her her sexual virtue as well. Though warned against the rake by friends and family, she insists on judging him by her own criteria and falls.

Foster's telling of Eliza's story contains significant discontinuities and silences. Foster splits Eliza's fall into two almost unrelated events: her rejection by the Reverend Mr. Boyer, her affair with the rake. Years separate the two. The second, the sexual fall, comes unaccompanied by either pleasure or passion.[22] The requisite physical decay, in fact, rather than following from her sexual seduction, precedes it by approximately a year (105, 110). If anything, Eliza's sexual seduction appears the formulaic conclusion demanded by the novel of seduction and needed to connect Hannah Foster's Eliza Wharton with Elizabeth Whitman, the woman who died of childbirth in a Massachusetts inn. We are drawn back to Cathy Davidson's suggestion that Hannah Foster deliberately wrote against an existing male narrative of sex and passion. Can the striking absence of sexual passion be explained, then, by the fact that Foster's Coquette, like Henry James's Daisy Miller, died not from lust but from the imprudent desire for an impossible social independence and the desire to assert her right to control her own body?[23]

Three letters that separate the two sections of the novel suggest an even more subversive reading—that Eliza's real seduction and fall occurred a year after Boyer's denunciation and long before her sexual fall with Sanford (101–6). At this point, realizing that no other man will propose, Eliza writes Boyer, acquiescing in his denunciation of her. He was right, she confesses; she had sinned. Indeed his letter of denunciation has led her to repent. She begs him to marry her. Boyer responds that he is pleased she now accepts his reading of her acts, but "Your letter came too late." He has chosen another, a "virtuous . . . amiable . . . accomplished" woman who will serve him better than the fanciful, extravagant, and independent Eliza. The tone of his letter is authoritative, judgmental, and assured (101–4).

It is at this point that Eliza cries out to Freeman: "O my friend, I am undone. . . . O that I had not written to Mr. Boyer!" She then reaffirms her submission to his text. "I blame not Mr. Boyer. He has acted nobly." From this submission comes not inner peace but ruin, inner torment, and decline. For a second time in the book, Eliza misappropriates language traditionally used to describe the sexual to discuss the social. She writes Freeman: "I approve his conduct, though it operates my ruin . . . and what adds an insupportable poignancy to the reflection is self-condemnation. From this inward torture where shall I flee? Where shall I seek that happiness which I have madly trifled away?" Eliza has finally accepted the fragmentation of virtue, independence, and happiness. She has been seduced not by the rake but by the minister's text of individual (especially female) submission to social consensus. It is the relinquishing of her social and intellectual independence, not of her sexual virginity, that constitutes her true fall. It is this fall, not her later sexual seduction, that she reports with all the anguish of a sexual fall and in the appropriate formulaic language – even to a discussion of the decline of her health. "My bloom is decreasing. My health is sensibly impaired," (105). Without the pleasures of independence and of "the exercise of my free will" Eliza's body wastes away.

It is at this point in Eliza's seduction by Boyer's text that the prudent Freeman, always Boyer's advocate, reverses her position. She chides Eliza on her fall from reason into sentimentality. To Eliza's lamentations, she sensibly responds: "Your truly romantic letter came safe to hand. Indeed, my dear, it would make a very pretty figure in a novel. A bleeding heart, slighted love, and all the *et ceteras* of romance enter the composition" (107). Eliza, she says, has given her heart to two imprudent texts – the text of religious prudery (Boyer's) and the text of the romance. Freeman recalls her to the better text of independence, reason, and strength, to the text of republicanism. It is that text that will lead her to happiness and virtue. "Where, O Eliza Wharton, . . . is that strength of mind, that independence of soul, that alacrity and sprightliness of deportment, which formally raised you superior to every adverse occurrence? Why have you resigned these valuable endowments and suffered yourself to become the sport of contending passions?" (107). Ironically, then, Foster does in the end agree with the male sermon and newspaper writers: reading romances led to Eliza's fall. Romances did so, however, not because they taught women sexual passion for men but because they taught women to renounce their own reason and independence. In this way, women lost their happiness. To cure Eliza from the excesses of male texts, Freeman tells her, a mutual friend, Julia, a sprightly, unmarried woman, will come to carry Eliza back to Boston and to her female friends. Freeman, in other words, in virtually her last letter in the novel, denounces the texts middle-class men use to construct gender and privileges the nontextual world of female friendship as a way back to the true text of republicanism.

But Julia comes too late. Eliza has already fallen victim, not to Sanford—he is secondary—but to the authoritative male discourse of her age. She has relinquished her quest to fuse independence and pleasure; she now accepts her community's definition of virtue. But such a definition, because it denies independence to women, brings neither happiness nor pleasure. "I frequent neither . . . the company [nor] the amusements of the town," she tells Julia. "Having incurred so much censure by the indulgence of a gay disposition, I am now trying what a recluse and solitary mode of life will produce. . . . I look around for happiness, and find it not. The world is to me a desart [sic]. And when I have recourse to books, . . . if novels, they exhibit scenes of pleasure which I have no prospect of realizing!" (135). Pallor, depression, an "emaciated form!" replace Eliza's gay independence (140). Only then, having lost independence, pleasure, and happiness, does Eliza relinquish her virtue as well.

Cathy Davidson reads Hannah Foster's Eliza Wharton as EveryWoman who, during years marked by political and economic revolution, lusted for independence. She sees *The Coquette* as a subversive novel which encourages the reader, against her reason, to applaud Eliza's desires and mourn her death.[24] I embrace Davidson's reading but suggest an additional layering. Eliza Wharton is Every*man* as well as Everywoman. Her career underscores the way economic change has transformed the independence of classical republicanism, making it highly individualized and economically risky. No longer securing social order, independence, tied to liberty and freedom, endangers the individual and society. Foster dramatizes the new impotence of family and community against the autonomy of youth and the power of the individual. Familial and community spokesmen have become spokeswomen, the feminized Greek chorus of Richman, Freeman, and Eliza's widowed mother, who, at the end, can only mouth hollow platitudes as Eliza is seduced in her mother's parlor and then disappears into the night.[25]

Reading in this way we see that Foster has in fact rewritten woman's place within the male texts of nationalism and class. Middle-class men had made middle-class women their alter egos, bearers of criticisms the gentry had directed against middle-class men and against the paper revolution. Middle-class women, not middle-class men, were thus depicted as incapable of civic virtue. Not only does Foster's text suggest that men, not women, are incapable of true virtue, but she also makes Eliza the ego, not the alter ego, of the new nation and the new class. It is Eliza, not Boyer or Sanford, who takes on the challenges the new capitalism thrusts upon the new American republicans. It is she, not they, who assumes tragic proportions. It is in her language that the dilemmas of her age are debated. The principal question of *The Coquette* is the principal question of the new nation and the new class: how can independence and individual happiness be made compatible with social order? In the end, Foster gives no answer. We are left to hypothesize that, in the late 1790s, Americans had yet to resolve the fundamental inconsistencies between their new capitalist and individualistic economy and the civic humanism they had inherited from their Augustan ancestors. Yet the subversive tone that runs through *The Coquette* suggests that old paradigms are about to crack open, that the next generation of writers will represent Elizas who do not have to die.

The middle-class construction of gender frustrated this anticipation. Everyman—whether he appears as "the Deerslayer" in Cooper's canonical text, as "the common man" in Jacksonian political rhetoric, as "the self-made man" in laissez-faire economic theory, as Davy Crockett in the scatalogical comic almanacs—a generation later has broken the old paradigms of civic humanism and fused independence and individualism. But not Everywoman. The freedom Foster subversively permits Eliza will recede in the face of the cult of true womanhood's growing hegemony, and a hundred years later Lilly in *The House of Mirth,* Edith in *The Awakening* will end, ironically, like Eliza—indeed, like ideal Revolutionary heroes—by giving their lives for their freedom.[26]

NOTES

This essay took form first as a paper at a conference on "American Democracy and *Democracy in America:* Tocqueville After 150 Years," University of California, Berkeley, November 1986. I am particularly indebted to the suggestions of Elaine Scarry, Alvia Golden, Toby Ditz, Phyllis Rackin, and Mary Poovey and most especially to those offered by Maureen Quilligan and by the literature graduate students at the University of Pennsylvania who were members of a graduate seminar on Language, Gender, and Power. Maureen Quilligan, assisted by those students, taught me the fundamentals of close reading. She contributed significantly to my analysis of *The Coquette.*

1. Over seventy novels by American authors were published between the 1790s and 1821 when James Fenimore Cooper's canonical novel, *The Spy,* became a best-seller, an event traditionally thought to initiate the American novel. During these same years, English novels circulated widely in America as well. *Charlotte Temple,* the first best-selling novel in America, was first published in 1791 and republished continuously and in large editions in America throughout the nineteenth century. Indeed, 104 separate American editions have been traced. See, for example, Susanna Rowson, *Charlotte: A Tale of Truth by Mrs. Rowson,* 2d ed. (Philadelphia: printed for M. Carey, 1794). Rowson considered herself a British citizen at the time she wrote *Charlotte Temple.* Hannah W. Foster, the author of *The Coquette,* came from old New England stock and was married to a New England minister at the time she wrote the novel, which first appeared in 1797 and was repeatedly republished into the 1870s. Page citations to *The Coquette* are to the most recent edition, edited with an introduction by Cathy N. Davidson (New York: Oxford University Press, 1986), and

are given parenthetically in the text. Charles Brockden Brown, a Philadelphia and New York merchant, was another prolific, widely published, and influential American author. His first American book, *Alcuin,* appeared in 1798. Six novels quickly followed, beginning with *Wieland* in 1798 and concluding with *Jane Talbot* in 1801. *Ormond* was first published in 1799; Ernest Marchand has edited and provided an introduction to a modern edition (New York and London: Hafner, 1937). For a brilliant analysis of the early American novel see Cathy Davidson, *Revolution and the Word: The Rise of the Novel in America* (New York: Oxford University Press, 1986). For an older survey see Lillie Deming Loshe, *The Early American Novel* (New York: F. Unger, 1958).

2. For classic studies of the revolutionary period which do not cite literary texts, see, for example: Gordon Wood, *The Creation of the American Republic, 1776–1787* (Chapel Hill: University of North Carolina Press, 1969); J. G. A. Pocock, *The Machiavellian Moment: Florentine Political Thought and the Atlantic Republican Tradition* (Princeton: Princeton University Press, 1975); Bernard Bailyn, *Ideological Origins of the American Revolution* (Cambridge: Harvard University Press, 1967); Jackson Turner Main, *The Social Structure of Revolutionary America* (Princeton: Princeton University Press, 1965); and Gary Nash, *The Urban Crucible: The Northern Seaports and the Origins of the American Revolution* (Cambridge: Harvard University Press, 1986). Richard Bushman is an exception to this list. See, for example, his essay "American High Style and Vernacular Cultures," in Jack P. Greene and J. R. Pole, *Colonial British America* (Baltimore: Johns Hopkins University Press, 1984).

3. Two important exceptions to this general rule among literary studies are: Emory Elliott, *Revolutionary Writers: Literature and Authority in the New Republic, 1725–1810* (New York: Oxford University Press, 1982), and Davidson, *Revolution.*

4. I have long been indebted to the work of Mary Douglas and Victor Turner in my reading of the physical body as a representation of the social body. Mary Douglas, *Purity and Danger: An Analysis of Concepts of Pollution and Taboo* (London: Routledge & Kegan Paul, 1964), and *Natural Symbols: Explorations in Cosmology* (New York: Vintage Books, 1970); Victor Turner, *Dramas, Fields and Metaphors: Symbol and Action in Human Society* (Ithaca, N.Y.: Cornell University Press, 1974), and *The Ritual Process: Structure and Anti-Structure* (Ithaca, N.Y.: Cornell University Press, 1969).

5. I am particularly indebted to Elaine Scarry for suggestions leading to this phraseology.

6. Davidson argues that subscription lists of early American publishers and printers as well as other items in early books indicate that women and men read many of the same books (Davidson, *Revolution,* esp. chaps. 3 and 4). Linda Kerber has been particularly influential in terms of underscoring the use republican male theorists and social commentators made of the mother's role in the new republic. See her *Women of the Republic: Intellect and Ideology in Revolutionary America* (Chapel Hill: University of North Carolina Press, 1980) and "The Republican Ideology of the Revolutionary Generation," *American Quarterly* 37 (Fall 1985):474–95.

7. J. G. A. Pocock, "Virtue and Commerce in the Eighteenth Century," *Journal of Interdisciplinary History* 3 (Summer 1972):122, cited by Joyce Appleby, "Republicanism and Ideology," *American Quarterly* 37 (Fall 1985):466. Indeed, I find one of John Pocock's most interesting contributions to the theoretical armamentarium of the historian to be his insistence that we conceive of and perceive our world using concepts and rhetoric inherited from past eras. This vision is fundamental to my own analytical approach in this essay.

8. See especially M. M. Bakhtin's arguments in "Epic and Novel" and "Discourse and the Novel," in *Dialogic Imagination,* ed. Michael Holquist, trans. Caryl Emerson and Michael Holquist (Austin: University of Texas Press, 1981).

9. See, for example, Bakhtin's comment: "Any concrete discourse (utterance) finds the object at which it was directed already . . . overlain . . . by the light of alien words that have already been spoken about it . . . entangled, shot through with shared thoughts, points of view, alien value judgments and accents. The word directed toward its object, enters a dialogically agitated and tension-filled environment of alien words, value judgments and accents, weaves in and out of complex relationships, merges with some, recoils from others, intersects with yet a third group" (Bakhtin, *Dialogic Imagination,* 276).

10. Few issues are as hotly debated among early national historians as the nature and sources of American republican political rhetoric. Two schools oppose each other. The older, led by Bailyn (*Intellectual Origins*), Wood (*Creation of the American Republic*), and Pocock (*Machiavellian Moment*), argues that American republican ideology is deeply rooted in the early eighteenth-century British gentry's transformations of earlier forms of civic humanism,

though all emphasize that economic change altered Americans' usage of the gentry's older rhetorical devices. Joyce Appleby (*Capitalism and a New Social Order: The Republican Vision of the 1790s* [New York: New York University Press, 1984] and "Republicanism and Ideology"), Linda Kerber ("The Republican Ideology of the Revolutionary Generation"), Drew R. McCoy (*The Elusive Republic: Political Economy in Jeffersonian America* [Chapel Hill: University of North Carolina Press, 1980]), and Isaac Kramnick ("Republican Revisionism Revisited," *American Historical Review* 87 [1982]:629–64) offer significant modifications to the Bailyn-Wood-Pocock thesis, stressing the disruptive influence of economic change. They argue that Americans used republican political terms in ways significantly different from the way in which the British gentry did earlier in the century. These new scholars stress the more individualistic and overtly capitalistic perspective of American theorists, as well as underscoring the influence of John Locke and Adam Smith on American republican thinkers. For a recent summary of the controversy see the special issue of the *American Quarterly* 37 (Fall 1985), edited by Joyce Appleby.

11. Isaac Kramnick in "Republican Revisionism Revisited" is particularly interested in the way the meanings the British gentry and American republicans assigned words changed. I find his essay most suggestive.

12. Charles Davenant, *The Political and Commercial Works of Dr. Charles D'Avenant,* ed. Sir Charles Whetworth, 6 vols. (London, 1771), cited by Pocock, *Machiavellian Moment,* 443. For a lengthy discussion of the gentry's ambivalent attitudes toward trade see Pocock, *Machiavellian Moment,* chap. 13, esp. 441–50. See also Wood, *Creation of the American Republic.* I wish to thank Toby Ditz for insisting on the ambivalence and contradictions that characterized the gentry's vision of trade and of the trader.

13. Kramnick, "Republican Revisionism Revisited."

14. For the influence of evangelicalism upon American republican thought see Ruth Block, *Visionary Republic: Millennial Themes in American Thought, 1756–80* (Cambridge: Cambridge University Press, 1985), and "The Gendered Meaning of Virtue in Revolutionary America," unpublished paper, Organization of American Historians, 1987 convention.

15. This is a central theme in fiction and in advice and sermon literature.

16. Bakhtin, *Diologic Imagination,* 300. See also Davidson, *Revolution,* 13 and 44.

17. Davidson has edited the most recent scholarly edition of *The Coquette*. Her introduction to this edition, as well as chapter 6 in *Revolution*, offers a highly suggestive analysis of the subversive nature of *The Coquette* as a female novel. Davidson is less interested in the relation between *The Coquette* and republican political ideology than she is in Hannah Foster's use of *The Coquette* to underscore the contradictions inherent in middle-class men's construction of the female role. Thus Davidson uses *The Coquette* to expand our understanding of women's experiences during the early national period. See, especially, "Introduction" *Coquette* (xi–xx). In this present essay, I am more interested in using the new middle-class discourse on gender to throw light upon the complexities and contradictions inherent in American republican ideology. Yet while they differ so in focus, I see our approaches as compatible, not contradictory.

18. See, for example, Clyde A. Holbrook, *The Ethics of Jonathan Edwards; Morality and Aesthetics* (Ann Arbor: University of Michigan Press, 1973). For British usage, see Edward A. Bloom and Lillian Bloom, *Joseph Addison's Sociable Animal in the Market Place, on the Hustings, in the Pulpit* (Providence: Brown University Press, 1971).

19. *The Compact Edition of the Oxford English Dictionary* (Oxford and New York: Oxford University Press, 1971).

20. The comments in the Declaration of Independence concerning the purpose of a just government can also be read in relation to Eliza's concerns about the government of marriage and the family. The Declaration follows its initial sentence that states that life, liberty and the pursuit of happiness are inalienable rights with its definition of a just government. "That to secure these rights, Governments are instituted among Men, deriving their just powers from the consent of the governed,–That whenever any Form of Government becomes destructive of these ends, it is the Right of the People to alter or to abolish it, and to institute new Government, laying its foundation on such principles and organizing its powers in such form, as to them shall seem most likely to effect their Safety and Happiness." Only then does the Declaration proceed to a discussion of prudence (referred to above). A subversive reading of *The Coquette* (and of the Declaration) might suggest the question: if marriage and the family do not promote the liberty and happiness of women, do women have a right to alter or abolish them?

21. Kramnick, "Republican Revisionism Revisited."

22. The absence of sexual desire from the process of sexual seduction or, indeed, of any mention of sexuality is one of the most striking aspects of this novel. Davidson pointedly remarks on it (*Revolution*, 149), as do most other readers.

23. Gayle Rubin argues that the most radical political assertion possible occurs when a young woman asserts her right to control the right of access to her body and her sexuality. Gayle Rubin, "Traffic in Women," in *Towards an Anthropology of Women*, ed. by Rayna Reiter (New York: Monthly Review Press, 1975).

24. Davidson, *Revolution*, 144–50.

25. Davidson points to Foster's construction of an impotent maternal figure in Mrs. Wharton. *Revolution*, 148–49.

26. James Fenimore Cooper, *The Deerslayer* (New York: New American Library, 1963). For an analysis of the Davy Crockett popular literature see Carroll Smith-Rosenberg, "Davy Crockett as Trickster: Pornography, Liminality, and Symbolic Inversion in Victorian America," in Smith-Rosenberg, *Disorderly Conduct* (New York: Knopf, 1985), 79–89. Edith Wharton, *House of Mirth* (New York: Scribners, 1976), and Kate Chopin, *The Awakening and Other Stories*, ed. Nina Baym (New York: Random House, 1981). Linda Kerber in *Women of the Republic* has already drawn attention to parallels between *The Coquette* and *The House of Mirth*.

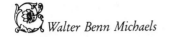 *Walter Benn Michaels*

The Souls of White Folk

The "Anglo-Saxons," says one of the black heroes of Sutton Griggs's separatist novel *Imperium in Imperio,* "have chosen our race as an empire."[1] He is speaking at the opening session of the Imperium's Congress, a session that takes place on the same day in April, Griggs says, "on which the Congress of the United States had under consideration the resolutions ... which meant war with Spain."[2] Shadowing the call to extend the American empire with a call to free blacks from it, Griggs insisted upon what Hazel Carby has recently described as the "link between internal and external colonization, between domestic racial oppression and imperialism."[3] The racism that justified Jim Crow could not be separated from the racism invoked to justify, say, the suppression of Aguinaldo in the Philippines and the replacement of his government with American rule. Like blacks and Indians, as Albert J. Beveridge put it, "The Philippinos are not a self-governing race."[4] Anglo-Saxons, on the other hand, were not only capable of self-government, as a "race of empire-builders," they were biologically destined to govern others as well: "The breed to which the Southern white man belongs," wrote Thomas Dixon in *The Clansman,* "has conquered every foot of soil on this earth their feet have pressed for a thousand years. A handful of them hold in subjection three hundred millions in India. Place a dozen of them in the heart of Africa, and they will rule the continent unless you kill them."[5] For Dixon, as for Sutton Griggs, imperialism began at home.

But if the racism of internal oppression and the racism of external conquest were not separable, they were not exactly identical either. For Jim Crow was perhaps even more compatible with a certain hostility to expansionism. Thus a Northern anti-imperialist could urge the American people to pause before undertaking "the task of giving the advantages of our civilization to the Negritos, Moslem pirates, and other mongrel Asiatics of the Philippines. These are all inferior races . . . [and] Wherever we have touched an inferior people we have, without exception, come into violent and bitter antagonism with them."[6] And thus the widow of Jefferson Davis could announce that her "most serious objection to making the Philippines American territory is because three-fourths of the population is made up of negroes," who, without "benefit of slavery," are a "semi-savage" and "predatory" people.[7] From this standpoint, Jim Crow might be seen not only as anti-expansionist but also as hostile even to internal imperialism. Thus one of the heroes of *The Clansman* (surprisingly enough) is Abraham Lincoln, whose freeing the slaves is understood by Dixon as the essential prerequisite not to making them citizens but to getting rid of them altogether. Just as the nation cannot exist "half slave and half free," it cannot exist "half white and half black" (47), says Dixon's Lincoln. "We must assimilate or expel" (46). And since assimilation is unthinkable, expulsion—a kind of visceral or emetic anti-imperialism—becomes essential. And in a more recent racist text, the proposed Pace Amendment to the Constitution which, by repealing the Fourteenth Amendment would seek to limit American citizenship to whites and would "repatriate" all nonwhites, expulsion rather than conquest remains the goal.[8]

Recently, however, many American racists appear to have given up the idea of repatriation as unrealistic and have begun arguing for secession instead. Andrew Macdonald's *The Turner Diaries* (published in 1978 and, as its own advertising boasts, described by the F.B.I. as the "bible of the racist right") goes beyond the Pace Amendment by depicting the impracticability of expulsion and beyond *The Clansman* by portraying civil war not just as a prelude to emptying America of blacks but as a prelude to emptying the world of all nonwhites. Even here, however, the racist impulse cannot be described as imperialist. For in the late twentieth-century world of *The Turner Diaries*, the earth has become so overpopulated that there is nowhere to send the blacks (and Jews, Mexicans, Chinese, etc.) and nowhere to hide from them; so they have to be exterminated. If, then, *The Turner Diaries* goes beyond *The Clansman* in ending with a triumphant vision not merely of a white America but also of a "White world,"⁹ it is a world created less by the hopeful possibility of expanding than by the gloomy impossibility of withdrawing.

There is, furthermore, an even more active sense – ideological as well as biological and geographic – in which American racism cannot be identified with expansionist imperialism. The Civil War, as Lincoln describes it in *The Clansman*, was a war of "self-preservation" rather than "conquest" (44). Indeed "The Constitution," he asserts (as if speaking in the voice of those who argued against the annexation of the Philippines), "makes no provision for the control of 'conquered provinces'" (42).¹⁰ Hence the federal government has no right to enfranchise the blacks, and hence, in *The Clansman*, Reconstruction is presented as the attempt, after the anti-imperialist Lincoln's death, to colonize the South. The Invisible Empire of the Knights of the Ku Klux Klan arises in rebellion against the "visible" empire of the North and its black soldiers like the rapist "Gus" who, as his full name – Augustus Caesar – makes clear, is to be regarded as an imperial storm trooper. In *The Clansman*, then, white Americans are understood not as imperialists but as the victims of imperialism.

This way of putting the point, however, doesn't quite get at the complexity of the situation. After all, Americans have characteristically imagined themselves the victims of imperialism, whether the empire in question is British – as it was throughout the nineteenth century – or Russian – as it is now (and as it was beginning to be then).¹¹ But in *The Turner Diaries*, the Russians aren't enemies, they are "racial kinsmen"; the enemy is what Macdonald calls "the System," whose black "Equality Police" (like Gus) rape and murder whites at the behest of their Jewish masters. This repetition in *The Turner Diaries* of the scene of Reconstruction makes clear the source of that scene's powerful appeal to the American imagination. Reconstruction not only enables white men to imagine themselves as victims of imperialism, it enables them to imagine the imperial power as their own government.

In the twentieth century, then, the evil empire is in its essence neither British nor Russian but American, and the task of resisting it becomes revolutionary as well as nationalist. For Reconstruction makes it possible to replay the revolutionary scenario of casting off the chains of empire and building a new nation even when there is no empire and when the nation isn't new. Thus, unlike, say, *Gone With the Wind*, *The Clansman* makes no appeal to nostalgia for the prewar South and for the more amicable race relations of slavery. As committed as any abolitionist to the impossibility of a nation half slave and half free, Dixon represents the Civil War not as the ultimate expression of sectional, political, and economic differences but as the site on which those differences are erased and replaced with racial difference. What he calls the "prejudices" of the Northern Phil Stoneman and the Southern Ben Cameron are "melted in the white heat of battle" (216), enabling them to see that a single man like either one of them "is worth more to this Nation than every negro that ever set his flat feet on this continent." Jim Crow thus marks not a return to but a final repudiation of paternalist prewar race relations, casting blacks out of the family so that Northern and Southern whites—Phil Stoneman and Ben Cameron look "as much alike as twins"—can finally become brothers. Insofar as the political, economic, and sectional differences caused by slavery had forestalled true nationhood, the racial difference rendered visible by abolition made the birth of a nation possible. For Dixon and, as Michael Rogin has shown, for D. W. Griffith and Woodrow Wilson, the Klan embodied the complete coincidence of racial identity with national identity.[12] In the past, the country had been divided on political, economic, and sectional issues; from now on, as Dixon wrote in his first novel *The Leopard's Spots*, "there could be but one issue—are you a White man or a Negro?"[13]

The identification of American with white (and the colonization or, failing that, segregation of blacks) marked, by its appeal to what the Supreme Court in *Plessy* v. *Ferguson* called "physical differences," a new development in racial thinking. For the doctrine of "separate but equal" affirmed racial distinction *as such;* it affirmed, that is, racial distinction independent of any other legal consideration so that the relation between black and white was radically distinguished from the relation between master and slave. Slaves, in principle, could become free; blacks could never become white. Thus the absence of any difference *grounded* in law became powerful testimony to the irreducibility of a difference *reflected* in the law; legal equality became the sign of racial separation: "A statute which implies merely a legal distinction between the black and white races—a distinction which is founded on the color of the two races, and which must always exist so long as white men are distinguished from the other race by color—has no tendency to destroy the legal equality of the races or reestablish a condition of involuntary servitude."[14] The transformation here of the difference between master and slave into the difference between white and black records the final separation of racism from slavery, racism's emancipation from the forms of a feudal economy. Freed from its embarrassing entanglements with the "peculiar institution," racism could now take its place as a distinctively modern phenomenon. Which is presumably what W. E. B. Du Bois meant by his famous remark, "The problem of the twentieth century is the problem of the color line."[15]

But, as *Plessy* v. *Ferguson* also made clear, the question posed by the color line—Dixon's question, Are you white or black?—and the questions on which this one depended—What makes a white man white? What makes a black black?—were not always easy to answer. In some states, the Court wrote, "any visible admixture of black blood stamps the person as belonging to the colored race."[16] But that test wouldn't do for Homer Plessy whose "mixture of colored blood was not discernible."[17] Hence one principle established by *Plessy* v. *Ferguson* was that "distinctions based upon color" weren't necessarily visible and therefore that it was up to individual states to determine what "proportion of colored blood" was necessary to constitute a colored man. "Legislation is powerless to eradicate racial instincts or to abolish distinctions based upon physical differences,"[18] the Court asserted. But the question of what race Homer Plessy actually belonged to and so of what ineradicable racial instincts might be his could be determined only under the laws of the State of Louisiana.

To put the case in this way is only to highlight what is already evident, the stunning incoherence of *Plessy* v. *Ferguson*. But it would, in

my view, be a mistake to understand this incoherence as fundamentally embarrassing to racist ideology. For to read the slippage between
Homer Plessy's color (white) and his race (black) as a reproach to
racism would be to miss the point of the Invisible Empire's invisibility.
The Clan is invisible partly because its organization is secret but more
importantly, according to Dixon, because its identity is based from the
start on a racial principle that transcends visibility—it consists of "the
reincarnated souls of the Clansmen of Old Scotland" (2). Or, as the
freedman Aleck describes the "Ku Kluxes" who persuade him to resign
his office as sheriff, "Dey wuz Sperits, ridin' white hosses wid flowin'
white robes, en big blood-red eyes!" (348). Identity in *The Clansman* is
always fundamentally spiritual. Thus, for example, marriage and "the
close sweet home-life" can make people more "alike in soul and body"
than can any physical relation. "People have told me that your father
and I are more alike than brother and sister of the same blood," Mrs.
Cameron writes to her daughter, "in spirit I'm sure its true" (118). This
is why the Civil War, customarily represented as turning brothers into
enemies, is represented in *The Clansman* as turning enemies into
brothers. The identity of soul that brings the Stonemans and Camer-
ons together transcends biology, replacing the natural unity of the
family with a spiritual unity that, unlike the family, is genuinely indi-
visible. And this is why the Klan is more than a clan. Aleck's account
of them as "Sperits" corroborates Dixon's; his superstitious fear of the
spirits must thus be understood as a response to the terrifying representation of an essentially invisible racial identity, an identity that
can't be seen in people's skins (it couldn't be seen in Homer Plessy's),
but can be seen in the Klan's sheets. The purpose of the sheets, then,
is not to conceal the identities of individual clansmen for, far from
making their visible identities invisible, the sheets make their invisible
identities visible. The Klan wear sheets because their bodies aren't as
white as their souls, because *no* body can be as white as the soul embodied in the white sheet.

There is an important sense, then, in which the question of the color
line—Are you white or black?—cannot be answered by an appeal to
color. And this sense is by no means confined to literary texts. Indeed,

it appears even more dramatically in the Supreme Court's decision in *Williams* v. *Mississippi* where the disfranchisement of blacks was legalized precisely by separating the question of race from color. The state supreme court that approved the notorious Mississippi Plan explicitly acknowledged the illegality of racial discrimination: "Restrained by the Federal Constitution from discriminating against the negro race," the Court wrote, "the convention discriminates against its characteristics."[19] And the federal Supreme Court could find no fault with this color-blind racism, ruling that "nothing tangible" could be "deduced" from such practices and hence that the "peculiarities of habit, of temperament and of character"[20] that distinguished blacks from whites were acceptable targets of legislation in a way that skin color was not.

In the hands of the Mississippi legislature, then, the invisibility of race (like the "intangibility" of racial character) became an opportunity not an embarrassment, an opportunity that would be put to even better use by writers less concerned with the reorganization of Southern politics. For if the identification of American with white made Reconstruction the necessary condition of an anti-imperialist nationalism, the transformation of skin color into "character" made the technology of racism available for a more general and more radical rewriting of biology as ideology. The "constructive ideas of our civilization are Anglo-Saxon ideas,"[21] as the reformer Washington Gladden put it. Where the new racism of skin color never tired of invoking the unchangeability of the leopard's spots, the new racism of ideas disdained such appeals: "You may change the leopard's spots," wrote the anti-imperialist Senator John Daniel of Virginia in 1899, "but you will never change the different *qualities* of the races."[22] The culmination of this process rendering race invisible was the creation of a new racial identity—one that transcended color while at the same time invoking its biological authority—Teddy Roosevelt called it "the American race." "Our object," he told the New York Knights of Columbus in 1907, "is not to imitate one of the older racial types but to maintain a new American type and then to secure loyalty to this type."[23] And, of course, strategies for securing loyalty to the American race—from congressional committees on un-American activities to cabinet-level defenses of the "Judeo-Christian" or "Western" "heritage"–have made a major contribution to twentieth-century American political life.

My point, then, in broaching the question of the *invisible* empire is to suggest a way of thinking about American identity, at least in the Progressive Era, that links it in principle to American racism.[24] In fact, insofar as the question, Are you white? has been and continues to be successfully replaced by the question, Are you American?–insofar, that is, as a question supposedly about biology has been preserved as a question supposedly about national identity–one might say that the very idea of American citizenship is a racial and even racist idea, racist not because it embodies a (more or less concealed) preference for white skins but because it confers on national identity something like the ontology of race. If, then, the problem of American imperialism was from the start a racial problem–a challenge to the racist identification of American with white–it was also, I have argued, an opportunity, the chance to create a new ideological entity–the American race. And this new entity (the American race) has substituted so successfully for its predecessor (the white race) that most Americans are genuinely shocked by any assertion of what looks like the old biological racism.

Which doesn't mean, of course, that skin-color racism has disappeared–no reader of the daily newspapers or, for that matter, of *The Turner Diaries* could imagine that. After a genocidal week in Los Angeles, for example, highlighted by the execution of the "race-mixing" U.C.L.A. faculty, the narrator of the *Diaries* rejoices in his vision of an all-white Southern California: "no Chicanos, no Orientals, no Blacks, no mongrels. The air seems cleaner, the sun brighter, life more joyous" (171). The commitment to a biological racism seems as strong here as ever, but its strength is at the same time a mark of its remoteness from middle-class American culture which, substituting character for skin, has largely repudiated biological racism. Even in *The Turner Diaries*, however, as in *The Clansman*, the characteristic invisibility of modern racism finds its place. Initiated into the highest levels of The Order, the secret organization that is running the new American Revolution, the hero of the *Diaries*, "knowing full well what was demanded in character and commitment" of his fellow initiates, is filled with pride: "These were no soft-bellied, conservative businessmen assembled for some Masonic mumbo-jumbo; no loud-mouthed beery red-necks letting off a little ritualized steam about 'the goddam niggers'; no pious, frightened churchgoers whining for the guidance or protection of an anthropomorphic deity. These were *real men, White men,* men who were now *one* with me in spirit and consciousness as well as in blood" (203). The project of eliminating black people is here transformed into a technology for identifying white people; spirit and consciousness not only supplement blood, they supplant it. As "white" becomes an adjective describing character instead of skin, the invisibility of race reappears, and the physiological obstacles to determining what race someone actually belongs to are transformed into ideological opportunities for finding "real white men."

Indeed, in *The Turner Diaries,* the term "technology" is taken literally; The Order defends itself against infiltration by administering injections of drugs and monitoring the responses with electrodes, a "method of interrogation" that "leaves no room for evasion or deceit" (72). In this test for whiteness, the difference between physiology and ideology (between, say, a blood test and a loyalty oath) evaporates, as both are subsumed by a "spiritual thing" (184) that is something "more" than biological and something more than political or social as well. To join the Order is thus, as Turner says, to be "born again" (74), and to die for it, as Turner does, is to accept its offer of "everlasting life" (204). In the nuclear holocaust that ends *The Turner Diaries,* the reincarnated souls of the Scots clansmen are reincarnated again.

THE SOULS OF WHITE FOLK

"'The Carraways are something of a clan,'"²⁵ Nick Carraway remarks in the opening pages of *The Great Gatsby,* and Nick's "something" marks a certain distance not only from the Ku Klux Klan but from the less ironic identification of themselves as members of "clan Cameron" (192) produced by the Southern heroes of Dixon's romance. It is worth remembering, however, that in 1924—the year *Gatsby* was written—Klan membership was at its peak and that the Klan's style of racism makes several nonironic appearances in *Gatsby*, primarily in Tom Buchanan's discussion of a book Fitzgerald calls *The Rise of the Colored Empires* by a man he calls Goddard: "The idea," Tom says, "is that we're Nordics . . . And we've produced all the things that go to make civilization," but that "if we don't look out the white race will be . . . utterly submerged" by "these other races" (13–14). The book Tom is speaking of was actually called *The Rising Tide of Color against White World-Supremacy*, and its real author's name was Lothrop Stoddard, but Tom's paraphrase, though crude, is essentially accurate. According to Stoddard, the world's population was divided into five major races—brown, black, red, yellow, and white—which could themselves be divided into "sub-species":[26] whites, for example, could be broken down into Nordics, Alpines, and Mediterraneans. Stoddard's mission in *The Rising Tide* was to teach white men the importance of a "true race-consciousness" (309) before it was too late, before, that is, the white world was overrun by browns, blacks, reds, and yellows.

Stoddard's racism, then, like Dixon's, was essentially anti-imperialist. He "regretted" the opening of the Far East which, although it had been "hailed by white men with general approval," had had the unfortunate effect of dragging till then "reluctant races" into "the full stream of world affairs" (19). The war between Russia and Japan had subsequently demonstrated that whites were not invincible in battle, and the Great War—Stoddard called it the "White Civil War"—had inopportunely weakened the white race in its preparation for what he envisioned as the great racial conflict to come. For although a political map of the world in 1920 revealed what looked like worldwide white supremacy, a racial map (Stoddard provided both) revealed how tenuous this supremacy was; on the political map, for example, India looked white, on the racial map, it was brown. Rereading the political map of Western imperialism as the racial map of colored imperialism, Stoddard ingeniously repeated Dixon's vision of white Americans as the victims of imperialism while at the same time inflating it to a vision of the entire white race victimized. Hence the appropriateness of Fitzgerald's title, *The Rise of the Colored Empires*, for a book that thought of itself as anti-imperialist on an international scale, written against "the imperious urge of the colored world toward racial expansion" (10).

At the same time, however, Stoddard's work represented not only an extension of but also a change in the racist discourse of the turn of the century. Writers like Dixon had been obsessed with blacks, which is to say that in the effort to produce a truly national identity they had conceived of the distinction between black and white as a distinction between people who couldn't be made American and people who could be. Thus Dixon's hostility to blacks was accompanied by an enthusiastic acceptance of more or less white (Stoddard would call it Alpine and Mediterranean) immigration. By 1920, however, blacks seemed only one aspect of the more general problem of the "alien," and the melting pot that Dixon had championed seemed only a "shibboleth" invoked by capitalists who, in search of cheap labor and personal gain, had plundered our greatest national treasure, the "magnificent racial treasure America possessed at the beginning of the nineteenth century" (261).

According to Stoddard, then, non-Nordic whites had their own role to play in the rise of the colored empires, a point missed by Jordan Baker when, in response to a diatribe by Tom that begins by attacking Gatsby and ends by predicting "intermarriage between black and white" (130), she murmurs, "'We're all white here.'" For Tom, as for Stoddard, Gatsby isn't entirely white, and his identification of him as in some sense black suggests the power of the new notion of the alien. Gatsby's love for Daisy seems to Tom the expression of something like the impulse to miscegenation, an impulse that Nick Carraway preserves by transforming it into "the following of a grail. [Gatsby] knew that Daisy was extraordinary, but he didn't realize just how extraordinary a 'nice' girl could be" (149). "Nice" here doesn't exactly mean "white," but it doesn't exactly not mean "white" either. Myrtle Wilson calls it "breeding" (35) when she is explaining why she married Chester instead of the "little kike" (34) who had been after her for years but who she knew was "below" her. Breeding, however, when applied to humans, is a term that tends to be used by people who are not themselves so nice, like Myrtle, or like Robert Cohn (another "kike," although he didn't become "race-conscious,"[27] Hemingway says, until he went to Princeton), who says of Lady Ashley in *The Sun Also Rises* that she is "fine and straight" and that she has "breeding" (38). Jake Barnes, on the other hand, says in response to Cohn, that Brett is "very nice," and he says it without even Nick's quotation marks, as a kind of reproach to Cohn.

"Nice" is a word Jake uses often to describe not only Brett but also cities and hotels; it is one of those words Hemingway deploys against the "abstract words" condemned in *A Farewell to Arms*. "There were many words that you could not stand to hear," Hemingway writes, "and finally only the names of places had dignity."[28] Nice isn't the name of a place, but it is a name for people who come from a place as opposed, say, to Gatsby, who is "Mr. Nobody from Nowhere" (130). Removing the quotation marks from "nice," Hemingway installs it— along with words like "good" and "true"—at the heart of a prose style that no longer needs the direct vocabulary of race (e.g., "Nordic") to distinguish those who have breeding from those who don't, in the way that, say, Jake's concierge distinguishes between visitors who are not to be allowed up and visitors like Brett, who is "very nice," which is to say, "tres, tres gentille," which is to say "of very good family" (52). "Nice" has its pedigree; indeed, pedigree is its pedigree. Or, as Muriel puts it, in Fitzgerald's *The Beautiful and Damned*, "if a person comes from a good family, they're always nice people."[29]

Robert Cohn, not a very good writer, doesn't "know how to describe" (38) the "quality" that Jake Barnes so easily finds a word for. To be nice—even better, to be able to *say* nice—is to identify yourself as neither Gatsby nor Cohn; the social point of Hemingway's prose style, I suggest, was relentlessly to enforce such distinctions, to rewrite race as an aesthetic. To be insufficiently "race-conscious," as, say, Robert Cohn had been before going to Princeton, was to be insufficiently alert to the irrevocable difference between people who really were nice and people who just looked or acted nice. The war had encouraged such inattentiveness; Tom can't understand how Gatsby "got within a mile" of Daisy unless he "brought the groceries to the back door" (132); the answer, of course, is that Gatsby was wearing the "invisible cloak of his uniform" (149) so that Daisy couldn't tell he was just Jimmy Gatz. Tom has to make what he calls a "small investigation" to clear up the confusion; in *The Sun Also Rises*, such questions are decided by "examination," like the "oral spiritual examination" (132) Jake has to pass to prove that he has *aficion*. "Aficion is passion," Jake says, an aesthetic passion since the difference between a bullfighter with it and a bullfighter without it is that the one gives "real emotion" while the other gives "a fake emotional feeling" (168). The bullfighter with aficion in *The Sun Also Rises* is Romero, who is to an "imitation" like Marcial as Nick is to Gatsby or as Jake is to Robert Cohn: "He knew everything when he started. The others can't ever learn what he was born with."

Aficion thus takes its place alongside niceness as another name for breeding. It may be "spiritual" but, like breeding, it is manifest in bodies; when aficionados see that Jake has it, too, they put a hand on his shoulder: "It seemed as though they wanted to touch you to make it certain" (132). But this doesn't exactly mean that aficion can be *reduced* to breeding. For one thing, as we have already seen, the term breeding when applied to people isn't itself very nice; Robert Cohn is reproved for using it to describe Brett, and when Brett herself urges Mike Campbell to "show a little breeding" (141) and behave better to Cohn, Mike answers her, "Breeding be damned. Who has any breeding anyway, except the bulls?" And, for another thing, even the bulls' breeding can't exactly be reduced to breeding. Only bulls have breeding, as Mike says, but, as Mike also says (several times), "bulls have no balls" (175, 176). Mike is drunk and he means to be insulting the bullfighter Brett is so attracted to, but there is an important sense in which Hemingway's identification of breeding with a literal inability to breed should be taken seriously, as should indeed the converse identification of literal breeding prowess with a lack of breeding.

"One thing's sure and nothing's surer," someone sings at Gatsby's house, "The rich get richer and the poor get—children" (96). Or, as the racist writer Madison Grant put it, "If we continue to allow [immigrants] to enter they will in time drive us out of our own land by mere force of breeding." Grant and Stoddard both worried that compared to the other races whites were the "slowest breeders," (7) but Stoddard worried even more about the sterilizing effect of immigration on whites: "There can be no question," he wrote later in the decade (after the Johnson Immigration Act of 1924 had put an end to mass immigration), "that every low-grade alien who landed prevented a native American baby or a North European immigrant baby from ever being born."[30] This contraceptive effect finds a weirdly literal echo in *The Sun Also Rises* where the alien Cohn is the only one with children and where, more tellingly, Cohn has an appropriately sterilizing impact on Nordic types like his girlfriend Frances who, having "wasted two and a half years" (47) on Cohn, imagines that her childbearing opportunities have passed: "I never liked children much," she says, "but I don't want to think I'll never have them" (47).

Frances, however, is hardly the most spectacular example in *The Sun Also Rises* of the inability to reproduce. Jake Barnes is the most spectacular example. The Great War, according to Stoddard, was a breeding disaster for the white race since, in killing millions of Nordic soldiers at an age when they were "best adapted to fecundity," it had (like immigration) "prevented millions more from being born or conceived" (185). Jake's war wound is often understood as a symbol for the Lost Generation's disillusion, but the testimony of writers like Stoddard and the "authorities" he cites gives new meaning to the wound and to the very term Lost Generation. War tends to "induce sterility" (184), Stoddard writes; "You . . . have given more than your life" (31), the Italian colonel tells Jake. The Great War, the "White Civil War," had induced sterility above all in members of the "Nordic race" since it was Nordic men who "went forth eagerly to battle" (183) while "the little brunet Mediterranean either stayed home or even when at the front showed less fighting spirit, took fewer chances, and oftener saved their skins" ("You, a *foreigner*, an *Englishman* . . . have given more than your life," the Italian colonel says), and since Nordic women were psychologically especially sensitive to the "disorders of a mental and sentimental nature" produced by the war. The war had thus "unquestionably left Europe much poorer in Nordic blood," or, as Madison Grant put it, "As in all wars since Roman times, from the breeding point of view, the little dark man is the winner." In *The Sun Also Rises* the little dark man is Robert Cohn, and one might say that Jake's war wound is simultaneously a consequence of the war and of unrestricted immigration since, as interpreted by the racial discourse of the twenties, immigration and the war were simply two aspects of the same phenomenon, the rising tide of color.

This is what it means for breeding and the inability to breed to be the same thing. If, for Thomas Dixon, being a white man had involved simultaneously the claim to a certain racial physiology and the claim to a racial identity that transcended physiology, for Hemingway, being "nice," having "aficion," simultaneously involved breeding and the transcendence of breeding. The whiter the Homer Plessys began to look, the more invisible whiteness became; to distinguish between people who looked white and people who really were white, the clan had to become a Klan. For Dixon, the reincarnated souls of the clansmen were a way out of acknowledging the inevitable impurity of one's own racial identity and a way into imagining a racial identity that could serve as the defining characteristic of one's national identity; Dixon was as eager to welcome immigrants as he was to repatriate blacks. By the twenties, however, the problem of the blacks seemed only a subset of the larger problem of "aliens" in general who, as Fitzgerald wrote in *The Beautiful and Damned,* "kept coming inexhaustibly" (75). Which is not to say that reincarnation lost its appeal. The threat of the alien was the threat of sterility; the "alien tide" was "killing American children by preventing them from being born" (153). Hemingway, I have been arguing, made use of this threat to imagine not so much a *race* whose purity would be defined by its sterility (this is what Dixon did in imagining white men who could reproduce themselves racially without reproducing themselves biologically), but an *aesthetic* defined by breeding without biology. His cult of aficion deploys the technology of race against the "false aesthetics" (i.e., the "imitations") of bullfighters like Marcial and writers like Robert Cohn.

Hemingway, then, may be understood as transforming racism into aestheticism. Fitzgerald, too, at least in his early novels, was attracted by racist schemes for both invoking and transcending biology. The hero of *This Side of Paradise* is introduced by the title of its first chapter as "Amory, Son of Beatrice," and is described as having "inherited from his mother every trait, except the stray inexpressible few, that made him worth while."[31] The comma after "few" and the fact that the only things he inherits form his biological father are his height and his "tendency to waver at crucial moments" suggest that Amory is exclusively his mother's son, except that as the novel wears on he begins to seem crucially the son of the Catholic priest, Thayer Darcy, who speaks of him as "the son of my mind" (159) and as "a reincarnation of myself" (160). And Gloria Gilbert, described by Fitzgerald as a "Nordic Ganymede" (106), enters *The Beautiful and Damned* as a soul in "paradise" waiting to be born and leaves it as a convert to her mother's crackpot religion, "Bilphism," which teaches what her husband calls the "silly rule of reincarnation" (303). "It was disturbing," he thinks, "to see this old belief, evidently assimilated from her mother, inserting itself again under its immemorial disguise as an innate idea" (304). But the disguise is no disguise; reincarnation has itself been reincarnated. "Celibacy," Monsignor Darcy says, "goes deeper than the flesh" (158); it transforms the reproduction of a body into the reappearance of an idea.

Thus Gloria Gilbert is represented by Fitzgerald as the incarnation of an "incomprehensible" beauty, incomprehensible because the incarnation is so successful—"the beauty of her body was the essence of her soul" (27). This is another version of what it means for celibacy to go deeper than the flesh; in these early novels, Fitzgerald was seeking to imagine the conditions of a culture that could be inherited without being learned—like Amory Blaine's "traits"—but that—also like Amory's "traits" or Gloria's "innate ideas"—could be more powerfully understood as repeated or extended than as inherited. Gloria isn't beautiful, she is beauty, an instance of what Fitzgerald calls, "that unity sought for by philosophers through many centuries" (27), the "incomprehensible" unity of body and soul.

"'Beauty is a sign of the soul,'" Dixon had written in *The Clansman*, going on to escalate signification to identify—"'the body is the soul'" (301). The body in question is Marion Lenoir's, soon to be raped by Gus and thus transformed into the sacrificial pretext for the origin of Klan; the words used to describe it are the remembered words of her dead father, a poet whose "incarnate soul" Marion is said to be. Such a description of such a body—a white body and hence, incomprehensibly, a white soul—reminds us of what it might mean for the "beauty" of Gloria's "body" to be the "essence" of her "soul." If Hemingway rewrites race as aesthetic, Fitzgerald might here be said to understand that such a revision was not, strictly speaking, necessary: the conditions of racial identity already were the conditions of aesthetic value, and the supreme condition of aesthetic value and racial identity both was identity itself, "unity," the requirement that, in Stoddard's words, a race "remain itself" (300).[32]

But how does a race remain itself? Or, to put the question a little differently, how could a race not remain itself? The best way for a race to "remain itself," Stoddard thought, was for it to "breed" its "best," which suggests that a race's failure to remain itself would be a biological one, a failure of breeding: "Civilization of itself means nothing," he wrote in *The Rising Tide of Color*, "It is merely an effect, whose cause is the creative urge of superior germ-plasm. Civilization is the body; the race is the soul. Let the soul vanish, and the body moulders into the inanimate dust from which it came" (300). But if this passage begins by asserting the priority of biology, it ends by suggesting that for Stoddard, as for Gloria, germ plasm isn't quite enough; the reason that civilization means nothing is that civilization is just "the body" whereas "the race is the soul." Civilization, defined first as a mere effect of the body (germ plasm) here becomes the body it was only an effect of, and the body that was a "cause" becomes a soul. Beauty in *The Beautiful and Damned* remains itself by not becoming anything else, a strategy that will seem unhelpfully tautological only if one fails to recognize the difference between being, as beauty is, "born anew" (27) and being, as ordinary people are, reproduced. Races, obliged to "breed" their "best," seem required to make do with reproduction, and so the white race, a breeding disaster, seems doomed. "'Civilization's going to pieces,'" Tom Buchanan tells Nick Carraway, "'I've gotten to be a terrible pessimist about things'" (13). But insofar as civilizations can become bodies and bodies can become souls, Tom's pessimism seems misplaced and his reading of Lothrop Stoddard mistaken. For what

The Rising Tide of Color really argues is that races, too, may be enabled to replace reproduction with reincarnation, and it thus plays its part, alongside *The Great Gatsby* and *The Sun Also Rises,* in the general effort to save the souls of white folk.[33]

THE MAKING OF AMERICANS

The Johnson Act allayed fears that America would be overwhelmed by an unassimilable "alien tide" that would turn the country into an Asian or Mediterranean colony, but it made available a new fear. By 1927, the "alien immigrant" who resisted assimilation by "withdrawal into the haven of his group, language, and traditions" seemed much less threatening than his son, the "New American": "The presence among us of a vast nondescript mass," Stoddard wrote in *Re-Forging America,* "with no genuine loyalties, traditional roots, or cultural and idealistic standards, is a real menace to our national life" (349). The purpose of this new book was to alert us to the danger and to propose new means of dealing with it. The Progressive attempt to Americanize the alien—rejected and replaced by the successful effort to exclude him—now reappeared as another effort of Americanization, the effort to Americanize not aliens but Americans.

"'We have a great desire to be supremely American,'" Stoddard wrote, quoting Calvin Coolidge, "'That purpose we know we can accomplish by continuing the process which has made us Americans. We must search out and think the thoughts of those who established our institutions'" (225). Stoddard called this "thinking historically" and urged Americans to discover how far back their "roots" went, "far beyond even the achievement of nationhood in the Revolution to the racial and cultural foundations of the early colonial period." Eliminating the alien—excluding Robert Cohn or killing off Jimmy Gatz—turns out to be only a first step; when Nick Carraway gazes across Long Island Sound at the "inessential houses" that melt away to be replaced by the "old island" that "flowered once for Dutch sailors' eyes—a fresh, green breast of the new world" (182), he begins to take the crucial second step. Nick replaces Gatsby's "wonder" in the face of Daisy's green light—the immigrant's desire for the "nice" girl *The Great Gatsby* will not permit him to have—with the Dutch sailor's "wonder" at the "continent" that is about to become his, or that, more powerfully, is about to become him. For the famous ending of *The Great Gatsby* is in this sense only a repetition of a passage several pages before, when Nick tells what it was like returning to Minnesota after a semester at prep school in the East, changing trains in Chicago, and then, as the new trains moved west, becoming "unutterably aware of our identity with this country for one strange hour, before we melted indistinguishably into it again" (177). The strangeness comes from our being identical to the country and yet sufficiently alien from it to become momentarily *aware* of that identity, to experience it as well as to embody it. It is this moment of alienation that makes possible what Coolidge called our "desire" to be American and that confers a certain plausibility on the Americanizing project, the project to make ourselves what we already are. Without the alien—the immigrant, the children of the immigrant, the "general spirit of *alienism*"—we could never properly encounter our own "Americanness," never take our proper place in what Stoddard calls "the spiritual unity, composed alike of the dead, the living and the unborn" (362) that is America.

The Great Gatsby—especially if it is understood as essentially Nick's story—is our great novel about the production of culture out of race, and—if it is understood, as it usually is, from Nick's point of view—it plays a powerful role in producing culture out of race. By the production of culture out of race, I mean that process by which a biological claim about identity is transformed into a cultural claim about identity without losing the immunity to cultural transformation embodied in biology. Distinguishing between Nick and Tom, *The Great Gatsby* distinguishes between a "physical" America and a spiritual one; preferring Nick to Tom, it uses Nick's disdain for Tom's racism as a way of making us supremely American. Coolidge urged Americans to rethink the thoughts of those who established our institutions; following Coolidge, Nick replaces the genealogical effort to trace our descent from the original Americans with the ideological effort to imagine ourselves identical to them. Lying on the beach at West Egg, watching the "inessential" "melt away," and coming to see the old island that "flowered once for Dutch sailors' eyes," we are "compelled into an aesthetic contemplation" of the essential America.

Fitzgerald calls this process of contemplation "aesthetic," but I have read it as if it were political, and indeed it might be objected that I have read both *The Sun Also Rises* and *The Great Gatsby*—aesthetic artifacts, novels—as if they were, like *The Rising Tide of Color,* political tracts. And, of course, I might defend myself against this objection by arguing, along with many recent critics, that aesthetic categories and aesthetic judgments really are political (gender-bound or class-bound), so that the explanation of aesthetic claims in terms of political interests is not only appropriate but also essential to an understanding of the real work—the political work—of aesthetics. But neither the objection nor the defense against it—and it will be recognized that the objection and the defense are, as I have described them, identical—seems compelling to me as an account of the relation between race and aesthetics in the texts I have been discussing, and so I would like to close by proposing an account that *will* seem compelling.

To begin with, the American race in the twenties was not really a political entity, a point which can be grasped most easily simply by contrasting it to the Progressive use of race. D. W. Griffith was right to redo *The Clansman* as *The Birth of a Nation* because *The Clansman* seeks to equate the expulsion or segregation of blacks with the creation of a new political entity, America. But in *The Rising Tide of Color,* Stoddard replaces a political map of the world with a racial map, and in *Re-Forging America,* he urges us to rethink the thoughts not of the founding fathers but of the earliest settlers. The birth of a nation is here replaced by what might be called the birth of a culture, and the racial ontology that for Dixon made possible the existence of a truly American state is invoked by Stoddard on behalf of a truly American culture.

Thus, in the best manner of the newly emergent cultural relativism, Stoddard, unlike Dixon, feels himself under no obligation to defend the "superiority" of the American race. The relevant factor, he asserts, is not superiority or inferiority, but "difference": "Let all parties realize that the problem is, at bottom, one of *difference,* for which no one is morally to blame. We Americans have built up *our* America, and we cherish it so supremely that no one should honestly blame us for our resolve that it shall be kept 'American.' Of course that is no reason why the alien should like our America, and no moral turpitude should attach to him if he voices his discontent" (253–54). If racial identity were political identity, then questions of "moral turpitude"—superiority and inferiority—would have their place after all; political systems can be more or less good, more or less just, more or less efficient. But Stoddard's relativism respects *difference* above all. Which is only another way of saying that it respects *identity* above all—we Americans desire to remain supremely American.

There is a sense, then, in which the relativism of race renders the very concept more aesthetic than political (in the way that we characteristically think of judgments of taste—chocolate instead of vanilla, Wagner instead of Brahms—as essentially relative), and it is in this sense that America may be described as the object of our aesthetic contemplation and that we ourselves may be powerfully said to "like" an America so described. But it may be that the conditions of this aesthetic contemplation are more important here than the affect. For we don't simply like America, we like "our America"; in other words, our aesthetic appreciation *of* America involves our participation *in* America, and our participation in America takes the form of our appreciation of America. To put this with only a little less circularity, our liking America is both an effect and a cause of our being American; making itself available for aesthetic contemplation turns out to be America's way of making more Americans.

There can be no question, then, of revealing the political interests that lie behind the deployment of aesthetic categories, no question, in particular, of revealing the racial unity that lies behind the claims for aesthetic unity, because both the ideal of racial identity and the techniques deployed for achieving that ideal are themselves already aesthetic. One might almost say that, from this perspective, I have been more concerned to reduce the political to the aesthetic than vice versa.

In the end, however, neither of these characterizations seems right; it is no more appropriate to think of American racism in the 1920s as fundamentally literary than it is to think of American literature in the twenties as fundamentally racist. Rather, I have argued, it is race and literature both that have contributed to the meaning of the term "American" that, in the preceding sentence, modifies them both and thus to the idea of a culture that—if it can no more be reduced to a certain racism and a certain aestheticism than they can be reduced to each other—can nevertheless not be understood and could not have been thought without them. In this respect, race and aesthetics may be said to have collaborated in the construction of American culture, and so, as students of that culture, we must begin by acknowledging that much of what we mean by American culture—what we mean by calling it American, what we mean by calling it culture—is a product of that collaboration.

NOTES

This essay was first presented as the 29th annual Joseph Warren Beach lecture at the University of Minnesota.

1. Sutton Griggs, *Imperium in Imperio* (New York: Arno, 1969), 218.

2. Ibid., 203.

3. Hazel W. Carby, "'On the Threshold of Woman's Era': Lynching, Empire and Sexuality in Black Feminist Theory," *Critical Inquiry* 12 (Autumn 1985):265.

4. Quoted in Thomas F. Gossett, *Race: The History of an Idea in America* (New York: Schocken, 1965), 329.

5. Thomas Dixon, Jr., *The Clansman: An Historical Romance of the Ku Klux Klan* (Lexington: University of Kentucky Press, 1970), 186. Subsequent references to this work will be cited parenthetically in the text.

6. Editorial from *City and State* (November 17, 1898), reprinted in *The Anti-Imperialist Reader*, vol. 1, ed. Philip S. Foner and Richard C. Winchester (New York: Holmes & Meier, 1984), 367.

7. Mrs. Jefferson Davis, "Why We Do Not Want the Philippines," *The Arena* (January 1900), reprinted in Foner and Winchester, *Anti-Imperialist Reader*, 237.

8. See Iver Peterson, "White Supremacists Meet in Quest for Homeland," *New York Times* (July 14, 1986), 8.

9. Andrew Macdonald, *The Turner Diaries* (Arlington, Va.: National Alliance, 1978), 210. Subsequent references to this work will be cited parenthetically in the text.

10. Compare this language with that in the *Platform of the Liberty Congress of Anti-Imperialists Adopted in Indianapolis, August 19,* which describes the conquest in the Philippines as a "war of conquest" and which denies that "either the president or congress can govern any person anywhere outside the constitution" (Reprinted in Foner and Winchester, *Anti-Imperialist Reader,* 309).

11. Anticipating the "consolidation of a Russian-Chinese empire," Franklin Giddings predicted a "gigantic struggle . . . between that empire and the power from which we have derived our own civilization and institutions, and which today is our truest friend and strongest ally," England (Franklin Henry Giddings, *Democracy and Empire* [New York: Macmillan, 1901], 288).

12. See Michael Rogin, *Ronald Reagan, the Movie* (Berkeley and Los Angeles: University of California Press, 1987), 192–98.

13. Thomas Dixon, Jr., *The Leopard's Spots* (Ridgewood, N.J.: Gregg Press, 1967), 161.

14. Plessy v. Ferguson, 163 U.S. 540–52 (1896), reprinted in *The South since Reconstruction,* ed. Thomas D. Clark (New York: Bobbs-Merrill, 1973), 159.

15. W. E. B. Du Bois, *The Souls of Black Folk* (1903; rpt. New York: Library of America, 1986), 372.

16. Plessy v. Ferguson, 167.

17. Plessy v. Ferguson, 167. Plessy, of course, was only one-eighth black and was, as Clark puts it, "so light of skin that he had some difficulty proving himself by Louisiana definition a Negro" (155).

18. Plessy v. Ferguson, 167. For an insightful critique of *Plessy* and an important account of the relation between racial identity and legal and literary fictions, see Eric Sundquist's unpublished essay "*Pudd'nhead Wilson:* Separate But Equal."

19. Williams v. Mississippi, 170 U.S. 215–25 (1898), reprinted in Clark, *The South since Reconstruction,* 175.

20. Williams v. Mississippi, 175.

21. Quoted in Gossett, *Race: The History of an Idea in America,* 317.

22. Quoted in ibid., 337.

23. Quoted in ibid., 319. Gossett's chapter "Imperialism and the Anglo-Saxon" is an invaluable survey of racist views at the turn of the century, one on which the preceding paragraph has drawn heavily. It tends, however, to treat racism as a relatively monolithic and unchanging phenomenon, and thus describes figures like Roosevelt and Gladden as exemplifying racist ideology rather than as transforming that ideology or, as I would argue, transforming race *into* ideology.

24. C. Vann Woodward describes the Progressive movement as coinciding "paradoxically" with "the crest of the wave of racism" but goes on to say that for some, racism was "the very foundation of American Progressivism" (Woodward, *The Strange Career of Jim Crow* [New York: Oxford, 1966], 91). The thrust of my own analysis here is only to insist on racism's foundational as opposed to paradoxical relation to Progressivism.

25. F. Scott Fitzgerald, *The Great Gatsby* (New York: Scribner's, 1925), 2. Subsequent references to this work will be cited parenthetically in the text.

26. Lothrop Stoddard, *The Rising Tide of Color Against White World-Supremacy*, with an introduction by Madison Grant (New York: Scribner's, 1920), 162. Subsequent references to Stoddard's work as well as Grant's introduction will be cited parenthetically in the text.

27. Ernest Hemingway, *The Sun Also Rises* (New York: Scribner's, 1926), 4. Subsequent references to this work will be cited parenthetically in the text.

28. Ernest Hemingway, *A Farewell to Arms* (New York: Scribner's, 1929), 185.

29. F. Scott Fitzgerald, *The Beautiful and Damned* (New York: Scribner's, 1922), 408.

30. Lothrop Stoddard, *Re-Forging America* (New York: Scribner's, 1927), 167. Subsequent references to this work will be cited parenthetically in the text.

31. F. Scott Fitzgerald, *This Side of Paradise* (New York: Scribner's, 1920), 3. Subsequent references to this work will be cited parenthetically in the text.

32. It may be worth noting in this context that Fitzgerald thought of *The Great Gatsby* as written "in reaction against" the "formless" novels of James's "imitators" and "in protest against" his own "formless two novels, and Lewis' and Dos Passos'" (*The Letters of F. Scott Fitzgerald*, ed. Andrew Turnbull [New York: Scribner's, 1963], 480). But by his own account, the protest was only partially successful since the character of Gatsby himself never achieved formal unity: "he started as a man I knew and then changed into myself—the amalgam

was never complete in my mind" (*Letters,* 358). "Amalgam" has, of course, a racial connotation; inveighing against the "melting-pot," Stoddard argues in *The Rising Tide of Color* that the "offspring" of racial interbreeding is a "walking chaos" because "there is no true amalgamation" (166). My point in citing this parallel, however, is to suggest not that Gatsby seemed to Fitzgerald a racial "mongrel" but instead that insofar as the mark of failure is the inability to achieve "true amalgamation," the criteria of success are simultaneously biological and aesthetic.

33. A more complete picture of the (white) discourse of race in the twenties could be drawn by including *The Sound and the Fury,* a novel which—replacing Jake and Tom/Nick with Quentin Compson, Brett and Daisy with Caddie, Gatsby and Robert Cohn with Dalton Ames—is structurally identical to *The Sun Also Rises* and *The Great Gatsby.* Which is not to say that the novels are in every way the same; Quentin's ability to imagine incest as a prophylactic device, for example, and then to turn little Italian girls into his "sister," both alters and extends the imagination of sterility that I have been discussing.